CHINA'S UNIVERSITIES and the open door

An East Gate Book

CHINA'S UNIVERSITIES and the open door

Ruth Hayhoe

M. E. Sharpe, Inc.
Armonk, New York
London, England

An East Gate Book

Copyright © 1989 by M. E. Sharpe, Inc.
Second Printing 1992

Available in the United Kingdom and Europe from M. E. Sharpe,
Publishers, 3 Henrietta Street, London WC2E 8LU.

Library of Congress Cataloging-in-Publication Data

Hayhoe, Ruth.
    China's universities and the open door / by Ruth Hayhoe.

        p.   cm.
    Includes bibliographies and index.
    ISBN 0-87332-501-X
    1. Education, Higher—China—History—20th
century. 2. Universities and colleges—China-history—20th
century. 3. Higher education and state—China—History—20th
century. I. Title.
LA1133.H37   1989
378.51—dc19   88-18347
                      ∞   CIP

Printed in the United States of America

To the colleagues in China's universities who have
been an inspiration over the years,
and to one in particular,
this book is affectionately dedicated

CONTENTS

LIST OF ILLUSTRATIONS

ABBREVIATIONS

AFP	Agence France Presse
ACCC	Association of Community Colleges of Canada
AUCC	Association of Universities and Colleges of Canada
BUIST	Beijing University of Iron and Steel Technology
BAU	Beijing Agricultural University
CAS	Chinese Academy of Sciences
CASS	Chinese Academy of Social Sciences
CAST	Chinese Assocation for Science and Technology
CEMA	Chinese Enterprise Management Association
CIDA	Canadian International Development Agency
CPC	Communist Party of China
CSCPRC	Committee for Scholarly Communication with the People's Republic of China
CUST	Chinese University of Science and Technology
DAAD	Deutscher Akademischer Austauschdienst
DIT	Dalian Institute of Technology
EEC	European Economic Community
FAO	Food and Agriculture Organization
IBRD	International Bank for Reconstruction and Development
IDA	International Development Association
IRDC	International Development Research Center (Canada)
IMF	International Monetary Fund
IUT	Institute universitaire de technologie (France)
JICA	Japan International Cooperation Agency
JSPS	Japan Society for the Promotion of Science
MAAF	Ministry of Agriculture, Animal Husbandry, and Fisheries
MBA	Master of Business Administration
MFERT	Ministry of Foreign Economic Relations and Trade (China)
MOE	Ministry of Education (China)
MOLP	Ministry of Labor and Personnel (China)
MOPH	Ministry of Public Health (China)
NAU	Nanjing Agricultural University
NEUT	Northeastern University of Technology
NIEO	New International Economic Order
ODA	Overseas Development Administration (Britain)
OECD	Organization for Economic Cooperation and Development
OISE	Ontario Institute for Studies in Education
SALT	Strategic Arms Limitations Talks
SAREC	Swedish Agency for Research and Educational Cooperation
SEC	State Economic Commission (China)

SEdC	State Education Commission (China)
SSHRCC	Social Science and Humanities Research Council of Canada
SPC	State Planning Commission (China)
SSTC	State Science and Technology Commission
UNDP	United Nations Develpment Program
UNESCO	United Nations Education, Science and Culture Organization
USIA	United States Information Agency
WHO	World Health Organization
WOMP	World Order Models Project

CHINA'S UNIVERSITIES and the open door

INTRODUCTION

China's adoption of an open door policy since 1978 represents an important historical turning point. It also has considerable significance for the world community, which China seems to be joining in a fuller way than has been the case since the Revolution of 1949. Both the political and economic aspects of China's reintegration into the international political economy have been treated at length in other studies.[1] This book looks at its educational implications, particularly the role of Chinese universities in the process. They set the tone for the whole educational system and provide the main channel for the inflow of new knowledge from other parts of the world.

There exists already a rich literature on Chinese education which, for good reason, has mainly focused on its achievements and special characteristics under socialism since 1949. One common approach has been to interpret educational change over the period in relation to broad political change, to policy debates within various factions of the Chinese Communist Party, and to the economic strategies expressed in successive five-year plans. Education is seen as an instrument used by political leaders to achieve desired social and economic change.[2] A second, more sociological, approach has centered on the concept of class and analyzed educational change in relation to the transformation of class relations within Chinese society under socialism. Access to higher education has been an issue of continuing interest in these studies.[3]

The new conditions of the open door may call for a fresh approach to looking at China's higher education, one in which the knowledge issue comes to the fore. It is universities and other higher institutions as a knowledge system that are now responding to the massive flow of knowledge coming into China. Their ability to adapt this knowledge to China's cultural, political, and economic needs will be crucial to the long-term success of the open door.

Recent sociological theory has been greatly enriched by a sustained concern with issues of knowledge and power, attempts to unravel the way in which what passes as legitimate knowledge is constituted and to explore its relations to social and political power. I have selected a few items from this literature that seemed to provide a useful starting point for reflecting on the ways in which knowledge has been constituted in the modern Chinese curriculum since 1911.

From a thorough understanding of both American and European systems of higher education,[4] the Israeli sociologist Joseph Ben-David did a special investigation into problems of research in the European university for the OECD in the 1960s. This led him to identify obstacles in the organization of knowledge and research that he saw as linked to power structures rooted in long tradition.[5] Basil Bernstein and Michael Young of the University of London Institute of Education have looked closely at school curricula, from the perspective of both language and science education, and identified patterns in the way in which school knowledge is structured and organized that are clearly linked to power relations within the school and the wider society.[6] From this literature I draw out a few provocative ideas as an entry point for a consideration of knowledge and power relations in Chinese society.

The scholar who is trying to examine a foreign culture through eyeglasses formed within her own culture must at least be aware of the nature of these glasses. This is the intention behind the brief summary of the European sociological debate in chapter 1. I do not pretend to offer an accurate summation of Confucian knowledge patterns from within, in spite of many hours spent with Chinese classical scholars trying to understand them. Rather, I start from a small selection of ideas in the Western literature that illumine issues of knowledge and power in the European historical experience. These provide an entry point for looking at the Confucian tradition and a perspective for understanding how European and Soviet knowledge patterns have harmonized with it. The Confucian knowledge construct is admittedly partial and limited, but it serves as an analytic tool for exploring how persisting Confucian knowledge patterns have affected China's modernization process.

Chapter 1 offers a broad historical overview of the modern Chinese university. Instead of considering changing political policies or social class formations, it looks simply at the historical record of how knowledge was structured and organized in the higher curriculum and identifies a fundamental contradiction that appeared in each period up to 1966, was briefly and unsuccessfully resolved in the Cultural Revolution transformation of the university, and reappeared in the post-1978 period. Sweeping reforms in the contemporary higher curriculum need to be understood against this broad historical background, rather than being seen as merely the expression of a new educational policy developed by the present pragmatically oriented leadership.

Chapter 2 depicts these curricular reforms as they affect the whole higher education system. Since the curricular patterns revived in 1978 were essentially those established in the 1950s under Soviet influence, the structure and organization of the knowledge system at its point of maturity just before the Cultural Revolution are first examined. Then the political-economic context of the 1985 reforms is sketched out and the reform documents are analyzed with a focus on the power implications of the dramatic changes envisaged for the structuring and organization of curricular knowledge. These power concerns become particularly evident in the debates over political structure reform and the subsequent student movement in the autumn of 1986. The final two sections of the chapter depict the ongoing process of curricular change and present policies toward the introduction of foreign-derived knowledge through various forms of educational collaboration with the industrialized world.

Chapter 3 moves from the systemwide discussion of changes in the structure and organization of higher curricular knowledge to the level of individual universities and their response to the present reform initiatives. In the regimented knowledge system of the 1950s, each institution was assigned a specific role as a comprehensive university of the pure arts and sciences, a polytechnical university, an agricultural or specialist engineering institution, a teachers' university, or an institution specializing in some other narrow knowledge area, with nationally standardized curricula in each case. Now Chinese universities are given some freedom in defining their own curricular objectives and curricular organization. The consequences are different for each type of institution, since each has a different starting point and different challenges and problems to face. Chapter 3 presents profiles of ten institutions and sums up the implications of the knowledge transformation underway at this level.

With chapter 4 the focus moves from the internal constitution of knowledge-power relations to the external issue of China's participation in a global community shaped by international knowledge-power dynamics. A view of global order is a necessary starting point for evaluative reflection on the flow of foreign-derived knowledge into the Chinese higher education system. Classical international relations theory, with its concern for the politics of national interest, international power balances, and global economic relations, fails to give serious treatment to the international flow of knowledge. By this unreflexiveness it serves to make contemporary international relations appear normal, even inevitable.[7] Marxism and dependency theory unmask the cultural and educational factors that help to maintain the striking inequalities of the present world order,[8] yet a certain doctrinaire determinism renders them ill-suited to an open-ended evaluative analysis. One knows in advance the conclusions that must be reached, and cultural dynamics tend to be subsumed under the political economy of global socialism set against global capitalism.[9]

My quest has been for a global framework that avoids the absolutism of these two poles and deals with knowledge and culture in a flexible way, taking into account their links to international power relations yet affirming cultural dynamics that elude economic or political determinism. The work of scholars associated with the World Order Models Project offers such a framework.[10] In chapter 4 I summarize the key ideas within this approach to international relations that may illumine the problems of China's reintegration into the global knowledge order. Two opposite ideal types work out the implications of a reintegration that allows China to play a transformative role as against one that results in China's conformity to the international status quo. The reality lies somewhere between these two poles, but the types provide an evaluative framework for the last three chapters of the book.

Chapter 5 deals with the policy of six major industrialized countries in their knowledge relations with China, depicting the range of programs for scholarly exchange, educational cooperation, and development aid that each has in place. These policies are seen as derivative on the conscious level from national political-economic policy toward China. They are also less consciously shaped by cultural tradition and a cultural vision unique to each nation. The differences of approach represented may affect significantly the kind of contribution each nation makes to China's universities.

Chapter 6 moves from the level of policy to practice and depicts various projects of educational cooperation on Chinese soil. Here the comparison is organized according to the broad knowledge areas represented, making possible an exploration of the particular challenge to cooperation posed by each field of knowledge. The fundamental evaluative question underlying the comparative analysis in this chapter is how far these forms of educational cooperation are instruments of political/economic penetration or expressions of mutuality.

Chapter 7 turns to the involvement of the World Bank in Chinese higher education development, which might be seen as the joint contribution of all OECD countries. With the huge amount of funding they provide, World Bank educational projects in China will almost certainly have far more wide-reaching effects than any of the national programs discussed earlier. In this final chapter these projects are critically reviewed and an attempt is made to assess their likely contribution in light of the internal transformation of knowledge-power relations that is going on and the potential of China's universities for a genuine interdependence with the world scholarly community.

Finally, a word about the sources used. In addition to specialist works on Chinese education, the bibliography includes books and articles on broader Sinological topics, international relations, comparative education, and sociology that have been valuable in the development of my theme. A second important set of sources has been documents and reports. Although many internal documents that have been consulted cannot be cited, those that are publicly available are listed.

Equally important as a source of material for this study has been the growing Chinese literature concerning China's universities. Since 1984, the Chinese State Education Commission has published three educational yearbooks, the first such publications since 1948. Other valuable reference materials include a handbook on Chinese higher institutions and two books of statistical data on education. In recent years Chinese university scholars have taken a great interest in the history of their institutions, and a whole series of institutional histories has appeared. Also, higher education has been recognized as a field of study, spawning a new literature in such areas as planning, management, and teaching and learning in higher education. The bibliography provides a select listing from this growing Chinese literature.

Chinese educational journals have also flourished in the period since 1978, and China's universities have often been featured in national newspaper reporting. This study has drawn upon both national journals and newspapers and some regional journals whose articles have been collected in a monthly compilation put out by People's University under the title *Daxue jiaoyu* (University education) and subsequently *Gaodeng jiaoyu* (Higher education).

Another major source of information for the study was interviews and visits carried out between the spring of 1984 and early 1987. In the autumn of 1985 I spent eight weeks in China under the sponsorship of the Social Science and Humanities Research Council of Canada (SSHRCC) and the Chinese Academy of Social Sciences, which enabled me to interview officials in the State Education Commission, personnel in the embassies of six OECD countries, and officials in some provincial higher education bureaus. I was also able to visit about twenty-five universities, including all of those profiled in chapter 3, and many of the cooperative educational projects detailed in chapter 6. In the spring of 1984 I had already completed interviews in Paris, Bonn, and London, and on six visits to Washington over the subsequent two years I familiarized myself with American cultural policy toward China and World Bank educational projects in China.

In all of these investigations, I have met with great courtesy and cooperation from the national and international civil servants involved in educational relations with China and been allowed to consult a large number of internal documents. In Canada, persons involved in CIDA activity in China and in other forms of educational cooperation with China have been generous in giving me their time and access to relevant documents. Above all I must express gratitude to SSHRCC, whose postdoctoral fellowship from 1984 to 1986 made the whole project possible.

The picture I have put together from these diverse sources is far from complete, but I hope it provides a context for reflecting on important policy issues in the involvement of OECD countries with China's universities and for anticipating both the benefits and the problems that lie ahead as China's universities become increasingly integrated within the world academic community.

Parts of chapters 1 and 2 were published in an earlier form as "China's Higher Curricular Reform in Historical Perspective," *The China Quarterly* 110 (June 1987), and an earlier version of chapter 6 appeared as "Penetration or Mutuality: China's Educational Relations with Japan, Europe and North America," *Comparative Education Review* 31, 4 (November 1986). I would like to express my appreciation to the editors of both journals for permission to use this material.

——— 1 ———

KNOWLEDGE AND MODERNITY:
THE EMERGENCE OF A CONTRADICTION

Central to China's traditional culture was a clear conception of the structure and organization of knowledge expressed in educational institutions that contributed to the remarkable continuity of the Chinese imperial system over many centuries. I would suggest that this aspect of Chinese scholarly culture persisted even after the imperial examination system was abolished in 1905 and the empire itself was overthrown in the Revolution of 1911. Its persistence created a contradiction within the Chinese modernization process that was to intensify in each subsequent period. Simply stated, Chinese political leaders wished to transform knowledge patterns within the higher curriculum to serve explicit goals of economic modernization. At the same time, they were reluctant to abandon a Confucian knowledge structure that was seen as essential to political order.

The introduction of foreign-derived knowledge patterns exacerbated this internal contradiction. In the early Republic European and Japanese patterns were emulated. With the establishment of the Nationalist government in 1927, a European structure and organization of knowledge was again favored in spite of strong political and economic ties with the United States. Finally, after the Liberation of 1949, Communist leaders adopted and implemented Soviet patterns for the structure and organization of the higher curriculum. These reinforced features of both the European and Confucian tradition, supporting a hierarchical and authoritarian sociopolitical order.

From this perspective, the Cultural Revolution of 1966 could be viewed as a violent resolution to this contradiction. A complete transformation of the structure and organization of knowledge within the universities concurred with a transformation of power relations in Chinese society. It was intended to make possible a lively grass-roots contribution to economic development as well as broad participation by the masses in political decision making. Although it failed to fulfill either the political or economic promise of its rhetoric, it may be important as a background for understanding the more gradual reforms that are being attempted in the eighties.

This chapter begins with some reflections on the relation between knowledge and power as conceptualized within Western sociology. From this sociological perspective the structure and organization of knowledge within traditional Chinese higher education and the classical social order are considered. Then each historical period since 1911 is discussed to see how the contradiction emerged and the ways in which it was exacerbated through European and Soviet influences. The chapter ends with a consideration of the way knowledge patterns were transformed during the Cultural Revolution period.

Knowledge and Power in the European Tradition

In a study carried out under the auspices of the OECD in the mid-sixties, the sociologist Joseph Ben-David investigated the structural obstacles to successful scientific research in European universities of the period.[1] In the European tradition he noted a set of relatively stable canonized disciplines, each having clearly defined boundaries and a sphere of authority linked to the hierarchical structure of European society. The reform of the higher curriculum up to 1850 consisted of changes in the content rather than the structure and organization of knowledge. The natural sciences and the new humanities found their way into the universities through a prolonged struggle, becoming new disciplines with clearly marked boundaries. Theology was replaced by philosophy, then by science, as the synthesizing discipline, but a rigidly hierarchical knowledge structure remained in place, sustained by the chair system of academic organization.

Between 1850 and 1950, little fundamental change took place in the structure and organization of the disciplines of knowledge, in Ben-David's view. University study tended to degenerate into scholastic study, disciplinary and authoritarian in its orientation. Science was in danger of becoming a tradition instead of a tool for the pragmatic investigation of the natural world. Ben-David linked this state of affairs with the hierarchical power structure of European society which depended on and reinforced these knowledge patterns. The solution he proposed was an adoption of American-derived patterns, where the free interplay of pure and applied sciences and the weak boundaries among knowledge areas would make innovation easier and encourage a broad and critical approach to science.

The theme of knowledge and power has been richly developed with relation to English education by the sociologists Michael Young and Basil Bernstein. In an article on curricula as socially organized knowledge, Young drew attention to two features of traditionally organized curricular knowledge in England: first, the purity of high-prestige knowledge and its separation from application to practice; second, the high level of specialization or compartmentalization of knowledge areas with strong boundaries among academic disciplines and between academic knowledge and ordinary life knowledge.[2] He explored the linkages between the high status of academic knowledge, preserved through the examination system in Britain, and the power of particular classes in British society. The same two emphases on theoretical purity and narrow specialization have also characterized the structure and organization of knowledge in the European university. Purity might be seen as central to the German definition of academic knowledge,[3] while specialization characterized the French.[4]

Basil Bernstein's work has mainly focused on linguistic codes, yet his seminal article "On the Classification and Framing of Educational Knowledge" has provided an analytical tool for considering broader linkages between the organization of knowledge within the curriculum and the power structure within the school.[5] He distinguished two polar types of curricular organization. The collection code constituted a group of knowledge areas that are closed and clearly bounded and insulated from one another, such as the European knowledge disciplines. Its opposite, the integrated code, had knowledge contents that stood in an entirely open relation to one another. Bernstein defined the degree of boundary maintenance between or among knowledge areas as classification. He characterized the European curriculum as having very strong classification.

The notion of framing relates to the degree of control possessed by teachers and students in the selection, organization, pacing, and timing of the knowledge being transmitted. Strong framing denotes a low level of teacher or student control over curricular knowledge and a sharp boundary between what may and what may not be transmitted in the pedagogical relationship, between academic knowledge and everyday life knowledge. In a situation of strong framing, the student is initiated into a specialized discipline that establishes a life identity and loyalty. Bernstein saw the European curriculum as having exceptionally strong framing.

After delineating these two curricular poles—the collection code with strong classification and framing and the integrated code with weak classification and framing—Bernstein asked what sort of power structures within the school each code was likely to promote. The collection code, organizing knowledge through well-insulated subject hierarchies, seemed likely to coincide with oligarchic control of the school characterized by vertical relations within departments and horizontal relations only at the level of senior staff. In contrast, the integrated code seemed to require strong horizontal links among teachers, also an explicit ideological consensus among teachers and between teachers and students.

This brief discussion of curricular knowledge and sociopolitical power in the European literature is intended to bring some clarity and precision to key terms used throughout the book in considering the Chinese higher curriculum. Drawing upon Ben-David and Young, I conceive the structure of knowledge in terms of the presence or absence of a relative ordering of prestige among different kinds of knowledge, for example, pure and applied knowledge, academic and practical knowledge, and such specific subject areas as physics, history, medicine, agriculture, and education. This structure may be vertical with a clearly delineated hierarchy of knowledge areas, or horizontal with all knowledge areas given equal weight and conditions for cross-fertilization or integration provided.

Drawing upon Bernstein, the organization of knowledge is understood in relation to the boundaries among different knowledge areas, and their institutional expression in the internal organization of educational institutions. Classification points to the relative strength or weakness of these boundaries, whereas framing calls attention to the pedagogical relations between teachers and students and the degree of control they possess over the definition of curricular content.

The consistent use of these terms in reflecting on persistence and change in the Chinese higher curriculum should draw attention to a dimension of China's modernization process that has not been carefully considered before. The importance of this dimension to the present open door in higher education justifies the central place it holds in the first half of the book.

Knowledge and Power in Confucian China

Approached from a European perspective, the Confucian curriculum has certain fascinating parallels with European educational traditions. Although China had no disciplines of knowledge as such, with clear boundaries delineating them, an absolute boundary existed between the pure classical knowledge worthy of inclusion in the imperial examinations and all other knowledge areas, such as medicine, mathematics, and engineering.[6] The former qualified a tiny meritocratically chosen elite for positions within the imperial bureaucracy,[7] while the latter were richly developed as techniques subject to the supervision of scholar-officials with examination credentials.[8] Pure knowledge, however, was less characterized by theoretical abstraction than by the notion of mental labor,[9] an absolute abstention from contact with the material world symbolically evident in the garb of the scholar.

The constituents of pure knowledge were not theoretical constructs but practical principles concerning the government and administration of society, interlinked with maxims of personal and family morality. Their source was a canon of texts, the Four Books and Five Classics, abstracted from Chinese historical experience by Confucius and put into final form by the neo-Confucian scholar, Zhu Xi.[10] It had the status of absolute and unquestioned authority, although limited debate was permitted over its interpretation and application to practical administrative tasks.

A further parallel exists in the notion of specialization and the initiation into a highly specialized knowledge area carrying with it a specific identity.

The Confucian scholar normally spent fifteen to twenty years mastering the classical texts and demonstrating his knowledge through participation in a series of centrally organized examinations at local, provincial, and imperial level. With the achievement of the third and highest traditional degree, he qualified to become a scholar-official within the imperial bureaucracy.[11] Thereafter he devoted himself to maintaining the hierarchical power structure that mirrored and took its justification from the order described in the classical texts.[12]

The coordination between the traditional knowledge system and the imperial power structure in China was more perfectly articulated than linkages between the medieval university and the church and civil states. The Hanlin Academy, whose membership gave prestige and standing to the upper echelons of the scholar-official class, was the final arbiter of all valid knowledge as well as the most important source of legitimation for the imperial system.[13] China's rigorous adherence to the principle of the meritocracy caused an English observer in the nineteenth century to make the following comment: "The whole of China may be said to resemble one vast university which is governed by the scholars who have been educated within its walls."[14]

The structure of knowledge in traditional China was thus characterized by a clear hierarchy of prestige with the pure knowledge of the classical principles of sociopolitical order holding absolute sway over such richly developed techniques as engineering, medicine, mathematics, and chemistry. As for the organization of knowledge, the boundary between pure knowledge and technique was very strong, institutionalized by the civil service examination system. Neither teacher nor student could make any contribution to the definition of the pure knowledge that both legitimized and reflected imperial order. While the notions of classification and framing would be anachronistic if applied to Confucian China, it is not difficult to see why European, and subsequently Soviet, curricular patterns, characterized by strong classification and framing, were so attractive to a modern Chinese leadership that relied upon Confucian values to preserve political order.

There was, of course, an alternative knowledge tradition that encouraged freer discussion and debates over the classical texts and their application to the task of government. The private academies or *shuyuan* made possible some innovation in traditional knowledge content through the study of unorthodox texts, such as those of Daoism and Buddhism. They were probably closer counterparts to the medieval universities of Europe than the Hanlin Academy and the official higher schools, yet they never achieved the same collective autonomy. Their fragmented individual autonomy was subject to either suppression or cooptation by successive imperial regimes,[15] limiting their influence on traditional knowledge patterns.

This brief comparative sketch of the European and Chinese knowledge traditions sets a perspective from which to view the development of modern higher institutions since the 1911 Revolution in China. I take as a focus in this historical overview the continuing contradiction between the desire of the Chinese leadership for modern knowledge patterns suited to economic development needs and their reluctance to abandon the Confucian patterns essential to political order.

Higher Curriculum in the Early Republic: The Contradiction Emerges

Considerable educational legislation passed in the first few months of the early Republic. Drawing upon earlier legislation of 1902-1903, it indicated current conceptions of a modern curriculum for higher education. A series of major subject areas were designated: arts, sciences, law, commerce, medicine, agriculture, and engineering. Within each subject area appropriate departments were defined with detailed guidelines for the courses in each specialist area laid down. Thus clear boundaries were established, and a collection of modern disciplines was created. The notion of the purity of theoretical knowledge and a hierarchy of knowledge areas was evident in the distinction made between the small number of institutions that should be entitled universities and the larger number of professional schools devoted to one specialist professional field. Universities were to have a higher status, and their curriculum was defined by three possible combinations: (1) pure arts and sciences; (2) arts plus law or commerce; or (3) sciences plus agriculture, medicine, or engineering.[16] The presence of a pure field of knowledge defined a university, and an exclusive commitment to pure disciplines of the first category came to represent the highest prestige. This legislation was strongly influenced by the German-educated Chinese scholar Cai Yuanpei, who was Minister of Education briefly in 1912.

When Cai became chancellor of Beijing University in 1917, his strong attraction to the Humboldtian university ethos was revealed in the way he restructured the curriculum of this leading national university. The applied areas of commerce and engineering were moved out, leaving only disciplines of the pure arts and sciences. Disciplinary boundaries between subject areas were clearly defined, and all students were required to take some courses in the core discipline of philosophy.[17] A traditional European conception of pure knowledge thus replaced the Chinese tradition of purity at this leading national university. The ferment of the May 4th Movement of 1919 demonstrated the intellectual vitality of this curriculum, yet I would argue that European knowledge structures were generally more amenable to political control than American ones.

New educational legislation in 1922 and 1924, which was American inspired, gave a much broader definition of the university.[18] Applied knowledge areas and cross-disciplinary fields were increased in response to economic modernization needs in such areas as business and commerce, psychology, agriculture, and rural sociology. The use of the credit system to facilitate curricular breadth was endorsed, and an American-inspired style of academic organization, with colleges between university and department, provided greater flexibility than the European chair system. Pure and applied sciences developed together, and the mingling of theoretical and practical aspects of the social sciences and humanities was supportive to the political activism intellectuals were involved in from the May 4th Movement onward. University scholars and students gave considerable support to the Northern Expedition of 1927, which overthrew the reactionary warlord government and established the first stable republican government under the Guomindang or Nationalist Party.[19]

Two distinctive approaches to the structure and organization of knowledge in the higher curriculum were thus available to the Chinese in the early Republican period. One was European inspired, had clear resonances with the Confucian knowledge tradition, and thereby offered the promise of service to economic modernization within authoritarian political structures. The other was American inspired, provided a more open and flexible approach to knowledge, and integrated theory and practice in ways relevant to both economic and political modernization. It resonated with aspects of the Chinese *shuyuan* tradition.

There were institutions on Chinese soil that provided clear exemplars of both the American and the European modes of knowledge organization. Qinghua University, founded through American government cooperation,[20] sixteen American missionary colleges,[21] and a host of Chinese institutions headed and staffed by American returned scholars[22] expressed a variety of American-inspired patterns. In contrast, Beijing University came very close to the Humboldtian pattern, while the German government supported Tongji University expressed the spirit of the German *Technische Hochschule*.[23] The French Jesuit university, Aurore, exemplified the excellence of French professional education in its faculties of law, medicine, and engineering.[24]

Significantly, European-inspired patterns were favored by early republican leaders seeking to establish centralized political control, while American patterns were promoted by Chinese scholars in the political anarchy of the twenties when regional warlords were unable to develop a coherent educational policy. In this situation educators took upon themselves the task of creating institutions that would contribute to economic development and political democratization. American knowledge patterns appeared most conducive to these ends.[25]

The emergence of a fundamental contradiction is evident between 1912 and 1927. On the one hand, there was an unequivocal commitment to modernization conceived as economic growth, requiring transformed knowledge patterns capable of solving practical development problems. On the other hand, a concern for political order meant that the Confucian knowledge tradition was not easily relinquished. The coincidence of a broad adoption of American knowledge patterns with political anarchy in the first half of the twenties must have left an impression on the Nationalist leadership that gained power in 1927. Their higher education policies were characterized by the same contradiction between a determination to transform knowledge patterns for the sake of economic growth and a need to preserve the Confucian structures that informed the very concept of political order.

Higher Curriculum in the Nationalist Period: The Contradiction Intensifies

When the Nationalist government came to power in 1927, the higher education system had a structure and organization of knowledge similar to American patterns. Most institutions embraced a wide range of pure and applied knowledge fields that were given equal importance. Broad curricular areas were organized within colleges, which consisted of several departments. The credit system was used to ensure that students had an exposure to a range of knowledge areas, and most had a general first year before following more specialized courses of study from the second year.

In legislation passed in 1929, the main contours of this pattern were confirmed, but emphasis was put on strengthening the pure and applied sciences vital to economic modernization. A university was decreed to be an institution of higher learning having at least three colleges, one of which must be in the pure or applied sciences.[26] The first concern of the new government was for the strengthening of science enrollments in order to meet economic development needs. The interrelation of pure and applied sciences, a sense of the permeability of the disciplines of scientific knowledge, and a problem-solving approach to the advancement of knowledge ensured a rather progressive style of curriculum suited to practical economic needs.[27]

The other side of this emphasis on the natural sciences, however, was a determination to reduce social science enrollments, which had demonstrated a parallel trend toward examining practical problems of the political and social order and were therefore seen as threatening to the political authority of the new government. Although student political activism had made an important contribution to Nationalist success in seizing power from the warlord government, it was now seen as a threat to the new government's authority. The approach to knowledge that sustained it had to be suppressed. In addition to a forced reduction in social science enrollments[28] and the closing of colleges and departments in these areas, the government legislated to abolish the National Union of Students and restrict student union activities to individual campuses and to academic issues. This latter policy was given an able intellectual defense by Cai Yuanpei, who based his argument on the German notion of academic freedom. He made the point that freedom to advance scholarship in a critical way depended on the university's abstention from political activism. A knowledge that advances through theoretical debate rather than through application to practice was implied in this classic European argument.[29]

The contradiction was thus clearly evident in the early Nationalist policies for higher education. American knowledge patterns might be valuable for science curricula that addressed important issues of economic modernization, but the Confucian knowledge structure was essential to political order and European modes of academic organization were more easily assimilated to it. Thus in 1931 a League of Nations Mission of Experts, all European, was invited to study the Chinese educational system and make recommendations for reform.

This was an enlightened and highly distinguished group of scholars, including the French Communist Paul Langevin, the British socialist R. H. Tawney, the former Prussian Minister of Education C. H. Becker, and the Polish scholar M. Falski. Many of their recommendations were valuable and practical, yet when it came to the higher curriculum, the reform measures they proposed clearly reflected a European view of knowledge. Emphasis was placed on the need to strengthen the basic disciplines and to centralize the administration of higher education in order that this could be achieved. Several measures were recommended to this end: the geographic and financial rationalization of higher institutions, the establishment of academic chairs in place of college and departmental organization, clear national procedures for monitoring all academic appointments, a final examination and a thesis for all graduating students to ensure strong initiation into a discipline, and the introduction of province- or city-wide academic examinations at the end of secondary school as a means of unified selection for university entrance.[30]

In legislation passed between 1933 and 1936, many of these measures were adopted.[31] This more absolutist and authoritarian approach to knowledge coincided with a need felt by Nationalist leaders to exert political control over the increasingly disaffected university community. It was complemented by a revival of Confucian teaching in the New Life Campaign, which was intended to raise the moral and spiritual tone of the nation by a renewal of the traditional social values upheld in the classical texts.[32] Both of these trends were seen by discerning intellectuals for what they were—a desperate effort to assert and maintain centralized political control over and through the educational system.[33]

The presence of certain foreign-supported institutions on Chinese soil intensified this contradiction in curricular policy. The French Jesuit university, Aurore, exemplifed most dramatically the potential of a French emphasis on specialization and high professional standards for supporting a rigid hierarchical authority structure and delivering graduates well prepared to support the status quo of the political regime. It boasted a large number of graduates in law who held high positions in the Nationalist regime, as well as engineering and medical graduates known for their high professional standards. The university's support for existing government authority was unquestioned, even when it came to the authority of the Japanese puppet regime during the war.[34] To a lesser degree Tongji University, with its high professional standards in engineering and medicine, made a substantial contribution to economic modernization without questioning political order.[35] On the other hand, an American missionary institution such as Yanjing, with its more flexible curricular organization, combined scientific productivity with a strong student and staff involvement in social and political issues.[36] In spite of American political support for the Nationalist government, American missionary institutions generally played a more progressive role than did European ones. I would argue that this was due to the structure and organization of their curricula.

Higher Curriculum in the Early Communist Regime:
The Contradiction Reaches Explosive Proportions

When the Communist Party formed a government in 1949, the approach to higher education that it had developed in the border areas was set aside for policies that were remarkably similar to those of the Nationalists.[37] There was the same determination to increase enrollments in the sciences and engineering to meet the needs of economic modernization.[38] At the same time, enrollments in the social sciences and humanities were drastically reduced, even though much of the student political support they had received in the revolutionary struggle had been inspired by work done in these fields.[39] The central concerns were very similar to those of the Nationalists: political order and rapid economic development. Once in power they had even less tolerance for the intellectual dissent that had been useful in the revolutionary struggle.

The higher education system inherited by the Communist government was close to the American one in its knowledge patterns, due to the Nationalist failure to implement policies legislated under European influence. Most institutions combined the pure and applied sciences with some social sciences and liberal arts and were organized into colleges and departments that allowed for the cross-fertilization of knowledge areas. Rather than strengthening the pure and applied sciences within this context, the new government chose to carry out a total reorganization of the higher education system in a close imitation of Soviet patterns.[40] These patterns held promise for an economic modernization that proceeded within a hierarchical and authoritarian political order.[41]

The structure and organization of knowledge in the reformed higher education system of 1952 did not reflect the Marxist commitment to the unity of theory and practice, which had become official dogma. It was much closer to those features of the European knowledge tradition noted earlier in the work of Ben-David, Young, and Bernstein: a rigid institutional separation of pure and applied fields of knowledge, with pure tending to hold high prestige; great stress on narrow specialization, now extended from the traditional disciplines to the new applied areas of knowledge related to socialist economic modernization; strong classification in the impermeable boundaries between disciplines and specializations; and extremely strong framing in the lack of any control by teachers or students over the knowledge transmitted in the pedagogical process. As in earlier periods, modern knowledge was structured and organized within the traditional patterns essential to political order.

Boundary strength between pure and applied fields and among the various disciplines and applied specializations now took on clear institutional expression. The pure arts and sciences, comprising the major disciplines of the European tradition, were isolated in 14 comprehensive universities (*zonghe daxue*) whose brief was to "train specialists for research and teaching in the theoretical and foundational sciences."[42] Within these, knowledge was divided by departments, which had a disciplinary identity, and even more narrowly by specializations within departments. Students were recruited to a given specialization, and there was little cooperation among either specializations or departments. The colleges, which had brought together several departments during the Nationalist period, were abolished.

The comprehensive universities devoted to pure knowledge in specialist disciplines formed an elite within the system, matched by the polytechnical universities (*zonghe jishu daxue*), which were also comprehensive in the sense of including a broad range of applied scientific fields in their curriculum. The latter were divided into narrowly defined departments in specific applied sciences rather than academic disciplines. The majority of institutions were specialist institutions in such areas as agriculture, highly specific engineering fields, medicine, and teacher training. With the exception of teachers colleges, their departments and specializations were even more narrowly defined.

Strictly speaking, the term university (*daxue*) was restricted to those institutions administered directly by the Ministry of Higher Education: the comprehensive universities, teachers universities, and polytechnical universities. All the specialist institutions administered by such national ministries as metallurgy, finance, agriculture, public health, light industry, railways, and so forth were termed colleges (*xueyuan*), although the academic level of their programs was no different than that of universities.[43]

Detailed teaching plans and course outlines for each specialization were set at the national level by the Ministry of Higher Education, ensuring high academic standards across the system and virtually no control by university teachers and students over the selection, organization, pacing, and timing of what was taught.[44] Teaching and the transmission of both specialist knowledge and appropriate professional skills were the main purposes of the system. While university scholars were expected to undertake some research, the main research tasks were delegated to institutes of the Chinese Academy of Sciences.[45] As a result, there was a tendency in the universities for knowledge to be viewed as a closed authoritative system rather than a changing set of tentative propositions.

The system produced technical experts who could be slotted into appropriate lifelong posts within the socialist bureaucracy and expected to apply their skills to socialist modernization, without raising fundamental questions in a broad or critical way. In the short term their contribution was very effective, as the record of industrialization in the fifties shows, but in the long term there were serious problems in adapting the knowledge and skills gained in the higher education to changing socioeconomic needs. Theorists and pure researchers were vulnerable to dogmatism while applied specialists lacked the depth of foundational theory needed to make creative adjustments to new work conditions.[46] The structure and organization of knowledge in the higher education system both contributed to and reflected a certain rigidity in the whole sociopolitical system. Not only were classification and framing extremely strong, but a hierarchical structure of curricular knowledge, with highest prestige going to pure fields, remained in place.

The parallels with the European dilemma, as analyzed by Ben-David, are not surprising, since European academic influences were seminal to the Soviet-inspired patterns of knowledge that have been described. On a deeper level, the dilemma might be analyzed in terms of the persistence of Confucian knowledge patterns, which exalted mental labor and defined it in terms of practical principles of benevolent government abstracted from the Chinese historical process. This pure classical knowledge had held absolute authority, with all other areas of knowledge in applied scientific fields subordinate to it. While Confucius and the classical texts had been fully and finally repudiated, a complete change in the content of high-status knowledge did not disturb its traditional structure. The science of history, Marxism-Leninism, replaced the Confucian classics as the knowledge of highest prestige. All other forms of learning were subordinated to it.

The new leadership intended that one particular institution exemplify a truly modern socialist university.[47] People's University was classified as a comprehensive university, yet its programs included only a set of social science fields closely patterned after the Soviet model.[48] This curricular content may not have represented pure knowledge in the European sense of theoretical academic disciplines, but it was pure in the traditional Chinese sense of the mental labor of scholar-officials. It was entirely separate from all other sciences, whose development it was to supervise, both by graduating cadres who would hold high positions in the bureaucracy and by forming political science teachers who would be distributed throughout the whole higher education system. Their watchdog role was to ensure that all other knowledge transmitted in the educative process was ideologically correct and would not undermine political order.[49]

An intense contradiction thus emerged. On the one hand, great emphasis was put on rapidly expanding the specialist fields that would contribute directly to economic modernization; on the other hand, the structure and organization of knowledge was tightly controlled within a framework that combined reactionary features of the Confucian and European knowledge traditions. The educational reforms of the Great Leap Forward represented a first challenge to these patterns,[50] but the early 1960s saw them reinstated. With the outbreak of the Cultural Revolution in 1966, the contradiction between knowledge for economic modernization and knowledge for political control had reached explosive proportions.

The Cultural Revolution: The Contradiction Resolved

The educational upheavals of the Cultural Revolution have been interpreted in relation to the policies of the political faction that gained ascendancy in this period.[51] They have also been analyzed from the more sociological perspective of concerns for equality in access to higher education and changes in the class composition of those who found their way into formal higher education.[52] In this section, however, I will focus exclusively on the Cultural Revolution rhetoric concerning the way in which knowledge was structured and organized.[53] At this point let me emphasize the fact that it is the rhetoric, not the reality of what happened, that is under consideration.

Soviet-inspired knowledge patterns had combined with residues of the Confucian knowledge tradition to create a sharply hierarchical structuring of knowledge and a curricular organization marked by strong classification and framing. Topping the hierarchy was a body of political, economic, and administrative theory that had the authority of science and emanated largely from People's University. It was both the main channel of Soviet influence and the main arbiter of the legitimacy of all lower forms of knowledge.

Given this situation, it is not surprising that the power struggle that went on in the early Cultural Revolution was paralleled by a struggle to transform the structure and organization of knowledge. After a period of debate, conflict, and struggle, all higher institutions were closed from 1966 to 1970, and students traveled throughout the country making revolution and learning from the experience of workers and peasants. The new approach to knowledge organization developed over this period could be understood in terms of Bernstein's integrated code with weak classification and weak framing. The structure was no longer hierarchical, nor could any differential prestige be attached to particular knowledge areas.

Neither pure theoretical knowledge nor abstracted mental labor, such as had characterized the major comprehensive universities in general and People's University in a peculiarly Chinese way, were countenanced. All theory, scientific and social, was to be integrated with practice. In the natural sciences, this involved close linkages with factories and farms. Scientific research projects were defined in relation to productive needs and as often carried out on factory premises as in higher institutions. In the social sciences and humanities, all society was to be taken as a factory, and student participation in class struggle and revolutionary mass activism was to ensure the linking of social theory with social practice.[54]

Knowledge had no existence on its own, separate from productive and social practice,[55] and no one body of theory could tyrannize a hierarchically structured knowledge system. Dramatic institutional evidence of this in the social sciences is found in the fact that People's University, that "great beehive of doctrinairism,"[56] remained closed for the full decade of the Cultural Revolution period, as did all other institutions of politics and law.[57] The Marxist-Leninist science of history was no longer seen as a distinct knowledge area relating hierarchically to subordinate fields of knowledge. It was rather a mode of thought and action which, in the medium of Mao Zedong Thought, ran through all knowledge and all activism, providing an integrating thread among disciplines, specializations, ordinary life knowledge, and action.[58]

As for the organization of the higher curriculum, disciplines and specializations were now to stand in an open flexible relation to one another. For the sciences, this was to be achieved by the application of specialist knowledge drawn from different areas to solving problems in production. In some cases, it involved the abolition of departments and a reordering of knowledge in direct relation to production. In the social sciences and arts, a similar focus on practice and the solving of social problems weakened disciplinary boundaries. The boundary between academic knowledge and ordinary life knowledge also receded. A major qualification for entry to higher institutions was a rich experience of ordinary life knowledge, gained by some years spent in a factory or rural production unit after secondary school, and this ordinary life knowledge was central rather than marginal to classroom discourse. Classification was thus greatly weakened.

Framing was even more dramatically weakened. The Ministry of Higher Education, which had been responsible for the planning and dissemination of nationally standard teaching plans, outlines, and textbooks for each specialization throughout the country, was abolished. All the old textbooks were criticized for their theoretical formality and narrow specialization and either discarded or radically altered. Three-in-one committees made up of students, teachers, and worker-peasant-soldier representatives took responsibility both for the administration of higher institutions at all levels and for the creation of new teaching materials that should reflect local needs. Teachers and students were to have control over the selection, organization, pacing, and timing of the knowledge transmitted in the pedagogical process. Worker-peasant-soldier representatives were also present on these committees to ensure strong links between academic and real life knowledge and the suitability of the knowledge being produced to local social and productive conditions.[59]

The rhetoric suggested a total transformation of the structure and organization of knowledge. This was both to reflect and to support the transformation of power relations in the wider society. The aim was mass-line democratic participation in government and an economic development that depended more on the creative involvement of the masses than on the input of experts. It was Mao's conviction that this transformation of superstructural social relations and culture would create conditions for even more rapid economic growth than had been possible under the hierarchically structured and controlled Soviet patterns. His writings formed the basis for the ideological consensus essential to an integrated curricular code.

Although many of the educational ideas of the Cultural Revolution were new, inspired by the intensity of opposition to entrenched traditionalism, there were echoes in China's historical experience, particularly that of the *shuyuan*. In his manifesto for the Hunan Self-Study University, written in 1923, Mao used the *shuyuan* model to criticize the so-called modern higher institutions of the time:

> In looking back at the *shuyuan*, although there were faults in their form of organization, they were not the faults of contemporary schools—lack of warmth between teacher and students, an authoritarian style of teaching that does harm to human personality, too many hours of class, and too complex a curriculum, so that students can't use their own ideas to initiate research. Secondly, there was no "academic government by professors" but a free spirit and free research. Thirdly, the curriculum was simple and discussion ranged broadly, it was possible to work in a leisurely and carefree way and to play a little.[60]

Residues of this progressive pedagogical tradition may well have informed some of the innovations of the Cultural Revolution period.[61] Aspects of American progressivism that had found their way into Chinese educational thought in the twenties also seemed to harmonize with some of the early Cultural Revolution rhetoric.[62]

This raises an interesting point, which was touched upon earlier. While American political and economic policy toward China in the late Nationalist and early Communist period was clearly reactionary from the Chinese perspective, American knowledge patterns apparently had liberating possibilities. It is fascinating, therefore, to notice how two institutions that had had a long-standing American orientation in the pre-Liberation period came to the fore in the Cultural Revolution period. Fudan, a leading comprehensive university, had been founded in 1905 and developed under the leadership of American-educated Chinese up till 1949. Qinghua, China's most distinguished polytechnical university, had a history going back to 1908 when American Boxer Indemnity funds were used to create a school for young Chinese preparing to study in the United states. Both became highly publicized exemplars of curricular transformation during the Cultural Revolution decade.

In the two sketches that follow, it must be remembered that this published rhetoric justified an unmerciful campaign against intellectuals who were associated with the old structures of academic authority.[63] Without in any way condoning the violence and cruelty, I think it is important to remember that there was a serious and often persuasively expressed rationale behind the transformations that were attempted.

When higher institutions were formally reopened in 1970-71, Qinghua University was taken as a model, and the *Red Flag* article "Strive to Build a Socialist University of Science and Engineering," based on Qinghua's experience, was widely discussed and emulated throughout the country.[64] Several significant points concerning the organization of the curriculum and the new approach toward knowledge emerged from Qinghua's experience. These might be best captured by quoting directly from the article:

> We broke the barriers of departments set in the past, merging some departments and adding new ones. On the basis of their relation with scientific research and production, the specialties are placed under the relevant systems of university-run factories, scientific research institutions or university-factory links, so that the specialists are guided by factories. At the same time we formed a new-type contingent in basic theory. . . . While using factories, we have accelerated the reform and construction of the laboratories. Closely linking the university-run factories and laboratories with society, we have turned the university into an important base for training students' ability in scientific experiment, energetically conducting scientific research, scaling pinnacles of technology, creating new technological processes and manufacturing new products, probing new theories and catching up with and surpassing advanced world standards. (pp. 18-19)

This account depicts how the knowledge formerly isolated in narrow specializations and departments became integrated in its application to production. New advances in scientific theory were seen to arise from practice and experimentation in this more open organization of knowledge. Classification was greatly weakened and the distinction between pure and applied sciences blurred. Significantly, in terms of aspirations at least, Qinghua was no longer termed a polytechnical university dealing only in applied fields, but a college of science and engineering.

A second significant aspect of the Qinghua experiment may be linked to the drastic weakening of pedagogical framing with knowledge being created by students, teachers, and workers, rather than arbitrated from above. The new teachers were young people drawn from worker-peasant-soldier backgrounds. They were described as follows:

> They have the courage to innovate and abolish misleading beliefs. And they have the ability to criticize. In addition they create close ties between schools and factories by bringing the inventions of laboring people into the classes. (p. 7)

The approach to teaching was laid down as follows:

> The college of science and engineering must enable . . . students to solve current problems arising in practical production and to undertake the tasks of designing and scientific research to meet the needs of their country's scientific and technical development. To achieve this aim, it is imperative to oppose the tendencies toward dogmatism and empiricism, persist in integrating theory with practice and train students' ability to analyze and solve problems. (p. 24)

This broad and critical approach to scientific knowledge may have seemed revolutionary in the Chinese context, where dogmatism had so long prevailed, but it has clear resonances with the nineteenth-century American transformation of the university. Due to its American roots, Qinghua's curriculum had from an early period included pure and applied sciences, together with social sciences and humanities. From the early 1930s engineering had developed with particular distinction, in a practical problem-solving response to China's wartime needs.[65] The integration of scientific theory with productive practice and the creation of strong linkages between the university and industry promoted during the Cultural Revolution thus had interesting resonances with the American historical experience.

If Qinghua University played a leading role in the transformation of science and engineering universities, Fudan was a recognized leader in the liberal arts and social sciences. In response to Mao's directive that "Liberal arts should take the whole society as a factory,"[66] Fudan made a special experiment in September 1969 with thirty worker-peasant-soldier students who were enrolled for two years. Considerable debate went on over the curriculum, with teachers wishing to preserve some of the clearly bounded academic specializations and students insisting on their full integration within the ideological framework provided by Mao Thought.[67]

> It is inconceivable that one who does not understand and apprehend dialectical materialism and historical materialism can learn any special field of liberal arts with success. Nor is it conceivable that a student of literature and art who knows nothing of the acute class struggle in the philosophical domain can learn his specialty with success. . . . If we confine ourselves to the narrow bounds of a specialty we shall not be able to understand thoroughly and master Chairman Mao's basic line, nor shall we be able to apply Mao Zedong Thought accurately in criticizing the bourgeois ideology in each sphere of learning.

The boundaries among disciplines and between pure and applied fields were eliminated and a new perspective on the status of knowledge became evident.

Didactic and authoritarian teaching methods were abandoned in favor of the following approach:

> Setting teaching in motion through revolutionary mass activism, conducting social surveys, summing up and exchanging experience, making self-study, and exercising teacher's supervision—these links were organically combined, centering on revolutionary mass activism.[68]

After participating in social activism of various types, students wrote critical articles, many of which were carried in the press or over the radio. This mastery of communication arts, combined with an activist social science and liberal arts program, culminated in the latter part of the Cultural Revolution decade in Fudan taking a leading national role in revolutionary activity and being very closely associated with the Gang of Four. The university's journal, *Study and Criticism*, which started up in 1973, was described as a comprehensive journal for the study of philosophical and social sciences, operating on the principle of "Let a Hundred Schools of Thought Contend."[69] Its editors wished to provide for the discussion of differing opinions related to scholarship and the participation of workers, soldiers, peasants, revolutionary cadres, and revolutionary intellectuals in their discussion. They published a wide range of articles between 1973 and 1976 and gained prestige equal to or even greater than that of the official party journal *Red Flag*.[70]

As in the case of Qinghua, the revolutionary role in knowledge production played by Fudan had some roots in an American approach to knowledge organization which had been introduced to the university as early as 1905. Fudan's social role had always been a revolutionary one, from its leadership of the May 4th Movement in Shanghai, through the various anti-Japanese student campaigns to the war years, when Fudan had a campus close to Chongqing. Its radical staff members kept in close touch with Yan'an through the journalism department, which had constant radio contact. Other progressive staff members published the journal *Wenzhai* (The digest), making available a large amount of information to the Chinese public which the Nationalist government would have preferred to suppress.[71] The mastery of communication arts demonstrated in the Cultural Revolution period was thus rooted in a long tradition of social and political activism.

In both the social and natural sciences, aspects of the American curricular tradition gave support to the revolutionary transformation of knowledge that was attempted during the Cultural Revolution period. This cultural influence, of course, is quite distinct from the political and economic relations between the United States and China; nor was it available to manipulation by either government.[72] It resonated with aspects of the teaching and learning style of the traditional Chinese *shuyuan*.

Conclusion

This chapter has dealt only with the rhetoric, not the reality, of the Cultural Revolution. In spite of the attractiveness of some Cultural Revolution ideas, there can be little doubt that the movement itself represented a major disaster in China's modern development. This is now being explained in terms of a vicious political power struggle and the senility of an aging leader who strayed from the correct and realistic path in his latter years.[73] This sort of explanation, however, does not account for the response of Chinese youth to Mao's leadership initiative, which created a sociological phenomenon of almost unprecedented proportions.

From the perspective of this chapter, the Cultural Revolution might be seen as a violent attempt to resolve a dilemma that went back to 1911. The transformation of knowledge patterns was essential if economic modernization was to be accompanied by political democratization. The Cultural Revolution leadership failed, however, to create institutional structures that could give enduring expression to concerns for mass-line democracy expressed in its rhetoric.[74] Rather, they opened the door for anarchy accompanied by an unprecedented vendetta in which intellectuals were among those who suffered most. There is a striking parallel in the correlation between transformed knowledge patterns and political anarchy in this period and in the early twenties, although the political context was entirely different.

The educational rhetoric of the Cultural Revolution decade thus needs to be understood as more than simply the political machinations of a far left faction that gained the support of the aging Mao and rewarded him with near deification. It relates to a popular perception of the regimentation of curricular knowledge and its use for purposes of political control that can be traced back to the Revolution of 1911 and the struggles over curricular policy that took place in each of China's subsequent modern regimes.

Present attempts to reform the higher curriculum express some of the same aspirations, even though the political context is entirely different. There is a concern for integrating applied and pure knowledge and for redefining narrow knowledge specializations in a broader way. There seems to be a move underway from a collection code with strong classification and framing toward greater integration. This is likely to take shape gradually within new attempts to forge ideological consensus around a shared commitment to the four modernizations (agriculture, industry, national defense, science and technology).

What is disturbing about the four modernizations formula is the fact that it reveals a continuing tendency in the Chinese leadership to focus on economic modernization and neglect questions of political democratization. The changes in the knowledge system now underway, which are described in detail in chapter 2, have brought in their train new demands for political democratization, which the leadership must face. Their willingness and ability to resolve a contradiction unresolved by all of their predecessors, except briefly and disastrously during the Cultural Revolution, may be crucial to the future of China's universities and the open door policy.

——— 2 ———

HIGHER EDUCATION REFORMS
IN THE EIGHTIES

With the fall of the Gang of Four in 1976 and the subsequent return to power of Deng Xiaoping and his sympathizers in 1978, a new era in Chinese politics began. The focus of this chapter is on higher education in the post-Cultural Revolution period. Yet it begins with a detailed depiction of the way in which knowledge was structured and organized in the early sixties, since these patterns have been basic to the post-1978 period. The political-economic developments of the 1978-1985 period are then briefly outlined as the background to a discussion of the major systemwide reforms in higher education.

The remarkable changes made in the higher curriculum have been clearly geared toward economic modernization needs, yet the leadership has remained ambivalent about their implications for political democratization. If Confucian patterns are finally being relinquished, as appears to be the case, it is not surprising that intellectuals and students have involved themselves in debates and marches over the issue of political structure reforms. The student movement and the repressive measures against intellectuals that followed it are a manifestation of the continuing contradiction within a leadership searching for curricular reforms that will serve economic modernization without pressing the issue of political democratization.

In spite of the vicissitudes of the political scene, a gradual change is already underway in the knowledge system. It can be seen in new modes of curricular decision making and in the opening of numerous channels for the inflow of intellectual material from abroad. These are examined in the last two sections of the chapter.

Several key questions run through the chapter as a whole. Are the changes taking place in the structure and organization of knowledge superficial ones, simply the cosmetic insertion of new content into traditional patterns? And is a new foreign orthodoxy giving the appearance of modernity in a way parallel to Soviet influences of the fifties? Or do these changes represent a genuine abandonment of the Confucian concept of knowledge regimentation for political order? Are new foundations being laid for political participation and for the critical assimilation of foreign things that can serve China?

New Content, Old Patterns

The organization of the Chinese higher curriculum in the early sixties maintained Soviet contours even though political relations with the Soviet Union had been broken off. A set of canonized disciplines and professional specializations linked to the hierarchical structure of the bureaucracy through the mechanism of the Five-Year Plan provided an effective tool for the maintenance of a hierarchical sociopolitical order. Their contribution to the socialist economy was direct yet tended toward sterility. Technical experts were formed for specifically anticipated slots, but there was little encouragement for creative thinking or problem solving. The conscious articulation of knowledge specializations to the socioeconomic structure meant that there was little external impetus for the transformation of knowledge patterns. Innovation consisted of adding new specializations (*zhuanye*), narrowly defined in accordance with specific sectoral needs, to old patterns. The separation of teaching and research, with major research isolated in institutes of the Chinese Academies of Science and Social Science, meant there was no strong internal dynamic for the transformation of knowledge patterns.

If we take 1965 as representative of the period, certain statistics relating to the higher curriculum are noteworthy: 65.5 percent of all students were enrolled in fields of the applied sciences, 15.2 percent in applied arts (mainly teacher training), 9.2 percent in pure theoretical sciences, 6.8 percent in the humanities, 2.7 percent in finance and economics, and 0.6 percent in political science and law. Those studying the theoretical human sciences concerned with issues of the socialist polity and economy thus made up only 3.3 percent of the total enrollment.[1]

Political science and law, the most select enrollment area, was highly unified, having only 1 specialization. In contrast there were 21 specializations in finance and economics, 72 in the arts, 55 in the pure sciences, 76 in teacher training and other applied arts, and 376 in the applied sciences. Engineering alone had grown from 107 specializations in 1952 to 315 by 1965.[2] The 601 specializations to which students were recruited matched needs identified in different sectors of the socialist bureaucracy, and annual recruitment quotas were decided in accordance with the guidelines of the Five-Year Plan for each sector. Four- and five-year programs leading to professional qualifications dominated with 644,000 (95.5 percent) enrolled in this type of program and only 30,428 (4.5 percent) enrolled in short-cycle practically oriented programs.[3]

The higher education system was closely integrated into the bureaucracy with around 200 higher institutions administered and funded by such central ministries as metallurgy, machine-building, light industry, agriculture and forestry, and public health. The Ministry of Education directly administered over 30 comprehensive, polytechnical, and teachers universities. Graduates from all these national-level institutions were given job allocations at the national level, within the sectors under the ministry to which their institutions were attached. A second echelon of higher institutions was administered and funded at the provincial level, and the graduates received provincial or local job allocations. Except for low-level teacher training institutions, higher education was not under the purview of local government authorities.

Control over all curricular content was centralized within the Ministry of Education. The "Decision on Unifying Management in the Higher Education System" passed by the State Council in May 1963 gave legal expression to this principle and was intended to promote unity of academic standards across the system.[4] In this document the Ministry of Education was given exclusive authority over decisions about the establishment of new specializations in all higher institutions, worked out through consultation with the State Planning Commission in light of needs defined in the Five-Year Plan. It had full responsibility for preparing teaching plans for each specialization, teaching outlines for each course, and textbooks that should be nationally standard and binding on all institutions. It was also responsible for political education in all institutions. In consultation with the State Planning Commission, which coordinated the manpower needs of all ministries, it decided on the enrollment quotas for each specialization each year, and the allocation of graduating students to posts throughout the system. It controlled the appointment of the leadership of all higher institutions and regulated the recruitment and promotion of staff.

A highly centralized system, not very different from that suggested by the European advisers of the 1930s, was given legal sanction through this document. It had a potential for maintaining excellent academic standards. These were defined, however, not in terms of creativity and practical problem solving, but in terms of fixed disciplines and narrowly defined specializations for which authoritative canons of true knowledge could be established. There was also the possiblity of an absolute political control over knowledge which was highly attractive to the Chinese leadership.

The second important document of this period, the Sixty Articles of Higher Education, expressed compellingly the combination of academic and political expediency represented by this structure and organization of curricular knowledge. It stated that the aims of higher institutions were to implement the Communist Party's educational policy and train the experts needed for socialist construction. Teaching was to be the primary task of higher institutions, and research, productive labor, and social activism were subordinate to the teaching function. All intellectuals were to be united in the service of socialist higher education and allowed free debates only over differences of a purely academic nature. Party leadership was to be strengthened through the central leadership role of the party committee in each higher institution, and its directives were to be implemented by the university president and academic council in a presidential responsibility system of management. Thought education was to be strengthened.[5]

These two documents were revived with minor modifications in the post-1978 period, which is the reason for this rather detailed consideration of their contents. In practice, they confirmed a structure and organization of knowledge in which European-Soviet patterns, superimposed on Chinese ones, gave an illusion of modernity but allowed no substantive transformation of the higher curriculum to take place. First the structure of knowledge is considered, that is, the hierarchical ordering of knowledge areas and the differential prestige attached to differing areas. Then the organization of knowledge is discussed using the concepts of classification and framing.

In chapter 1 it was noted how pure knowledge in the European tradition was defined in terms of the theoretical disciplines, while purity in the Chinese tradition was associated with the mental labor of scholar-officials who administered the imperial system on the basis of authoritative classical texts. Applied social sciences were the high-prestige knowledge which dominated and regulated all other knowledge areas in traditional China. In Communist China, political science and law constituted the knowledge area with the smallest enrollment of all fields (0.6 percent) yet a high potential for entrance into influential positions in the socialist bureaucracy. Its task was defined as "to adapt to the developing political-legal work of the socialist system by training in a planned way cadres and legal experts with specialist knowledge of politics and law, a devotion to the motherland and socialist construction and working class consciousness."[6]

The creation of institutions that would preserve the high status and directive role of political-legal knowledge was an interesting process. Between 1949 and 1965 a series of readjustments were made to ensure institutional patterns that gave a special position to this field of knowledge. University departments of political science and law, which had flourished in the pre-Liberation period, constituting 24.4 percent of the total higher enrollment in 1947,[7] were removed from the universities and combined to form four specialist institutions exclusively devoted to political science and law: the Beijing Institute of Political Science and Law, the East China Institute, the Southwest Institute, and the Northwest Institute.[8] By 1965 there were still only six such institutes.

The leading role in developing this field of knowledge was given to People's University in Beijing, whose law department hosted a number of Soviet experts and held major responsibility for translating Soviet materials and developing teaching plans, course outlines, and textbooks to be used throughout the country.[9] In addition to People's University, and the four specialist institutes, a few other comprehensive universities kept or reestablished departments of law and political economy which played a supportive role in educating political and legal cadres for the socialist system. These institutions also trained political educators and developed the theoretical material used in the foundation courses on politics required by all students of higher education. Three standard courses have remained the core of higher study over several decades: history of the Chinese Communist Party, political economy, and philosophy, taking up 10-15 percent of curricular time for all students.[10]

Second in importance to political science and law was finance and economics, which had a select, if somewhat larger, enrollment of 2.7 percent of the total in 1965, and a more diversified knowledge content embracing twenty-one specializations. People's University was again the leading institution for this area, combining Soviet academic materials with Chinese practice in the total reconstruction of the field needed for a socialist economy. Six specialist institutions of finance and economics were established in 1953, serving broad regional areas, and the economics departments of certain comprehensive universities were reformed to suit new needs.[11] By 1965 the number of these specialist institutes had grown to eighteen.

These two fields, small as they were in enrollments, produced experts who were the mental laborers par excellence of the new socialist system, guiding its development in accordance with the classics of Marxism-Leninism which provided a unified and authoritative body of theory. The institutional distribution of this high-prestige knowledge is significant. People's University was clearly the center, and it combined politics and law, finance and economics in a curricular content that covered in a modern form the high-prestige social sciences of Confucian China. As the arbiter of correct theory, its role was similar to that of the Hanlin Academy in traditional China.[12] It formed teachers and prepared textbooks for the other two kinds of institution: the specialist institutions of political science and law and finance and economics, training cadres for broad regional areas, and the departments of law, political economy, and economics in the comprehensive universities, whose curricular focus on pure arts and sciences preserved intact the ancient European definition of academic purity.

If one thinks of curricular knowledge in terms of a pyramid, then applied social sciences, first politics and law, then finance and economics, created the peak. Next beneath them on the pyramid were the pure theoretical sciences and arts, the disciplines of traditional Europe, concentrated in a small number of so-called comprehensive universities. These were equaled or even surpassed in prestige by the new technological specializations essential for industrialization and represented most powerfully in the great polytechnical universities. Below these were the specialist institutions, training experts in agriculture, forestry, medicine, specialist engineering areas, and finally at the bottom of the pyramid the teachers colleges. This structure, if examined closely, represents a fascinating combination of features of the Confucian and European traditional structuring of knowledge. For all the new content introduced, with its value for modernization tasks, the traditional structure remained unchallenged.

As for the organization of knowledge, clear boundaries between specializations were maintained through the teaching plan, the teaching outline, and the textbook. These were designated as the responsibility of the Ministry of Education in the 1963 Decision outlined above. The teaching plan for each specialization included four points: the purpose of formation in that specialization, the organization of time, the structuring of all the required courses (there were no electives), and the arrangement of the teaching environment. Four types of courses were distinguished: common courses (political science, physical education, productive labor, and foreign languages), foundation courses in basic disciplines, specialist foundation courses, and specialist courses.[13] Each specialization was self-contained, with students being given all their instruction under its auspices, having little contact even with other specializations in the same department.

The teaching outline ordered the knowledge content of each course, arranging the subject material to be transmitted according to the structure of the discipline and according to Marxist-Leninist theory.[14] It included a statement of aims and requirements for the course, a list of the important content areas in appropriate order, a list of basic reference texts, and teaching guidelines. It was the responsibility of the Ministry of Education to maintain the high standards of the teaching plan, teaching outline, and textbook and ensure that the latest scientific findings were incorporated into them. In this it had assistance from academic subject committees whose members were usually professors of the most prestigious institutions.

Teachers were thus the transmitters of authoritative knowledge which had been determined elsewhere. They themselves were organized within even more narrowly defined categories than students. Each specialization had several teaching and research groups (*jiaoyanzu*) responsible for different levels and types of courses within the teaching plan. The research carried out by these groups largely consisted of investigation into methods for transmitting authoritatively defined knowledge as effectively as possible.

This situation was very close to the traditional European one, particularly the French, with firm boundaries delimiting specializations that were in turn institutionally organized in a similar way to the old academic chair system. In China's special circumstances political authority was explicitly integrated with academic authority. Departments existed, but the main unit of curricular knowledge was the specialization, and it was this that was controlled at entry and exit point by the Ministry of Education and tightly linked to the socialist bureaucracy as a whole.[15] This might be described as strong classification, supporting both a hierarchical pattern of governance within the higher institution and a hierarchical ordering of society. Even stronger framing is evident in the central control over each aspect of the teaching process, textual content, ordering of subject matter, and timing for each segment of a course. No discretion over the pacing or timing of the knowledge being transmitted was allowed to teachers, and students had even less opportunity for creative participation in the pedagogical process.

The attitude toward knowledge expressed in this organization of the curriculum was revived in the post Cultural Revolution period. It might be illumined by a small anecdote. A student of mine in the English specialization of the Department of Foreign Languages and Literatures at Fudan University became greatly interested in philosophy. She located in the library Bertrand Russell's *History of Western Philosophy* and tried to borrow it. The library staff member quizzed her on which specialization she belonged to, and when it was discovered to be neither history nor philosophy, she was denied the book. This is an extreme example and should not be taken to represent general policy in Chinese university libraries, but it shows how the system made possible the policing of the boundaries of disciplines; it also indicates the narrowness of the contribution expected of university graduates.

A few statistics on the ratio of enrollments among subject areas, and the ratio between four-to-five-year professional programs and two-to-three-year short-cycle programs, will fill out this sketch of the patterns of the early sixties. Enrollments in political science and law dropped from 37,682 in 1947 to 7,338 in 1949 and continued to fall, reaching 4,144 in 1965. Enrollments in finance and economics dropped from 19,362 in 1949 to a low of 11,395 in 1959 and were back up to 18,119 by 1965. These two fields of the social sciences, which contributed most to the definition of China's new development model, were thus restricted to a tiny elite and actually dropped absolutely in enrollment in the face of a huge expansion of enrollments in all other knowledge areas. Engineering grew from 30,320 in 1949 to 295,273 in 1965, agriculture from 9,820 to 66,862, medicine from 15,234 to 108,470, teacher training from 12,039 to 137,561, arts from 11,829 to 40,098, pure sciences from 6,904 to 88,433.[16]

The burgeoning numbers and the rapid growth of specializations in these fields took place within the strict control of definition by narrow academic discipline and narrower professional field. The number of specializations proliferated from 215 in 1952, when the system was introduced, to 601 in 1965.[17] They produced technical experts or pure academic specialists who were not encouraged to think creatively about the political and economic development needs of the country. Their specialist diploma assured them a particular place within the socialist hierarchy where their skills could be directly useful and they would pose no threat to political order.

The second aspect of interest in the curricular structure is the striking imbalance between four-to-five-year regular (*benke*) programs offering professional qualifications and two-to-three-year short-cycle (*zhuanke*) programs for mid-level manpower needs. A balanced proportion of both types of graduates would have been appropriate for economic development needs, yet the lower qualification held far less promise for political influence and prestige. It was thus less attractive to students, higher education leaders, and ministries, all of whom wanted to see their particular knowledge area gain greater prominence.

Engineering is a good example of this situation, since huge enrollments made polytechnical and engineering universities among the most powerful in the new system. In 1949 there had been 23,118 enrolled in regular programs and 7,202 in short-cycle programs. By 1965 regular enrollments had been increased to 292,680, while short-cycle enrollments had dropped to 2,593. The higher qualification was much more desirable, with the result that short-cycle programs were virtually abandoned, in spite of pressing economic needs for this type of manpower. Not surprisingly, political science and law had an almost nonexistent short-cycle enrollment, and finance and economics had a very low one. The only fields in which there was any success in developing short-cycle programs were areas of least prestige in the pyramid depicted earlier: medicine, teacher training, and humanities. By 1965 there was a ratio of 9,952 short-cycle enrollments to 72,909 regular enrollments in medicine, 7,320 short-cycle to 86,948 regular enrollments in teacher training, and 5,905 short-cycle to 40,053 regular enrollments in humanities. The total short-cycle enrollment in 1965 was 30,420, contrasting with 644,088 in regular programs.[18]

These statistics, representing the situation on the eve of the Cultural Revolution in 1965, reveal the intense contradiction created by Communist higher education policy. On the one hand, there were remarkable achievements in the number and academic quality of personnel trained in the various applied scientific areas needed for economic modernization. On the other hand, those social sciences seen as having a directive role, most notably political science and law, were kept under a very tight rein. They were used to transmit an unquestioned political orthodoxy that drew in spirit, though not in content, on the Confucian knowledge tradition. Following a Soviet model, the Communist government thus achieved what the Nationalist government had tried to do when they reduced social science enrollments and introduced curricular reforms based on the European model in the 1930s. Both regimes were unconsciously reproducing features of the Confucian social order that held promise for political control.

The Cultural Revolution represented a dramatic attempt at resolving this contradiction. The lines along which curricular content was transformed have been sketched out in chapter 1. Political science and law as fields of specialist study were abolished with People's University and the four regional institutes closed down for the full ten-year period.[19] Economics and finance went into an eclipse almost as serious. All students were to be involved in studying the political and economic development needs of Chinese society, and some studies of the period suggest they learned very little else. All regular programs were abolished, and short-cycle programs became the norm. This was intended to break the linkages between the higher education system and the hierarchical power structure of the socialist bureaucracy as well as to meet the real economic needs of development. The very definition of knowledge areas by specialization was discontinued, and students were recruited to broad knowledge areas.[20] A strong emphasis was placed on knowledge for practical economic development and direct political participation.[21]

A few statistics for enrollments during the Cultural Revolution period reveal the change in knowledge emphasis. After the lacuna between 1967 and 1971 when most institutions were closed, enrollments for political science and law, which had been 4,144 in 1965, only reached 410 by 1976. Those in finance and economics, which had been 18,119 in 1965, were 6,569 in 1976. Total enrollments in 1976 were 564,715, contrasting with the figure of 674,436 in 1965. While there were considerable decreases in engineering, natural sciences, and humanities, enrollments in two lesser prestige areas showed considerable growth: teacher training from 94,268 to 109,731, medicine from 82,861 to 98,336.[22]

Interestingly, present curricular reforms address some of the same issues as did the Cultural Revolution reforms, though in very different ways. In contrast to the radical abolition of the social sciences as ruling disciplines in 1966, these fields are now being given their place alongside of other curricular areas with their content diversified and their enrollments rapidly increased. The direction seems to be toward an integration of the social sciences with other knowledge areas in more broadly defined programs, a more gradual way of moving toward an integrated curricular code than what was attempted in the Cultural Revolution period. Equally, the importance of short-cycle programs for mid-level manpower needs is now being recognized. The intention is to achieve a balance in higher enrollments of half regular and half short-cycle students, with most of the increase being in short-cycle programs. Before considering these reforms in detail, I turn to a discussion of the political context that has made them possible.

The Political Economic Context of Reform

The Third Plenum of the Eleventh Central Committee of the Communist Party, held in December 1978, is now widely regarded as the turning point in

favor of Deng Xiaoping's pragmatic policies for China's internal development and the maintenance of an open door to the advanced capitalist world
externally. This was affirmed in the "Resolution on Certain Questions in the
History of Our Party since the Founding of the PRC" adopted by the Sixth
Plenum of the Eleventh Central Committee in June 1981. This document
acknowledged Mao's central role in the Chinese Communist movement
while condemning unequivocally the ultraleftism of the Cultural Revolution
period and attributing it to arrogance and arbitrariness in the aging Mao,
the persistence of feudal autocratic thinking among other powerful party
cadres of the period, and the party's failure to create a legal structure for effective democratic institutions. Four fundamental political principles were
laid down as the nonnegotiable context of the post-1978 movement toward
"emancipating the mind and seeking truth from facts": upholding the
socialist road, the people's democratic dictatorship, the leadership of the
Communist Party, and Marxism-Leninism Mao Zedong Thought.[23]

Both the external exigencies of international involvement and the internal rationale given for the Cultural Revolution debacle have meant that one
of the the most compelling political trends of the post-1978 period has been
the drafting of legislation and the strengthening of socialist democratic institutions. A new state constitution was passed in December 1982,[24] and a
whole series of new legislation has been passed in the areas of criminal justice, the family, internal economic activity, taxation, and foreign economic
relations.[25]

Elections have been revived at the local government level, with the selection of members for local people's congresses at the township and county
level by direct popular election. Another important political development
has been the revitalization of the right of appeal to the party for the redress
of past injustices, which has led to the rehabilitation of both intellectuals
and party cadres whose problems go back as far as the Antirightist movement of 1957. Perhaps the most remarkable evidence of political democratization is to be found in the Chinese press, which has become more
frank in depicting China's social problems than at any time since Liberation
and provides a forum for debate and discussion over differing views and
policies.[26]

All of these developments, however, must be seen within the context of
the four fundamental principles, which assure the absolute control of the
Communist Party. The harsh treatment of participants in the democracy
movement of 1979 and the extensive use of capital punishment in dealing
with aberrrant elements left over from the Cultural Revolution decade indicate that the concept of democracy has to be applied with some reservation
to the Chinese situation.[27]

On the economic side, changes have been even more dramatic. The rural
responsibility system, in which land is contracted to the peasant household

and specialized households are encouraged to develop a diversified rural economy, has demonstrated spectacular success in raising agricultural productivity in the short term at least.[28] This has been succeeded by plans for urban economic reform presented in detail in the CCP Decision on the Reform of the Economic Structure adopted by the Third Plenum of the Twelfth Central Committee in October 1984.[29] In this document, reform is seen in terms of a contradiction between the relations of production and the forces of production and a need for the superstructural relations of production to be reformed so as to promote the growth of the forces of production.

This superstructural reform is discussed on two levels. The first is a readjustment of relations between urban enterprises and the state that gives enterprises both greater economic flexibility and decision-making power and a greater responsibility for economic success or failure. The second is a readjustment of the relations between the enterprise and its workers such that elected representatives of the workers participate in democratic management of the enterprise. Fundamental to the success of this urban responsibility system is a reformed managerial group able to take responsibility for economic decisions at the enterprise level. In the education of this group, the document states that "we must draw on the world's advanced methods of management, including those of developed capitalist countries, that conform to the laws of modern socialized production."[30]

Parallel to this enhancement of enterprise autonomy has been a limited enhancement of regional autonomy, especially for those areas that are seen as leading the way in economic relations with the industrialized world—the special economic zones and the fourteen coastal cities, which have been given considerable commercial autonomy to enable them to attract foreign capital.[31] The encouragement of economic cooperation between coastland and hinterland in order that development inequality should not be too blatant is based on an economic more than a political rationale.[32]

Higher Education Policy since 1978

Higher education has been seen as vital to economic success in this new political context. In his speech at the National Education work conference in April 1978, Deng Xiaoping affirmed the importance of education in transforming China "into a powerful modern socialist country" and spoke of the need to "master and advance modern science and culture and the new techniques and technologies of all trades and professions."[33]

The first approach to higher education reform under the new leadership, however, amounted to a revival of the patterns of the early 1960s, described earlier in this chapter. In 1979, the Central Committee affirmed the "Decision on Unifying Management in Higher Education" of 1963 as correct, and once again the Ministry of Education was given the role of regulating nationally standard teaching plans, teaching outlines, and textbooks.[34] The introduction of new knowledge content linked to modernization requirements was achieved by simply adding new specializations to existing patterns of organization. The total number of specializations grew from 601 in 1965 to 1,039 in 1980.[35] This process was centrally controlled by responsible bureaus within the Ministry of Education. While it administered only 38 higher institutions directly, it made all major curricular decisions for the 226 institutions administered by other national ministries and the 411 administered by provinces, municipalities, and autonomous regions.[36]

The Sixty Articles were also revived and circulated for discussion among higher institutions. After some modification they were accepted by the Ministry of Education as the correct guidelines for the development of the higher education system. However, four important changes in these articles hold promise for a new direction in Chinese universities. First, there is a new emphasis on research, with universities called upon to give equal importance to research and teaching. Second, intellectuals have been officially recognized as part of the working class, which suggests greater freedom for them than the mere guarantee of academic debate in the earlier version. Third, university presidents are to have greater powers in the internal administration of higher institutions vis-à-vis the Party Committee's supervisory role. Finally, political education is redefined in a more open way.[37]

With the revival of the patterns of the early sixties and the reaffirmation of the two documents that gave them legal form, the contradiction between transformed knowledge patterns for economic development and traditional ones for political control seems to have reemerged. A firmly reestablished central authority regulates the expansion of specializations within the same narrow, controlled framework that had been established in the 1950s under Soviet influence. However, the "Decision on the Reform of the Education System" adopted by the party's Central Committee at a National Education Conference in May 1985, has opened up a whole range of reform possibilities. The seeds of change hinted at in the revision to the Sixty Articles are more evident in this document.

The document envisages higher institutions as having two main responsibilities: training advanced specialized personnel and developing science, technology, and culture. The first reflects the persistence of the Soviet orientation of the 1950s, which dictated the service of higher education to specifically projected manpower needs in highly specialized fields. The second indicates the restoration of the research function to universities, which could provide an internal dynamic for curricular transformation.

The main rationale for reform given in the decision is "to change the management system of excessive government control of the institutions of higher education, expand decision making in the institutions under the guidance of unified educational policies and plans of the state, strengthen the connection of the institutions of higher education with production organizations, scientific research organizations, and other social establishments, and enable the institutions of higher education to take the initiative and ability to meet the needs of economic and social development."[38]

This rationale clearly follows the theme of the documents on the reform of the economic structure, which stressed the autonomy and responsibility of enterprises. It is also related to the reform of the science and technology system, discussed at the National Science Conference of March 1985. A more flexible scientific research system is emerging, with more direct and lively linkages between research and teaching as well as research and production. The new Science Fund accepts applications from universities and research institutes of the academies equally, and these are judged through peer review, giving higher institutions the opportunity to develop their research function more fully.[39]

Several measures are indicated in the educational reform document that will make possible a new independence for higher institutions. First, the links between the higher education system and the socialist bureaucracy are weakened in that enrollment and job allocation according to the state plan no longer hold a monopoly. Higher institutions may now enroll additional students on the basis of contracts with enterprises for particular types of formation. Private, fee-paying students can also be enrolled, and these will be responsible to find their own jobs on graduation. Also, universities are being given a more direct role in the job assignment of students under the state plan.

Furthermore, higher institutions can now participate in the definition of the curriculum, as indicated in the new powers given to them: "power to readjust the objectives of various disciplines, formulate teaching plans and programs, and compile and select teaching materials; the power to accept projects from and cooperate with other social establishments for scientific research and technological development, as well as setting up combines involving teaching, scientific research, and production; the power to suggest appointments and removals, to dispose of capital construction investment and of funds allocated by the state; and the power to develop international educational and academic exchanges by using their own funds."[40]

These remarkable new powers are hedged around only by the affirmation of the role of the newly established State Education Commission in giving overall guidance to the system. Three major changes in the structure and organization of the higher curriculum are envisaged as part of this national policy. The ratio between natural and social sciences is to be changed, with a considerable increase in finance and economics, political science and law, and management. Second, the overspecialization of knowledge areas and categories is to be reformed and provision made for the growth of new and frontier science courses that are interdisciplinary and interspecialization in nature. Third, the ratio between regular and short-cycle programs is to be changed by a rapid acceleration of short-cycle programs and the stabilization of regular enrollments.[41] The redefinition of regular specializations and large increases in short-cycle enrollments, where innovative curricula are more easily introduced, should mean a considerable weakening in the classification of curricular knowledge.

Other reforms touch upon the framing of curricular knowledge and open the possibility of much greater control by teachers and students over the pedagogical process. Curricula are to be refined and updated and a greater element of practice is to be introduced. Teachers and academic departments will have considerable discretion over the formulation of teaching plans and course outlines and the selection of textbooks. Students, for their part, can exercise some choice through a partial elective system which is now widely used. Also, the reduction in the required number of course hours in favor of self-study arrangements should make possible greater student initiative.[42]

In short, there seem to be possibilities for reforming the organization of knowledge along lines reminiscent of the Cultural Revolution rhetoric discussed in chapter 1: the breaking down of the boundaries between disciplines and specializations, increasing links between academic knowledge and the real-life knowledge of productive practice, a general localization of control over the creation and transmission of knowledge with teachers and students playing a participant role, and an increased emphasis on short-cycle programs for the training of mid-level manpower.

In the Cultural Revolution, curricular reforms were achieved through intense ideological struggle. In the present situation, there seems to be a balance between central political guidance, which is to ensure that the overall manpower needs of the economy are met, and the initiative of administrators and scholars at the institution level. For administrators, there is the economic incentive of market forces in the demands of thriving enterprises for graduates and for research results. Knowledge has become a commodity. As for intellectuals within higher institutions, they are allowed to express their natural propensities in the new freedom given them to participate in curricular development. Historically this group has had a predilection for the more open, pragmatic approach to knowledge organization that characterizes the American system, an orientation rooted in the values of the *shuyuan* of traditional China. It seems, therefore, that both the politico-economic and cultural conditions for a gradual transformation of knowledge patterns are present.

What in fact is happening to the higher curriculum in the present period? Between 1980 and 1985, the number of higher institutions increased from 675 to 1,016. About 140 of the new institutions are vocational universities with short-cycle programs administered by city governments, the new administrative echelon that has emerged. It is in this type of institution that the major future growth is expected to take place. Another high growth area is teacher training institutions, which increased from 172 in 1980 to 253 in 1985. Institutions of political science and law grew from 7 to 24, institutions of finance and economics from 30 to 62. Comprehensive universities increased from 38 to 43 while institutions in the applied sciences showed more moderate growth rates.[43]

The beginning of a change in the ratio between natural and social sciences is already evident. The number of students admitted to humanities rose from 4.6 percent of the total to 7.3 percent over this period; finance and economics from 4.3 percent to 8.7 percent; and political science and law from 1.0 percent to 2.1 percent, representing a growth from 5.3 percent to 10.8 percent in the theoretical social sciences. Engineering and forestry also increased both absolutely and proportionately, while the natural sciences and other applied sciences fell slightly. The number of specializations over this period began to decrease, indicating a redefinition of knowledge areas already under way. In 1980 there were 1,039 specializations, and by 1985 this had fallen to 823, with a drop from 537 to 368 in engineering, on the one hand, and a growth from 7 to 11 in political science and law, on the other. The ratio of regular to short-cycle students admitted in 1980 was 77,088 to 264,142, and by 1985 it was 301,598 short-cycle to 317,637 regular.[44] Thus a fair balance between these two types of program had been achieved by the autumn of 1985.

Progressive aspects of Chinese scholarly tradition, especially those related to the *shuyuan*, favor the curricular reforms that envisage greater interdisciplinarity, the integration of theory and practice in a problem-solving approach to knowledge, and a larger and more diversified enrollment in the applied social sciences. There is, however, little prospective support in the intellectual community for short-cycle programs leading to less prestigious certificates and job assignments. The Chinese leadership has dealt with this situation in an interesting way. In June 1985, shortly after the promulgation of the educational reform decision, the Ministry of Education was transformed into a state commission and put under the leadership of then Vice-Premier Li Peng.[45] This raised its status to equivalence with the State Economic Commission and the State Planning Commission and was intended to enhance its authority in educational policy making in relation to the other national ministries that administer the many polytechnic and specialized higher institutions. Thus its authority was reaffirmed at the very time that its control over detailed curricular decision making, enrollments, and finance was reduced.

The State Education Commission has retained the key decision-making power over the establishment or cancellation of a regular specialization and over annual enrollment figures for each specialization in accordance with the state plan. Provincial institutions or national institutions under other ministries must apply through the appropriate bureau of higher education to the State Education Commission for permission to establish a new regular specialization. National and regional needs as well as academic considerations are taken into account by the commission in these decisions. However, the establishment of new short-cycle specializations and enrollments for these are left completely to the initiative of provincial and local authorities.[46] This seems to have encouraged their proliferation in response to practical needs of the local area.

Consequences of Curricular Reform

The economic promise of the higher education reforms that have been described seems to be without question. The greatly increased number of young people trained for mid-level technical posts will fill a serious gap in the structure of the work force. The integration of theoretical and applied scientific studies in more broadly defined specializations at the higher level as well as the new research linkages between higher institutions and productive enterprises should enable young professionals to have a creative, problem-solving orientation in their work assignments. The large increase in the social sciences, especially in the areas of finance, economics, and management, and the integration of new courses in these fields into such programs as engineering should make possible the training of a management contingent suited to the new approach to enterprise management outlined in the Economic Reform Document.

There are, of course, some problems in regulating the new situation so that economic needs are served in a balanced way. Thus the State Council promulgated provisional regulations on the management of higher education in June 1986 to give more specific guidelines concerning financial profits gained through contract research and contract training of personnel for enterprises or other units, limiting these activities within bounds that will not prejudice the academic quality of higher institutions.[47] Similarly, the new freedom given to higher institutions to participate actively in the job assignment of graduates through linkages with enterprises and other employing units has had to be curbed.[48] While only 23.6 percent of all graduates in 1985 were assigned posts within the state plan, this percentage was raised to 63.8 percent in 1986, since "the system did not ensure that key industries and government units, especially those in remote and backward regions, received much needed graduates."[49] Nevertheless, a long-term move toward the abolition of unified university graduate allocation has been reaffirmed.[50] Over time, it seems quite likely that the greater flexibility and mobility of the work force at both high and mid-levels, seen as desirable for economic development, will be realized.

The political implications of higher curricular reform may be the more serious issue at stake in the present period. The growth in enrollments in the key social science areas of political science and law, economics and finance from 43,111 (5.8 percent of the total) in 1980 to 183,672 (10.8 percent of the total) in 1985 represents a near fourfold increase in young persons formed in these areas of key importance for the future direction of Chinese socialism. In addition, general social sciences electives have been introduced into many other programs, and young people studying the sciences and humanities are encouraged to reflect in a critical way on problems of the socioeconomic system. Furthermore, required political education courses have been modified in a more liberal direction.

Generally, both the structure and organization of knowledge have been substantively changed. The curricular pyramid of the sixties has now been considerably flattened with the social sciences taking their place alongside of other knowledge areas, experiencing a parallel diversification and adopting a more empirical and experimental orientation.[51] As for the organization of knowledge, a redefinition of disciplines and specializations has weakened classification, and new possibilities for teacher and student contribution to the definition of curricular content have modified framing. These changes in the structure and organization of knowledge have implications for both the internal power structure of the university and the wider political power structure.

A speech made by Vice-Premier Wan Li at the National Education Conference in May 1985 reveals the continuing ambivalence on the part of China's political leadership over the transformation of the curriculum. He expatiated at length on the need to abolish a traditional educational theory and teaching method of the closed type, with contents fixed and ossified and products obedient and docile. This must be replaced by creativity, the opening up of new fields of knowledge, attempts to understand and transform the natural environment rather than passively adapting to it, the ability to sum up new experience and develop new theories, and so forth. Wan Li warned, however, that "one should never think that discipline can be disregarded and a deaf ear can be turned to the word of higher authorities or even the Party Central Committee, whenever the ability to think independently and the spirit of making innovations are stressed." This warning was expressed in direct connection with the "ten chaotic years of the Cultural Revolution."[52]

One year later in the spring of 1986, the thirtieth anniversary of the Hundred Flowers Movement of 1956 provided an opportunity for Chinese intellectuals to raise fundamental questions of intellectual freedom. In the lively discussions that accompanied this celebration, three distinctive positions on intellectual freedom were put forward. The first, very close to the European-Soviet definition of academic freedom, suggested that it was possible to make a clear demarcation between political and academic issues, and that complete freedom for debates and differences of view should be guaranteed within the university community on academic issues.[53] The second view was that freedom for debates on academic issues within the university community required a democratization of the internal structure of university life, since the democratic centralism of the state socialist system did not provide a suitable milieu for intellectual debates in the university community.[54] The third and most radical position was that it was not possible to draw a clear demarcation between political and academic issues, and that the only effective guarantee of intellectual freedom was the democratization of the political system.[55]

Interestingly, the terms in which the subsequent call for political structure reform were couched coincided precisely with the general line of analysis developed in this volume—the sense of a contradiction between the transformation required by economic reform and the resistance of a rigid political system. "The high tide of China's economic reform is now sweeping over the structures and functions of the noneconomic social systems. The reform and building of the political structure are put on the agenda and have attracted the attention of theoretical workers," stated a commentator for the progressive Shanghai publication, *Shijie jingji daobao*.[56] By the autumn of 1986 there seemed to be a widely shared perception among the intellectual community that if the profound effects of economic change were to continue in the desired direction, changes had to be made in the political structure toward greater flexibility and participation. Party rule since 1949 was seen as informed by aspects of feudal autocratic traditions not easily eliminated. These must now give way before the floodgate of economic transformation.[57]

The call for reform generally involved four aspects, all under discussion at different times since the early 1980s. The first was the strengthening of people's congresses at all levels from the local to the national, so that the people's representatives could speak out on behalf of the electorate and address inquiries to or even impeach government officials when necessary. New electoral laws, published in November 1986, stipulated that deputies from township and county congresses could be nominated by ten voters, and the number of candidates should exceed that of places by between 50 and 100 percent.[58] The second aspect of reform called for a clear demarcation of tasks between the party and the government with policy and general leadership separated from the day-to-day running of government institutions which should draw more and more on the expert personnel and soft scientific research results produced by higher institutions. Third, a further reform in the cadre system was called for, with firmer implementation of limits on terms of office and a more effective supervision of the work of cadres by both state organs and people's representatives. Finally, emphasis on the strengthening of the legal system drew attention to the need for both legislation in many areas and new attitudes toward the law. The rule of law should replace the rule of man, and party personnel and organizations should be as fully subject to the law as ordinary citizens.[59]

These broad debates over political structure reform were mirrored by parallel debates on the reform of internal administration in Chinese higher institutions toward greater flexibility and participation. University presidents complained that none of the new freedoms promised by the educational reform document were fully realized, and various forums were used to press for greater autonomy.[60] The higher institution that led the way in internal administrative reforms was the Chinese University of Science and Technology, established in 1958 under the Chinese Academy of Sciences and a leading institution in both the basic and applied sciences. During October and November 1986, the *People's Daily* carried a series of five articles featuring the reforms being carried out in the internal administration and governance of this university.[61] A representative assembly with members elected from faculty and technical and support staff was organized to supervise the work of the executive committee responsible for general leadership and the evaluation and academic degrees committees, which also operated at the central level. Academic heads of departments were also given greater say in decision making. Conditions were provided for open discussion of academic questions, matters of university administration and budget, and broad political questions among faculty and students.

The atmosphere created was one in which scientific and intellectual leadership was harmonized with party supervision in such persons as Fang Lizhi, the distinguished astrophysicist and party member, who was vice-president of CUST. He gave several widely publicized interviews in the autumn of 1986 calling for the strengthening of China's intellectuals as a social group and their development of an independent mentality so that they "do not always yield to power and link their prospects with an official career."[62]

Lively discussion over political structure reform and intrauniversity administrative reform culminated in a massive outbreak of student activism, the largest such movement since the Cultural Revolution period, in December 1986. At least seventeen Chinese cities were the scene of student marches, in some cases involving up to five thousand students. The intellectual conditions for such a movement can be seen taking shape in the curricular reforms analyzed earlier, particularly the large increases in social science enrollments and the more open and flexible approach to the organization of knowledge. The more specific concerns that sparked it off seem to have been threefold.

Agitation over issues of political structure reform took concrete form in Hefei and Tianjin, where university students protested the illegal interference of party authorities in the nomination of deputies for local and provincial people's congresses. In other cases specific institutional issues took precedence, with students campaigning for a greater voice in their own affairs. Finally, increasing material pressures upon students and faculty in a period when other groups in Chinese society are experiencing increasing prosperity were the main cause of discontent in provincial and local universities. Efforts at improving efficiency and using more cost-effective management practices, suggested by World Bank advisers among others, are making themselves felt.[63] Students at local-level institutions have to pay modest fees, and the guaranteed stipend for students of provincial and national institutions is being changed into a system of scholarships, bursaries, and loans which expects a much greater individual and family contribution to the cost of higher education.[64]

Of the three kinds of issue, the key and most disturbing one for the leadership relates to the legitimacy of the political power of the party, which was brought into question by students in the powerful universities of Shanghai and Beijing. On December 18, the mayor of Shanghai went to Jiaotong University to calm students down on the eve of the massive protests of December 19-22. One student dared to ask whether he had been elected by the people of Shanghai, and another raised the question whether the constitutional changes of 1982, which denied the rights of the people to put up large character posters and engage in great debates, had been endorsed by the people. This was a direct questioning of the actual representativeness of delegates to the National People's Congress who are elected by lower-level congresses. In the election of deputies to these congresses students have protested against party manipulation on numerous occasions since 1980.

Close upon the Shanghai movement followed demonstrations of students in major Beijing universities—People's, Beida, Qinghua, and Beijing Teachers University. In this case the municipal government was prepared in advance with a ban on all demonstrations that did not have prior permits. This limited their scale without effectively quashing them. In defiance of the ban, students marched on the Great Square of the People on New Year's Day. Some were arrested under the terms of the ban, and the rest returned on January 2 to demand the release of those being held, a demand very quickly met. The movement culminated on January 5 in a public burning of the *Beijing Daily* and the *People's Daily*, which were accused by the students of misrepresenting their genuine concerns for political democratization and institutional reform. By this action, students called into question the legitimacy of official ideology and its organs, the party-controlled press.[65]

Up until the end of December, the response of party and university leaders to students' criticism and demands were relatively compliant. Election processes were rescheduled at both Hefei and Tianjin in recognition of the validity of students protests. When Vice-Premier Wan Li visited Hefei at the end of November he cautioned the need for maintaining discipline but did not question the general orientation of the institutional reforms at CUST.[66] The dominant view during December seemed to be that students' concerns were justified and should be given attention, even though the disruption to normal economic life in the major cities caused by their marches was reprehensible.

Deng Xiaoping, however, finally spoke out for greater firmness in controlling students and intellectuals in early January, and intensive intraparty discussions at the highest level culminated in the resignation of Hu Yaobang as general secretary of the Chinese Communist Party and his replacement by Premier Zhao Ziyang.[67] In the wake of Hu's resignation after a self-confession of inadequate firmness in dealing with tendencies toward bourgeois liberalization within party ranks, there followed a reshuffle at the top level. This was accompanied by public reproof of certain intellectuals within the party, who had spoken out on the issue of political structure reform. For some persons, such as Fang Lizhi and the writers Liu Binyan and Wang Ruowang, this rebuke involved explusion from the party.[68]

If we return to the three views on intellectual freedom outlined earlier, it seems clear that students and intellectuals were lobbying for the most radical position—an intellectual freedom guaranteed by the visible democratization of socialist political institutions. The response of party authorities suggests a position close to the first and most conservative view. Freedom for scholarly debates over purely academic subjects, especially in the areas of science, technology, and economics, is likely to be maintained, because it is seen as essential to economic reform needs, but central political control must be reasserted.

This reassertion of political control poses a problem for the leadership in that it is still committed to rapid economic modernization[69] and to the curricular changes that hold promise for economic reform needs. Thus the gradual transformation in the structure and organization of knowledge described earlier is almost certain to continue, as is the open door for an inflow of foreign-derived expertise. The next two sections describe the process of curricular change already in motion and review policies and practices relating to the open door in China's higher education. The continuation of these two trends is likely to mean continuing tension between knowledge transformation for economic development and knowledge regulation for political control.

The Process of Curricular Decision Making

Within the State Education Commission, the first and second departments of higher education are responsible for decision making across the major fields of knowledge. In 1985 the first department had six bureaus responsible respectively for (1) the humanities as taught in comprehensive universities; (2) finance and economics and political science and law; (3) foreign languages; (4) the sciences as taught in comprehensive universities; (5) both humanities and science specializations in teachers universities; and (6) fine arts. The second department was responsible for the curricula of engineering universities, agricultural and forestry institutions, and medical universities.[70] In 1987 responsibility for the basic science specializations in comprehensive and normal universities was also moved to this department.[71] General political education in higher institutions is the responsibility of a separate department, as is the case with physical education.

The second department of higher education seems to have gone farther toward establishing new patterns of activity than the first, so I begin with a discussion of curricular developments in engineering and agriculture. Between 1978 and 1983, a whole series of meetings was held involving officials of this department, representatives of higher institutions and the ministries administering them, and the major enterprises that employ engineering graduates. These meetings culminated in the creation of an entirely new list of specializations (*mulu*), amounting to a total of 210 in contrast with the 537 in place in 1980.[72] The main principles for this adjustment process were strengthening the theoretical foundation of each specialization, broadening its definition with reference to professional activity, and linking it to the manpower development needs of the Sixth and Seventh Five-Year Plans.

While the traditional engineering specializations have been radically redefined in much broader terms, greatly reducing their number, new specializations have been added in three important areas: six or seven specializations in aspects of management as related to engineering; several theoretical specializations such as applied physics, applied mathematics, and applied optics; and several in the computer field. These changes reflect three important trends—a broader definition of knowledge area with greater emphasis on foundation theory, a new emphasis on the social sciences integrated within the applied natural sciences, and a response to the new technological revolution in the development of new high technology areas. Young graduate engineers should thus be creative, thinking people, with a potential for political and social leadership as well as technical expertise.[73]

Each of the 210 specializations in the list is defined by a brief introduction (*jianjie*) which states the main purpose, principles, and key required courses for a specialization. Within these general guidelines, each university has the freedom to create its own teaching plan and course outlines and to select the text and reference books it wishes. The same pattern holds true for the agriculture-forestry list, which was completed in May 1986 and includes a new stress on management fields, as well as a broader definition of specializations including some in engineering.[74]

Parallel changes are going on in the first department, where the Bureaus of Economics and Finance, Political Science and Law seems to have moved most quickly. In 1979 a national meeting was held to discuss economics and finance, coordinated by the Ministry of Education, the State Planning Commission, and the ministries of Finance, Banking, and Foreign Economic Relations and Trade. Teaching plans for ten to fifteen important specializations were drafted, but these are regarded as reference materials in contrast to the law-like status of the teaching plans of the fifties and sixties. A new list, including forty-seven specializations, was still under discussion in June 1987. During that summer, a national planning meeting was held to develop guidelines for programs in economics and management with the involvement of some distinguished Western academics supported through one of the World Bank projects discussed in chapter 7. For political science and law, the number of specializations had grown to twenty-three by 1987, representing quite a remarkable diversification of knowledge content from the unified one-specialization situation of the 1960s.[75]

In the humanities, a meeting was held in Wuhan in 1978 in which general guidelines for major disciplines were set, and since then meetings within specially defined fields have been held to discuss curricular content. The main principles for reform are the strengthening of foundation theory in all specializations, a focus on the development of applied fields such as journalism, archives, and museum studies, an attempt to ensure young successors for esoteric fields such as minority languages and cultures, and an intention to improve quality in the major disciplines of history, literature, and philosophy, but not to increase enrollments.[76]

The department sees its role as assisting in the development of a new and more precise definition of specializations in an approved list and regulating the establishment of new specializations throughout the system on the basis of general manpower needs, the regional situation, and the ability of particular institutions in terms of faculty and resources. Rather than producing authoritative teaching plans and outlines, they help to organize teaching material committees (*jiaoyu ziliao hui*) that will develop new curricular materials. They envisage the professional associations for major disciplines and specializations taking an increasingly active role in future curricular development. However, this department must mediate the tension between professional educators bent on strengthening the theoretical and disciplinary aspects of their programs and enterprises and ministries desiring a precise definition of knowledge area suited to their manpower needs.[77]

At the level of the provincial, municipal, and city bureaus of higher education, curricular decision making has two aspects. For all academic (*benke*) specializations, the bureau must channel applications from provincial institutions to the appropriate departments of the State Educational Commission. However, for short-cycle programs the bureau has the authority to respond to all applications directly and to set guidelines for curricular development that are consonant with the development needs of the province or city. In discussions with the leadership of the provincial bureau of higher education in Liaoning and Jilin provinces, one of the most compelling trends evident was the increasing provision for management education. In Jilin, about 14 percent of the total enrollment in 1985 was in new management departments that had been added to various types of higher institutions.[78] In Liaoning province, about half of the engineering and agricultural universities had new management departments, and there was a new school of management in the provincial comprehensive university.[79]

In this sketch of the process of curricular change it is already possible to see some transformation taking place in the structure of knowledge. The applied social sciences, political science, law, economics, and management are being reintegrated within a broad spectrum of higher institutions, while still developed in a certain number of specialized institutes. The general attitude accompanying this change in structure is that law, political science, management, and economics are now everyone's concern, not just that of an elite group of the party faithful. Hierarchy still exists, to be sure, mainly in terms of the greater prestige attached to well-known national institutions as against lesser known or provincial ones, but the rigid pyramid-like structure of knowledge areas has been modified.

The organization of knowledge is also being transformed toward a weakening of classification and framing. Specializations are being more broadly defined, the credit system is being widely adopted, allowing students to chose up to 30 percent of their courses,[80] and there is a general reduction in the number of class hours required, allowing more time for individual and small group study.[81] The present curricular patterns are still a long way from an integrated code, but it may be of interest to ask what sort of ideological conception provides the unifying thread for this more flexible and open organization of knowledge.

For this, we must turn to the politics courses that are required foundation courses for all higher students and which till recently have included three standard courses: history of the Chinese Communist Party, philosophy, and political economy. These courses are now in the process of reformulation.[82] History of the Chinese Communist Party is being replaced by Chinese revolutionary history, including all revolutionary movements, rather than exclusively those under party leadership. The standard philosophy course used to focus on *Das Kapital*, but now it is to consider Marxism-Leninism much more broadly in its philosophical, economic, and historical aspects. Finally, the course on political economy is being renamed "the problems of socialist construction" and expanded to cover a range of socio-economic issues in China's development experience.[83] New courses in Communist ideals and professsional morality are also being developed.[84]

The reform of political education now under discussion calls for a new type of political instructor with a wide grasp of sociopolitical issues and an understanding of moral psychology.[85] To this end the State Education Commission has set up twelve special departments in social studies at well-known comprehensive, normal and engineering universities, offering a two-year graduate program without thesis for such instructors. Courses include psychology, sociology, philosophy, and literary theory as well as political science. Provincial higher education bureaus are setting up parallel programs, providing two-year training for graduates of short-cycle programs. The graduates of these programs are expected to form a new group of younger political instructors whose approach will be less dogmatic and more rooted in psychological theory and sociological understanding.[86] In fact it is very difficult to recruit talented young people for this kind of work, even among young party members. Political instructors lack academic prestige, even with recent attempts to give them a similar career structure to academic faculty,[87] and they face a difficult challenge in the conditions of 1987. The increasing sophistication and critical spirit of the student body they deal with will require all their skills, if political consensus is to be forged in a noncoercive way and young people are to be adequately motivated to give their best to national development needs.

It is in this situation, where fundamental changes in the structure and organization of knowledge are under way, that doors have been opened wide to cooperation with the advanced capitalist world. The introduction of knowledge content and patterns from Europe, Japan, and the United States must be analyzed in relation to the changes that are going on within the Chinese higher curriculum. How do foreign knowledge transfers affect the contradiction that has reemerged between measures to transform knowledge patterns in the service of economic development and the concerns of the leadership about the implications of knowledge transformation for central political authority?

The Open Door and Knowledge Transfer

One of the most important channels for the introduction of foreign knowledge to China is that provided by the large number of Chinese scholars and students studying and doing research in Japan and the West, then returning to work in Chinese institutions. Beginning from 1979, 2,000 scholars and students were sent abroad each year by the Ministry of Education. This number increased to 3,000 a year in 1983, in accordance with explicit guidelines within the Sixth Five-Year Plan.[88] Between 1979 and 1985 a total of 29,000 were sent through various official channels at central, provincial, and local level, and an additional 7,800 were thought to have gone through institution-level linkages or private channels of various types.[89]

Each year the State Education Commission, State Economic Commission, and State Science and Technology Commission deliberate about the number to be sent abroad by field of study, level, and type, with the State Science and Technology Commission having the strongest say over the visiting scholar program and the State Education Commission making most decisions over the student program. The plan for each year is part of the overall annual plan for development worked out in relation to the five-year plan. Implementation of all programs is carried out by the State Education Commission.[90]

In practice this means that the State Education Commission prepares quotas for all other units, within which scholars and students are selected for study abroad. Each of the thirty-eight universities directly administered by the State Education Commission gets a quota, as does each national ministry that has responsibility for specialized higher education and each provincial bureau of higher education. The Chinese Academy of Sciences (CAS) and the Chinese Academy of Social Sciences (CASS) also get quotas to divide among their institutes. It is not possible to get exact figures on these yearly quotas, but scattered information drawn from numerous interviews makes possible a general picture. Universities directly administered by the State Education Commission, especially the more prestigious ones, are most favored, in some years receiving quotas of up to 30 or 40 places. The Chinese Academy of Sciences typically gets a quota of about 150 places to be divided among its many institutes. This is supplemented by places it provides through direct linkages abroad and its own financial support.[91] The CASS quota of 20 each year rose to 30 in 1985.[92] Other ministries typically get quotas of between 50 and 150 places, in accordance with the relative priority of their knowledge area with the current plan. This is divided among the universities they administer and often favors a few prestigious institutions. Finally, the provinces and municipalities typically get quotas of between 5 and 20 places to be divided among 25-50 provincial-level institutions. It is clear that national-echelon institutions are highly favored, and there is and will continue to be a concentration of foreign returned scholars in these institutions.

Provincial and municipal bureaus of higher education, however, have begun to take action in this situation. Seeing within their provinces a situation where a few national-echelon institutions singly command more opportunities for study abroad than the entire quota given to the province for its institutions, many of them have made their own plans for sending scholars abroad. Shanghai was one of the earliest in this regard, from 1983 sending fifty each year and planning to send one hundred each year from 1986.[93] Jiangsu province decided to send fifty as early as 1981, but it was only in 1984 that all of this group had been sent. This delay was due to the difficulties of language preparation and appropriate linkages with foreign institutions.[94] Liaoning and Jilin provincial bureaus were both seeking financing from the provincial government for a policy of sending fifty scholars per year in 1985, but this had not been approved due to the economic problems caused by flooding in that region.[95]

At both national and provincial level part of the financing for these official programs to send scholars abroad comes from bi-lateral exchange agreements, or provincial-level ties with foreign provinces or states. Also World Bank funding, which will be discussed in detail in chapter 7, is channeled through the State Education Commission in the provision it makes for study abroad. This forms a part of the annual plan. While the combination of the active efforts of provincial bureaus and recent World Bank projects supporting provincial-echelon institutions has made possible greater participation by these institutions in opportunities for study abroad, national-level institutions are still far ahead in their contacts with foreign institutions.

National policy on sending scholars abroad has changed in significant ways between 1978 and 1986. Initially the greatest emphasis was on visiting scholars, who were sent for one- or two-year periods to upgrade their teaching and research skills and familiarize themselves with work in their field abroad. In addition, a small number of undergraduates were sent for degree programs. Starting in 1980, the emphasis moved to sending promising young graduates for masters and doctoral programs. By 1985, about half of those going abroad were visiting scholars and the other half graduate students.[96] In 1986 it was decided that only doctoral and postdoctoral students would be sent in the second category, since China's own masters programs were already able to meet needs at that level.[97]

Whereas visiting scholars normally return to the institutions they came from, graduate students will be assigned posts by the State Education Commission on return. There is great concern at present over the issue of how best to make use of talented Ph.D. holders, and a series of postdoctoral centers have been established by discipline or research area in prestigious national universities. Promising returnees are allowed to work at one or two of these centers for up to two two-year periods before a final decision is made on where they are to work. Their own research interests and ongoing research work are to be taken into account in the final assignment.[98]

As for field of study, there have also been interesting changes in policy since 1978. Initially, the concern was for upgrading the level of faculty in higher institutions, with an emphasis of around 60-70 percent on the natural sciences. In 1982, there was an adjustment in favor of the engineering sciences, bringing the proportion of pure and applied to about 50-50. More recently, especially with the decision to learn from the advanced management practice of Western countries, the applied social sciences have gained greater relative importance than the initial cautious intent in the Sixth Five-Year Plan to "survey and study politics, economics, law, education, and languages of foreign countries."[99] Another aspect of the change in policy is a desire from the Chinese side to gain access to industrial research centers, enterprises, and government offices so as to make possible a deeper practical knowledge of the applied natural and social sciences in Western society.[100] There has been some frustration in implementing this policy, due to a reluctance or inability on the part of some foreign governments to open up this sort of opportunity. Others, such as Canada, Japan, and West Germany, have been supportive of this type of initiative, as chapter 5 indicates.

In May 1986 a conference was held to review the work done between 1978 and 1986 and chart a course for the future. At this conference it was agreed that the number of students and scholars sent abroad under the Seventh Five-Year Plan (1986-1990) would be kept at the current level of about three thousand per year, but that provincial and municipal governments and central ministries would be encouraged to increase the number they sent, provided they could find the funding. Better planning to meet actual social and economic development needs was stressed, and the idea of joint doctoral programs with foreign countries was put forward. Greater care in the selection of candidates for study abroad, including moral qualities as well as academic and linguistic preparation, was also emphasized. The distribution of government-sponsored awards to grass-roots institutions and potential employers was suggested as a means to ensure a more appropriate choice of candidate.[101]

In June 1987 the most comprehensive regulations published so far made clear the official position on sending scholars and students abroad. Concerns about the brain drain are evident in the requirement that all who go abroad at public expense sign legally enforceable contracts with their units promising either to return or to repay the government for the full cost of the study period.[102] In addition, all university students and faculty who have found their own funding abroad are required to go under the new category of unit-sponsored candidates and to sign similar contracts undertaking to return or repay the cost of their higher education in China.

By early 1988 persistent rumors and student protests suggested that quotas had been imposed to limit the number of people being allowed to go to the United States, a measure that infringes on the autonomy promised to higher institutions over their international exchanges in the 1985 reform document.[103] In early April a senior official within the State Education Commission, Huang Xinbai, affirmed in a public interview that the central government would continue to send three thousand students and scholars each year, of whom about six hundred go to the United States. In addition, he stated that unit-sponsored students and scholars were expected to be at about the same level in 1988 as 1987, that is, about five thousand. Of these, four thousand went to the United States in 1987, and the same figure was expected in 1988.[104] It thus remains to be seen whether official fears of a brain drain will in fact prevent the continued flow of students and scholars to the United States.[105]

Besides the scholars abroad, who probably represent the most significant channel for foreign knowledge transfer into the Chinese higher education system, there are other important channels. Foreign curricular materials and foreign educational systems in general are being intensively studied both by Chinese comparative educationists and by officials who have a more practical and direct concern with curricular reform.[106] The State Education Commission has an office responsible for the preparation of teaching materials, and it makes great efforts to obtain the latest material from abroad in specific fields. This material is vetted, and that considered most valuable is given out to specialist research centers to be translated. With the help of comparative educationists, the office has identified particular foreign institutions in the Soviet Union, Japan, Germany, and France whose work is considered of high quality and whose curricular materials are widely used in these rather centralized systems of higher education. These materials are given special attention in the preparation of new learning materials for China.[107]

Other channels of knowledge transfer are the cooperative educational projects, organized and funded bilaterally between China and various OECD nations. These are discussed in detail in chapter 6. Probably the channel having the most widespread impact over the whole higher education system is that of World Bank higher education projects, analyzed in chapter 7. Other, more diffuse channels of knowledge transfer include the media, particularly television, the many economic linkages such as joint ventures, and the increasing tourist presence in China. These lie outside the scope of this book.

Conclusion

This chapter has probed in some depth the contradiction between traditional knowledge patterns which served centralized political control and transformed knowledge patterns which hold promise for economic development and political democratization. An understanding of the intensity of this contradiction in the early 1960s sheds some light on attempts in the early Cultural Revolution to create alternative curricular forms that came close to an integrated code. Post-1978 curricular reform also comes into perspective against this background. A gradual transformation toward a less hierarchical structuring of knowledge areas and greater permeability among disciplines and specializations in the organization of knowledge is definitely under way. Yet the leadership remains ambivalent about the implications of this transformation for the political power structure. Lively intellectual debates over political structure reform and the subsequent student movement with its demands for the implementation of this reform were subsequently condemned as "the outcome of the rampancy of ideas of bourgeois liberalization over the years and the irresoluteness of some comrades within the party in dealing with them."[108]

Nevertheless, scholars within the higher education system have greater authority than ever before over the definition of curricular knowledge both within individual higher institutions and at the national level, where many participate in teaching material committees. It is they also who are the main mediators of the flow of knowledge coming into China through the channels described above. Since the open door has been reaffirmed by the Chinese leadership, the role of the scholarly community will continue to be of crucial importance.

The internal aspect of this role is primary. A dual tradition of Chinese scholarly culture has been discussed briefly—the highly centralized, control-oriented imperial examination system and the diffuse, more independent tradition of the *shuyuan*. Residues of both remain a part of contemporary scholarly culture, and the question is whether intellectuals will stay with a safe pattern of orthodoxy that harmonizes with the political leadership's predilection for the control of knowledge or will launch out along the more open and innovative lines of the *shuyuan* tradition and seize the present opportunity being given to them to create a new ethos for China's higher institutions. This was clearly the direction of Fang Lizhi's efforts at the Chinese University of Science and Technology. While the condemnation of the student movement has brought its particular leadership role into question, other higher institutions are developing their own distinctive ethos, as chapter 3 will demonstrate.

The kind of internal role adopted by Chinese institutions will affect in turn the way in which they operate as channels for foreign derived knowledge. If they stay with the orthodoxy of Confucian patterns for the regulation of knowledge, they could provide the Chinese leadership with newer and more sophisticated means for political control, legitimated by Western science, especially the science of management. A new hierarchy of knowledge areas could emerge in China that reflects not only the internal power structure but also international power relations.

However, if the intellectual community draws on the strength of its own scholarly traditions, both those of the *shuyuan* and those of such liberal institutions of the Nationalist period as Beida and Qinghua, it may succeed in an eclectic and critical selection of foreign materials, and their reinterpretation for the Chinese context. It could open up an understanding of foreign knowledge and technology that makes possible their creative and liberatory use. The task of selection and assimilation has different dimensions for different knowledge areas—the sciences, where China already has a well-developed indigenous base, the humanities, where the richness of Chinese culture assures a certain resilience, and the applied social sciences, particularly management science, where China is probably most vulnerable. The Soviet domination of this area in the fifties provides a cautionary lesson of how the so-called advanced management theory and practice of the capitalist West and Japan could be used by the Chinese leadership.

The chapter closes with a sense of China at the crossroads. Curricular reform could easily be subverted toward knowledge patterns that directly serve both internal political control and the international status quo. However, a resilient Chinese ethos of modern scholarship would be the best antidote to this. To get a sense of whether and how this is being created, chapter 3 moves from systemwide curricular reforms to the individual experience of ten different kinds of higher institutions. It presents a view from within of how curricular changes are affecting each institution.

3

A NEW ETHOS
FOR THE CHINESE UNIVERSITY

Since a university is primarily a knowledge institution, the range and organization of knowledge areas in its programs and the knowledge orientation of its members should reveal its ethos, or *xuefeng* (scholarly style), to use the Chinese term. Added to this might be their sense of history as a scholarly community and their plans for the future development of their institution.

In the Soviet-derived higher education system put in place in 1952, Chinese higher institutions each had a specific identity assigned to them. With centrally standard teaching plans and texts and central control over recruitment to each specialization and over all courses taught within each, there was little opportunity for members of these institutions to create a distinctive institutional ethos. This situation proved to be an optimum one for Soviet political and cultural penetration, most evident in the role of People's University, which has been described in earlier chapters.

While People's University focused on Marxist-Leninist social sciences, all other comprehensive universities were limited mainly to academic disciplines in the natural sciences and humanities, a pattern very close to the nineteenth-century German idea of the university. Polytechnical universities embraced a range of applied sciences but had neither theoretical scientific disciplines nor social sciences. Engineering universities, administered by such national ministries as metallurgy and machine-building, reflected the precise manpower needs of the ministry in the product-oriented definition of their specializations. Agricultural universities under the Ministry of Agriculture, Animal Husbandry and Fisheries (MAAF) had a range of precisely defined agricultural specializations linked to manpower needs.

The stereotyping of institutions according to a division of knowledge areas largely derived from the traditional European disciplines, extended under Soviet socialism to new professional specializations, was first challenged in the Hundred Flowers Movement of 1956 and the subsequent Great Leap Forward. It was at this time that several universities of science and technology were established, bringing together the pure and applied sciences, which had been separated under the Soviet model, as well as many new provincial-level comprehensive universities. The reforms going on now have interesting parallels with that first post-Liberation attempt to create a higher education ethos that had Chinese characteristics,[1] and in some ways they build upon the curricular reforms of that period. The extreme radicalism and overenthusiastic expansionism that accompanied the 1958 reforms made their demise and the return to Soviet patterns in the early sixties almost inevitable. In contrast, the present reforms have a sounder economic basis and are proceeding within a political climate of greater moderation and maturity.

For each institution the challenges are different, since the starting point is a different one. To capture this diversity, the experiences of ten higher institutions of six different types will be explored. Each is developing in a unique way, and some are conscious of their role as models of reform.

Fudan University in Shanghai is one of China's most prestigious comprehensive universities. It rivals the somewhat older and equally prestigious Jiaotong (Communications) University, a polytechnic institution. Both are under the direct administration of the State Education Commission. The Beijing University of Iron and Steel Technology and Northeastern Technological University are both administered by the higher education bureau of the Ministry of Metallurgy, while Nanjing and Beijing Agricultural universities are under the MAAF. In this range of national-echelon institutions, fundamental differences in the reform process reflect the different knowledge base each institution brings to reform, the different constraints experienced under its administrative linkage, and the changing needs of the sectors of society served by its graduates.

Provincial-echelon institutions, all administered by the higher education bureau of the province, reflect a specific geographical orientation and respond to provincial manpower needs. In this study two provincial comprehensive institutions, Heilongjiang and Liaoning universities, are considered. Finally, at the local level under city governments, vocational universities represent a new echelon and type of institution, which has a unique curricular identity and is responsible to meet city manpower needs. Two of these, Shenyang Vocational University and Jinling Vocational University, are described.

While the general hierarchy of the system established in 1952 remains in place, there is much greater freedom for each institution to develop an ethos of its own. Universities under the State Education Commission continue to enjoy highest prestige, with their scholars dominating the teaching material committees that continue to set national guidelines. Institutions administered by other ministries have the support of a now more powerful State Education Commission in broadening their knowledge base and emphasizing scholarly criteria as well as the professional manpower criteria of their respective ministry. Provincial institutions are limited only by the need for central approval in the establishment of a new academic specialization and thus can respond freely to provincial priorities and needs in their curricular reforms. Vocational universities are entirely free to establish new short-cycle specializations without central approval, and to respond to urban development needs. In high technology areas they have the conditions to move ahead more quickly than regular higher institutions. The old hierarchy could thus be gradually challenged by advanced institutions at the provincial or local level.

The second area where changes can be expected is in the internal administration of higher institutions. In the administrative patterns established under Soviet influence, the Academic Affairs Office (*jiaowu chu*) was responsible for overall curricular planning for each institution. Below it were the departments, organized at the discretion of university authorities. Each department normally had several specializations. The specialization was the unit subject to greatest central control. Quotas were given according to unified state plans for recruitment to each specialization each year. All aspects of students' lives were regulated within the context of the specialization to which they belong. Faculty belonged to even more narrowly defined units, the teaching and research group, of which there were often several serving each specialization. These patterns of internal organization are now being challenged in different ways, as the sketches below will show. They are drawn from visits made to each institution and interviews with faculty, department heads, and personnel within the academic affairs office.

Fudan University

Fudan University's history might be seen as a microcosm of the struggle for the transformation of knowledge depicted in chapter 1. Created in 1905 as an expression of Chinese patriotic revolt against a French-imposed academic curriculum and an authoritarian style of institutional government in l'Université l'Aurore, it was dedicated to scholarly independence and intellectual freedom from its earliest days. Its curriculum was remarkably open to innovation over the years, starting with programs in the arts and sciences, adding commerce in 1917; engineering in 1923; education, psychology, and other social sciences in 1925; journalism in 1927; and finally agriculture during the war years when it relocated to rural Sichuan. These developments were clearly a response to China's modernization needs, both economic and political. Fudan led the May 4th movement in Shanghai and was subsequently in the forefront of many anti-Japanese movements. Its commitment to intellectual freedom ensured fierce debates and struggles among faculty members adhering to the Nationalist regime, progressives, and Communists.[2] The school song summed up its ethos in this line: "independent scholarship, free thinking, no educational or political stranglehold."[3]

With the success of the 1949 Revolution, Fudan's revolutionary role was recognized in the standing given to it as one of the major comprehensive universities in East China. Ironically, this very recognition changed its character dramatically. Many of the fields in which it had excelled, such as commerce, engineering, and agriculture, were removed in order that it could fit the Soviet-European sterotype of a university devoted to the pure arts and sciences. Distinguished scholars in mathematics and natural sciences as well as traditional humanities were transfered there to enhance its scholarly reputation. The one applied field of knowledge that remained was journalism. This department had gained high repute under the leadership of the literary figure Chen Wangdao, who had come to Fudan after the May 4th movement in 1919, became its president in 1952, and remained in this post till his death in 1977.

In a speech to the Shanghai People's Congress in May 1959, Chen developed the notion of intellectual freedom in the context of the Hundred Flowers movement of 1956-57. He stressed the importance of free intellectual debates for cultural as well as scientific progress in the nation and remarked that some intellectuals had become timid since the Antirightist movement, hesitating to take the antithetical position in a scholarly debate for fear of being accused of an incorrect political standpoint. Chen insisted that scholarly errors could not be simplistically explained in terms of political standpoint and condemned as remnants of bourgeois scholarly thought, but must be analyzed in a concrete way according to differing conditions and dealt with appropriately in each case. A strict distinction should be drawn between problems of scholarly standpoint and those of political standpoint, involving opposition to the party, the people, or socialism. Only the latter could be regarded as contradictions between the people and their enemies.[4]

This was an interesting attempt to develop a working principle of intellectual freedom within Mao's theory of contradictions, which is quite distinct from the European notion of academic freedom. However, the question of boundaries to scholarly involvement in political affairs remained a sensitive one. Fudan's Cultural Revolution role, depicted already in chapter 1, culminated in a very close association between the university and the despotic rule of the Gang of Four.

In a recent attempt to redefine Fudan's long-standing commitment to "independent scholarship and intellectual freedom," Xie Xide, the American-educated physicist who is now president of Fudan, spoke of Fudan's Cultural Revolution experience as a baptism. Her new interpretation of the old motto includes the tasks of "fully developing each person's intellect and ability and scaling new heights in science, technology, and the social sciences."[5] These tasks must be pursued, however, under the disciplined guidelines of the party's national development plans for the year 2000, and each person should be asking what they can do to contribute. Xie thus attempted to bring together individual scholarly development and the collective, a commitment to scholarship and service to advancing socialism. The highly academic role of transmitting pure knowledge given to Fudan in the Soviet-imposed patterns of the fifties is modified by possibilities of a practical social and technological role within disciplined service to national development plans.

A parallel scholarly caution combined with a long-term view of curricular development was evident in the rationale for Fudan's curricular development given by Qiang Lianqing, head of the Academic Affairs Office. He described how the Fudan community had approached the challenge of reform with a determination to maintain and enhance scholarly quality and to create their own model gradually rather than adhere to any model selected from outside. They saw their role in Chinese society as nurturing people who should be leading figures in the basic disciplines of knowledge. In widely publicized debates with Jiaotong University over whether the university should be a center of research and teaching or of research, teaching, and direct service to economic development, Fudan held firmly to research and teaching. At the same time they recognized that the Soviet comprehensive model, with its exclusive focus on the pure disciplines of knowledge, was no longer appropriate. Therefore they decided to build on the strengths they already had, taking into account the needs of China's long-term modernization program.

This in turn called for an assessment of their own strengths and weaknesses. The four areas of strength they identified were high teaching quality, a more or less complete representation of the disciplines of knowledge, a good library, and a good laboratory and scientific equipment for teaching needs. Four weaknesses were a tendency to obsolescence in teaching and research, the absence of applied fields related to the theoretical disciplines, and the inadequacy of the library and labs for the needs of high-level research. In light of this inventory of the practical situation, they decided they did not have the conditions for a fully comprehensive university within an American definition. Rather, they should build on what they had, seeking to maintain quality and to expand the curricular offerings on the basis of three principles: *jiaocha*—creating new programs at the intersection of two or more old ones; *shentou*—osmosis, or the cross-fertilization of the natural and social sciences; and *lao zhuanye dai chu xin zhuanye*—old disciplines spawning new ones.

Qiang Lianqing gave examples of each of these forms of innovation. As an example of *jiaocha*, he took the mathematics department, which has a high reputation for scholarship. It had the practical problem of appropriate work assignments for its graduates. Therefore it gradually developed the areas of computer science and statistics, the latter in cooperation with the State Statistical Bureau, in order to produce graduates who could make a practical contribution as well as theoretical mathematicians. Two new departments, Operations Research and Computer Science, came into being. In addition, the mathematics department made a strong contribution to the new department of management science.

As an example of the cross-fertilization of social and natural sciences, Qiang took the case of linguistics, where mathematical theory had greatly enhanced its strength as a scientific discipline within the Chinese and foreign language departments, and theoretical political economy, where new courses in statistics and quantitative research methods broadened it to a study of socialist economic development. The demography specialization within the new department of management science was another example of a true blending of the natural and social sciences, with both arts and science students recruited to study there. In such areas as world economy, international politics, and journalism, students were being recruited from science as well as arts entry streams. The journalism department has a new specialization in international journalism that offers a double degree program; 60 percent of those who applied to it were second-year science students who would combine expertise in international journalism with the science specialty of their main degree. In addition to the breadth provided by a double degree option for a small number of students, a modified version of the credit system allows for all students to elect freely anywhere between 10 and 25 percent of their courses, depending on their specialization.

Finally, the idea of old disciplines giving birth to new ones has been richly developed at Fudan within a new school of technological sciences that grew out of the major theoretical science disciplines. It now has six departments: biological engineering, operations research, applied mechanics, statistics, computer science, and genetic engineering. These departments have close links to factories and play an important research and development role.[6]

All in all, the curricular reform process at Fudan is a gradual one, guided by the principle of maintaining and building upon present strength rather than rapid innovation or the adoption of a new model to guide reforms. In light of extensive foreign contacts (over sixty university-level linkages with Japan and the West) and the fact that several hundred of its faculty have gone abroad for research or higher degrees since 1979, Fudan is bound to be an important channel for foreign-derived knowledge to be introduced into China. Its own well-established knowledge tradition and its cautious determination to build slowly on the strengths it already has should provide conditions for a serious and thorough reinterpretation of knowledge introduced from abroad.

The channels for the dissemination of this knowledge are many. Both undergraduate and graduate students are recruited nationwide and given job allocations nationwide. By 1990, Fudan plans to have 15,000 students, 8,400 undergraduates, 2,000 graduate students, 750 students in refresher courses (many of them teachers from other institutions), and 450 in short-term cadre training courses. These are all part of the national plan, while the remaining 2-3,000 will be students trained under contract with the city of Shanghai and with certain national ministries.[7] The posting of these graduates throughout the country will be one sure form of knowledge dissemination. In addition, there are certain cooperative research and teaching efforts with other parts of the country. One cooperative project that has had some press attention is that with the open city of Shenzhen near Hong Kong in the fields of science and technology, economic management, law, and journalism.[8]

Jiaotong University

The history of Jiaotong University has striking contrasts with that of Fudan. Established in 1896 as Nanyang Gongxue by Qing statesman Sheng Xuanhuai, its early curriculum included engineering sciences, social sciences, and humanities. It was an official attempt to introduce modern knowledge for China's self-strengthening.[9] By 1902, however, the modern ideas derived from such authors as Rousseau and the Chinese reformer Liang Qichao were perceived as threatening to the imperial government and suppressed. The resultant student storm, in which the young lecturer Cai Yuanpei took an active role, led to the closing of the school.[10] When it reopened in 1905, it was placed under the new Ministry of Commerce (Shang Bu) and given a curricular focus on the applied sciences that would minimize the likelihood of future social or political ferment.[11] After the 1911 Revolution it was administered by the Ministry of Communications, and subsequently in the 1920s by the Ministry of Railways. Its school song gives an insight into the ethos it developed over the years: "Wide awake and clear, its spirit always responds to the challenge of seeking practical knowledge with a practical heart and strength, serving practical concerns with a practical heart and strengh."[12] Jiaotong students and staff took part in the various patriotic movements from May 4th onward, but their curricular focus on applied sciences and tight administrative control by the central government meant that they did not have as prominent a political role as Fudan. They did make an important contribution to China's economic development and to defense efforts during the Sino-Japanese War.[13]

In 1952, Jiaotong University was made one of the group of fourteen major polytechnical universities administered directly by the Ministry of Higher Education. It had a fairly broad range of applied sciences, including marine power, automatic control, shipbuilding, electrical engineering, engineering physics, elecronic engineering, metallurgy, machine-building, and locomotives. Its spirit of practical commitment to practical development needs was put to the test in 1956, when Zhou Enlai personally oversaw a transfer of the whole university inland to the city of Xi'an in Shaanxi province, as part of the drive to develop the hinterland. In 1957, the Shanghai campus was reopened and the two branches of the university were jointly administered until 1959, when the State Council recognized Xi'an Jiaotong and Shanghai Jiaotong as two separate universities.

In the post-1978 climate of reform for higher education, Shanghai Jiaotong has managed to capture and hold the national spotlight more compellingly than any other higher institution. The focus has been on the reform of its management system and its success in streamlining both faculty and staff, with less competent people moved to other units and a new, younger group drawn largely from its own graduating classes. Jiaotong has also pioneered a contract system for its teachers and a salary scale reform closely linked to workload.[14]

Although management reform has been the main focus of interest in the Jiaotong model, it has gone hand in hand with a reform of the structure and organization of knowledge in the curriculum. In 1980 a research bureau in teaching and learning was established within the Academic Affairs Office; its head, Mr. Dong Yinchang, gave an account of its activities in an interview in October, 1985:

Between 1978 and 1980 Jiaotong faculty redefined the then existing twenty-seven specializations to constitute twelve specializations, one or two at most per department. This experience proved useful when a committee was established with representatives of the fourteen polytechnical universities under the Ministry of Education to discuss the reform of engineering curricula. At its first meeting in Chongqing in 1983, the discussion focused on how to break away from the Soviet patterns in which engineering specializations had been defined in terms of products rather than technological or disciplinary knowledge. A set of principles and guidelines were developed for the redefinition of specializations based on considerations of technology, basic scientific disciplines, and the needs of the reformed economic system. This led to the creation of the new national list (*mulu*) of engineering disciplines with 21 broadly defined specializations replacing the former 537, a development discussed in chapter 2.

At a second meeting of this committee in 1984, intensive discussions were held concerning the levels at which various knowledge areas should be taught (short-cycle, undergraduate degree programs, and graduate degree programs) and the length of time appropriate for various programs. The next meeting of the committee in 1985 focused on the preparation of teaching plans, and the 1986 meeting looked at teaching methods and educational thought.[15] Jiaotong University personnel have continued to play a leading role in these meetings.

Between 1978 and 1985, Jiaotong University's own curricular offerings grew from nine to fourteen departments, with new departments in applied mathematics, applied chemistry, computer science, industrial management engineering, materials science, and foreign languages. It sees itself gradually developing into a comprehensive university by building on the strengths of its engineering sciences. The range of new departments in basic sciences are the first move toward a more comprehensive coverage of knowledge areas, while industrial management and foreign languages departments represent the beginnings of programs in the social sciences and arts. A department of social sciences for training political educators opened in 1985, and a department of literature and the arts in 1986.[16]

A modular approach to the organization of the teaching plan has been developed which calls for all students to have exposure to five modules of knowledge (*zhishi mokuai*):

1. Basic and foundation courses as well as technological ones in their own field, 70-75 percent.

2. Specialist courses related to their own field, 8-10 percent.

3. Frontier scientific and technological knowledge, 5-10 percent.

4. Human and social sciences, 3-5 percent.

5. Economics and management, 3-5 percent.

Over a four-year period, formal class time has been reduced to 2,400 hours maximum, from the former 2,800-3,000 hours. Also, foreign language work, computer applications, and lab experimentation have been made part of the program throughout the four years. The teacher's role is no longer one of transmitting knowledge but of creating a suitable learning environment. A tutorial system in the third and fourth years makes possible an informal learning relationship between students and faculty.[17]

Another reform of great interest is the change of locus of curricular decision making. The Academic Affairs Office no longer channels uniform, centrally decided teaching plans to the departments, but coordinates the teaching plans that are now the full responsibility of each department. Not only is the department's role enhanced by new powers vis-à-vis the Academic Affairs Office, but it is also taking over the administrative responsibilities of the former teaching and research groups and specializations. Now that specializations are more broadly defined, there is often only one for each department, which means their effective replacement by the department. Teaching and research groups normally responsible for the salaries, housing, political organization, and educational work of the faculty have also been abolished. These administrative responsibilities are now carried out at the more impersonal level of the department.

Faculty are encouraged to group together informally with others who have similar teaching and research interests into much smaller academic discipline groups (*xueke zu*) which have no administrative function. In 1985 there were 143 of these groups in place of the former 60 teaching and research groups. The organization of knowledge is thus being separated from the mechanics of administrative and political control over the lives of faculty members. A more lively intellectual atmosphere and greater research enthusiasm among faculty should result, as scholars work in small collectives dedicated to solving shared intellectual problems and advancing knowledge in their fields of common interest.[18]

With the specialization and the teaching and research group both disappearing as organizational units, academic departments are being grouped together under schools or colleges, which in turn will be responsible to the Academic Affairs Office. Already there is a school of management with three departments—industrial engineering, decision science, and international industrial trade. There is also a college of electric and electronic engineering which groups together departments of computer science, automatic control, electrical and power engineering, and electronic engineering.[19] These parallel the new school of technological sciences at Fudan.

Interdisciplinary research is encouraged through five all-university research committees covering the areas of thermal engineering, systems engineering, bioengineering, environmental engineering, and ocean engineering. In biotechnology, there is considerable cooperation with Shanghai No. 1 Medical School.[20]

The picture that emerges of Jiaotong University from this brief outline of the reforms in its knowledge structure is one of considerable vitality. Both a greater breadth of programs and a more flexible organization of teaching and research hold promise for a scholarly environment in which knowledge is advanced in an open, creative way. The greater emphasis on fundamental theory is likely to make possible the continuous development of frontier areas. This lively environment provides the conditions for a creative reinterpretation of the knowledge and technology introduced from abroad by the three hundred faculty who have been abroad since 1978 and the many cooperative projects with foreign countries.

What about the dissemination of knowledge from Jiaotong throughout China? The flow of students recruited on a national basis as well as teachers and cadres participating in short-term programs ensures channels similar to those of Fudan and other national universities. In addition, Jiaotong has put a special emphasis on knowledge dissemination through a direct contribution to economic development. While Fudan's ethos stresses the primacy of teaching and research over service to economic interests, Jiaotong has made university-enterprise linkages part of its ethos. Its Nanyang Corporation has been highly successful, entering into contracts with industrial and commercial agencies nationwide and abroad and generating a large amount of profit for the university. The principles laid down for these industrial linkages are equal participation in planning, research and development, investment, management, risk taking, and profit making. Jiaotong's enthusiastic promotion of this economic role for the university contrasts with Fudan's more cautious academicism. The different history of the two institutions and the difference in their knowledge base are partially responsible for clear differences in the present ethos. It has also been a matter of different choices made by the scholarly community in each institution.[21]

Two Universities of Metallurgy

Beijing University of Iron and Steel Technology (BUIST) and Northeast University of Technology (NEUT) were established in the post-Liberation period, and their identities reflect very clearly the view of higher education prevalent in the early 1950s. An important priority of the new Communist state was rapid industrialization within a socialist framework, with a greatly expanded capacity in heavy industry seen as the key ingredient. Each of the major government ministries was empowered to create its own system of higher institutions which could be shaped to respond directly to the manpower needs of those sectors of the economy under its control. Thus the Ministry of Metallurgy set up a system of institutions comprising eight universities of iron and steel, seven technical colleges, twenty mid-level technical schools, two mining colleges, and forty-six factory-run colleges. BUIST and NEUT are two of the most prestigious of this group of institutions. They recruit students from the whole of China, and their graduates have been allocated posts in the iron and steel industry across the nation, creating a network that keeps close contacts with the universities.[22]

The curricular histories of the two institutions have broad similarities. BUIST came into being in 1952, with the mining and metallurgy departments of several prestigious universities including Qinghua and Beiyang brought together to form a new institution with four departments: mining, metallurgy, metal materials, and heat treatment and metals forming. In 1957, an attempt was made to strengthen the theoretical base of the field by the addition of departments of physical chemistry, materials science, and electronics. Since 1978, a much more dramatic broadening of programs has been taking place, with new departments in automation and control engineering, energy engineering, physics, chemistry, mathematics and mechanics, foreign languages, and social sciences.[23] The main role of the social science department is the formation of political educators. In addition, it provides courses for the whole university in politics, psychology, philosophy, law, and the history of science.

Curricular reform has followed the main lines of the new list of broadly defined engineering specializations. In the metallurgy department, for example, the original five specializations were adjusted over a period of four years into two much broader specializations. The major curricular decisions, such as the teaching plan and course outline, are made at the department and specialization level. A limited form of the credit system was adopted in 1985, to make possible student access to courses in other departments.[24]

A central focus of curricular reform has been on the transformation of teaching methods. Formal classroom hours have been considerably reduced and great stress placed on self-study under supervision. It is estimated that 60 percent of the courses have seen reforms in the approach to teaching. One of the ways this was brought about was by the creation of an internal journal on teaching and learning which had already had twenty-nine issues by March 1985, and which published articles by faculty reporting their experiments with teaching reform.[25] In addition, the education bureau of the Ministry of Metallurgy has a ministrywide contest each year for which faculty are encouraged to submit new teaching materials along with an analytical essay evaluating the outcome of the innovation.

This focus on teaching reform seems to be directly connected with a long-standing cooperation agreement between BUIST and McMaster University in Canada and coincides with efforts made in Ontario in the late 1970s to support the reform of teaching in higher institutions across the province. Two McMaster science professors have spent periods of time at BUIST lecturing and giving demonstrations on the teaching process rather than on their specialist professional field. This has given BUIST a national profile in the area of teaching and learning, with faculty from other institutions coming to participate in these courses.

Another aspect of leadership in higher education reform is the development of a strong center for higher education research at the university. It works in close cooperation with the National Society for Research into Higher Education and also publishes its own journal.[26] National manpower planning and aspects of the reform of management in higher education are its main areas of research.

Northeast University of Technology is located in Shenyang, the capital of the northeastern province of Liaoning. It has its roots in the engineering college of Dongbei University, founded in 1923. After Liberation a number of strong departments of engineering were combined with this college to form the Northeast College of Engineering, which had programs in mining and metallurgy and in a broad range of pure and applied sciences. It thus started out as a polytechnic institution. In the Soviet-inspired reorganization of 1952, however, its programs were greatly narrowed, leaving only four departments: metallurgy, mechanical and electric engineering, mining, and construction. In 1955 the department of construction was moved to Xi'an to develop the hinterland, and other departments were redefined more narrowly to create seven departments in all. As many as eleven Soviet specialists worked at NEUT over this period, making it a center of Soviet-inspired reform in the engineering sciences. It pioneered the graduation engineering project, which subsequently became a standard part of the teaching plan in engineering specializations throughout the country.[27]

In 1958, the curriculum was broadened by the addition of departments of sciences, engineering physics, engineering mechanics, and electronics. Since 1978, new departments in mathematics, chemistry, mechanics, computer science and engineering, management engineering, the social sciences, and foreign languages have been established. Although there are as yet no full-time students in social sciences and foreign languages, these areas are being strengthened as part of the formation of engineering graduates.

Like BUIST, NEUT is playing an important role in the struggle for higher education reform. It has close links with the provincial higher education research society which is headed by one of its former distinguished professors, Tao Zengpian. He explained the constraints placed on curricular reform by what he described as the phenomenon of universities being the property of ministries (*buwei soyou zhi*). While the university leadership sees the vital importance of strengthening basic science and broadening the formation of young engineers, the ministry's interest is in having highly specialized personnel who can immediately move into the jobs to which they are assigned on graduation. The practical result of this conflict is that the university has great difficulty in getting financial support from the ministry for its new departments in the basic sciences and for research that is not specifically related to current problems of the steel industry. Applications for the establishment of new specializations must be channeled through the higher education bureau of the Ministry of Metallurgy to the State Education Commission. Those not perceived by the ministry as being directly in its interests are given very little support.

The kind of fragmentation of knowledge areas that results from this structural situation is particularly evident in the field of management. Tao Zengpian pointed out that there are three distinctive approaches to management theory in China which bear little relation to one another. In engineering institutions such as NEUT, management departments are related to the specific needs of explicit engineering areas, in this case metallurgy. In the comprehensive universities they are rooted in the discipline of economics. In the institutes of finance and economics they have a strong professional identity. This fragmentation militates against the possibility of collectively developing a coherent theoretical approach to management with Chinese characteristics. As a result, Western theories and practices are making an impact on uncoordinated Chinese efforts toward the development of this important area.

In addition to limitations placed on curricular reform by the controlling ministry, the State Planning Commission's hold on the quota of students to be recruited to each specialization is another important restriction on the reform of higher curricula. It is extremely difficult to get permission to recruit students outside of the narrow curricular areas designated to institutions by specific ministries.

In the face of this situation, professors within the eight universities under the Ministry of Metallurgy have joined to form a Metallurgical Higher Education Society to discuss curricular reform and ways of enhancing the autonomy of their institutions. Before the educational reform document of May 1985 was finalized, a strong lobby tried to persuade the highest authorities to institute a unified educational leadership of national higher institutions and disband the higher education bureaus of the various ministries. The ministries were not prepared, however, to give up this power. Their control of the essential revenue for these institutions made this reform impossible. A further difficulty has arisen for the metallurgical universities in that the Ministry of Metallurgy has recently been divided into two ministries, one for steel and the other for other metals. This has happened just when the universities are seeking to broaden their curricula and embrace a wider range of fields.[28]

Officially the reform document gives individual higher institutions the right to curricular decision making and to the allocation of financing within each institution. For scholars within ministry-controlled institutions such as BUIST and NEUT, however, the struggle to broaden curricula and gain financial support for new areas faces greater constraints than those experienced by universities such as Fudan and Jiaotong under the State Education Commission.

Two Agricultural Universities

Eight national keypoint agricultural universities, in addition to a range of other colleges and schools, are administered by the Ministry of Agriculture, Animal Husbandry and Fisheries. Like the metallurgical universities, they constitute a self-contained system of higher education relating to a particular sector of the economy. However, two important differences have created an even greater challenge for these agricultural universities as they seek to develop a new ethos suited to the new situation. First of all, they suffered more extensive disruption and damage than most other institutions during the Cultural Revolution decade. In most cases they were required to leave their campuses on the outskirts of major cities and move to remote rural areas, in some cases becoming peripatetic institutions. The destruction of research equipment and the requisitioning of buildings for other purposes has made the restoration of these institutions a slow and arduous process.

At the same time the reforms in the economic system were instituted in the agricultural sector long before the industrial sector. The rural responsibility system has been in place since 1978 and has proven its effectiveness through rising agricultural production. Therefore a whole new set of needs must be addressed by the programs of agricultural universities, both in the graduates they produce and in the agricultural extension work that has been an important part of their role since 1949. Small-scale agricultural machinery rather than more highly mechanized equipment is needed, new skills in food processing and marketing are required to deal with agricultural surpluses, and general economic and commercial skills quite different from those suited to the command economy of an earlier period.[29] The recruitment of students willing and able to work in agriculture is another serious problem. Up to 1978, it was estimated that more than half of those students educated in higher agricultural institutions had found their way into urban postings unrelated to agriculture.[30]

In this section I look at developments in two national agricultural universities, Nanjing Agricultural University (NAU) and Beijing Agricultural University, to get a sense of how they view their role in the current situation. NAU had its roots in two distinguished pre-Liberation institutions, National Central University and Jinling University, an American missionary institution. Both had colleges of agriculture founded in 1913 and 1914 respectively and were nationally prominent for an agricultural education along lines drawn from the American Land Grant University experience. These were combined to create a specialized agricultural university in 1949, with departments in agronomy, plant protection, horticulture, soil chemistry, agricultural economics, and animal science.[31]

Given the university's national eminence as a center of agricultural teaching and research, it was not surprising that Wu Zhaojing, head of the Academic Affairs Office, presented the university's view of curricular reform within a broad framework. He recounted how Vice-Premier Wan Li invited seven American specialists in agricultural education to China in 1983. After consultations at Nanjing and Beijing agricultural universities, an intense forty-day meeting was held in Hangzhou at which the Americans introduced all aspects of higher agricultural education in the United States and gave their comments on the problems of Chinese agricultural education.

They had three major criticisms of the Chinese system. They saw the curriculum as far too narrow and suggested that the Chinese should reunite their agricultural institutions with the comprehensive and engineering universities from which they had been separated in the reorganization of 1952. A multicampus comprehensive university was suggested. The second criticism was lack of creativity and student participation in the learning process. They recommended greater opportunity for student electives and a more lively approach to teaching and learning. Third, they criticized the inbred nature of the agricultural university, particularly the fact that most of the staff recruited in the post-Liberation period had been educated solely in agricultural institutions and so lacked a broader exposure to the basic sciences.

The Chinese discussed these criticisms and suggestions. They decided not to pursue the idea of a large-scale reorganization of higher institutions toward a more comprehensive style of university, but rather to build gradually on the strengths they had in their present institutions. Certain principles were set out to guide this development. The first was an intention to strengthen the basic sciences, particularly mathematics and biology. Four required mathematics courses now replace the original one in the foundation program. Also, science graduates from the comprehensive universities have been recruited as young teachers and graduate students to work in the basic sciences.[32]

Second, the specializations are being redefined in much broader terms. One example of this was pest control, which is now called agricultural environmental studies and includes all aspects of protection for the rural environment. The department of agricultural economics has been redefined as agricultural economics and management, with new courses in marketing, finance, economic law, land planning, and foreign commerce. It sees its role as summing up and developing a historical understanding of the new economic relations emerging in agriculture, and introducing new ideas and materials to meet these needs. The new economic cooperatives, created by households grouping together to solve problems of transport and marketing, require a knowledge and skill that was not called for in the old system.[33]

NAU sees itself as moving in two directions at once—first toward the strengthening of scientific theory in its teaching and research programs and, second, toward a more flexible and practical service to changing agricultural needs. The university's role within the agricultural extension system makes for well-established channels for the dissemination of new knowledge and techniques. This practical aspect is being reinforced with the gradual development of contract programs in which the university trains rural youth for the specific needs of certain areas, on condition that they return and serve these needs on graduation. There were two such classes in 1985, one in food processing, another in agricultural economics. In addition, a new short-cycle program in agricultural finance is training people specifically for the needs of the agricultural bank. Complementing this practical aspect is the recruitment of highly qualified students and staff in the basic sciences to strengthen theoretical research and teaching.

Beijing Agricultural University (BAU) has a history similar to that of NAU, with agricultural colleges from several distinguished universities brought together in 1949: Beijing University, Qinghua University, Furen University, and North China University. With the reorganization of 1952, its programs were narrowed, forestry and agricultural mechanization being separated to create independent institutions. In 1957, the reform movement was expressed at BAU in the creation of new theoretical specializations in the areas of biophysics, biochemistry and plant physiology, biochemistry and animal physiology, and agricultural microbiology.[34]

After extremely severe disruptions in the Cultural Revolution period,

BAU has moved energetically since 1978 toward reestablishing its programs. Curricular developments between 1978 and 1985 reflect a similar emphasis to that of NAU, both the strengthening of theoretical courses and a new emphasis on a practical, flexible response to the rapidly changing agricultural economy. The key theoretical area of biology has been strengthened by the creation of a college of agricultural biology that brings together biochemistry, biophysics, and microbiology. In addition, new colleges of veterinary medicine and agricultural economics have been created, indicating the importance of these two fields. To the long-standing departments of agronomy, horticulture, plant protection, soil chemistry, and animal science have been added new departments of agricultural meteorology and food processing. Also, the Central College of Agricultural Administration provides short-term training courses for agricultural cadres on a nationwide basis.[35]

BAU recruits students nationwide within the national plan and is also beginning some contracts for training students to meet needs in particular areas. Long-term curricular planning is under intense discussion, and the introduction of foreign materials suited to Chinese needs forms part of this planning. An agricultural education center of the State Education Commission, whose role is to identify and translate foreign teaching materials in the field, is located on the BAU campus, giving its faculty a particularly strong role in the adaptation process.[36]

The concern for raising the theoretical standards to international levels is balanced by a strong emphasis on the integration of practice into all programs. In the first year, all students are required to spend a month living on the experimental farm and learning basic agricultural concepts. Throughout the second year, students spend half a day every week on the farm, observing specific agricultural phenomena and keeping a detailed record. In the third year, students spend two days a week on their own research project, collecting data that will be used in the graduation thesis. Finally, in the second term of the fourth year, they spend two and a half months at an agricultural extension station, before the graduation thesis is completed and written up.

Curricular reform is also characterized by a reduced number of teaching hours, greater breadth with the strengthening of mathematics and biology, and a partial credit system that allows students to take courses in such areas as rural sociology, literature, and music appreciation. At the graduate level, BAU is putting serious efforts into the development of new courses, many of them inspired by the experience of their over three hundred faculty who have done research abroad in recent years, others by new developments in China. Cooperative research projects with foreign universities—Guelph in Canada, Hohenheim in West Germany, Massey in New Zealand, Tokyo Agricultural University, and the University of Minnesota—as well as training projects supported by the FAO have created a lively environment. The new ethos was summed up by a member of the Graduate School who is responsible for its curricular development as "broad knowledge, an international perspective, and a strong emphasis on experimentation."[37]

Two Provincial Universities

In the higher education system put in place in 1952 on the Soviet model, the system of higher institutions administered by each provincial higher education bureau was intended to meet the specific manpower needs of the province, as worked out in provincial five-year plans. Although national-level higher institutions under the State Education Commission or central ministries are subject to some supervision from the provincial bureau in the province where they are located, a maximum of 30 percent of their graduates are given job allocations within the provincial plan. The majority of the manpower needs have to be met by provincial institutions, and these were organized in a way that expressed a similar regimentation of knowledge to that of the national-level system described in chapter 2. Specialist engineering and agricultural institutions related to the specific production emphasis of the province, while commerce, medicine, foreign languages, economics and finance, political science, and law were also organized in specialist institutions. Up until 1957, the only institutions with any breadth of knowledge areas were the teachers universities and colleges, which embraced the major arts and sciences disciplines, education, psychology, fine arts, and music.

An important part of the educational reforms of 1958 in many provinces was the creation of provincial comprehensive universities that were to exercise intellectual leadership for the province. In most cases one specialist institution of quality was turned into a comprehensive university by adding new departments or borrowing departments from other institutions. This development of the late 1950s is of particular interest at present, since many specialist institutions are now trying to become more comprehensive in their curricular provision.

Provincial comprehensive universities differ from national ones in their more local orientation. Student recruitment and job allocations are limited to provincial boundaries, and the curricular emphasis is determined by local needs. In addition to regular students recruited according to specifications of the provincial plan, they tend to have a large complement of correspondence and evening students, and they are rapidly developing various forms of contract-programs to meet specific needs. Thus, well-developed channels exist for a widespread dissemination of knowledge throughout the province.

In the early years of educational exchange with Japan and Western countries provincial universities tended to participate only in a limited way. Provincial bureaus of higher education were typically given quotas of around twenty for sending scholars abroad within the national plan, and these had to be divided among thirty to fifty institutions. This situation is now changing, however. Some provinces have developed special linkages with counties, provinces, or states in Japan, Europe, and North America, involving educational exchanges. A few are financing their own programs to send scholars abroad. In addition, one of the World Bank educational loans focuses on key comprehensive and normal universities in each province and provides funding for their faculty to study and do research abroad. Thus provincial universities are starting to become part of the filter through which foreign knowledge is introduced and applied to Chinese needs.

How do they see their role in the present situation, and what kind of an ethos are they building? To answer these questions, I give brief sketches of Heilongjiang University and Liaoning University, which sum up the views of their leadership on the new spirit that is emerging.

Heilongjiang University (Heida) has its roots in the famous Resistance University (Kangda) of Yan'an days, specifically the specialization for teaching Russian set up in 1941. In 1946 it was moved to Harbin and became a specialist Russian language school. In 1954 it was broadened into a Foreign Languages Institute and in 1958 was made into a comprehensive university with departments of Chinese, philosophy, English, Russian, Japanese, mathematics, physics, and chemistry. Its role up to that time expressed a spirit of flexibility and service to the special needs of each period. As part of Resistance University it served the Liberation effort. In the early 1950s it served national construction needs by training over a thousand teachers and interpreters of Russian whose role in mediating Soviet expertise was important. Its transformation into a comprehensive university in 1958 suited the greater maturity and assurance of that period. Present leaders, however, see this transformation as having been limited by the Soviet model of the comprehensive university.

Since 1978, new departments and new specializations have been added that express the new guiding idea of a comprehensive university with a curricular orientation relevant to local needs. New departments include law, computer science, information science, economics, and biology. New specializations in journalism, archives, accounting, statistics, international commerce, and banking add a practical dimension to existing theoretical disciplines. Plans are also being made for the development of engineering sciences, specifically those related to the light industry applications of the oil and coal resources of the province. It is envisaged that by 1990 the university will have five colleges: Arts, Foreign Languages, Science and Engineering, Law, and Economic Management.[38]

The history of Liaoning University has parallels with that of Heilongjiang University. It was created in 1958 by a merger of the Northeast Institute of Finance and Economics, Shenyang Teachers University, and the

Shenyang Institute of Russian.[39] From the Soviet comprehensive university model of that period, with its focus on pure disciplines, it has moved toward a strengthening of applied fields since 1978. A newly established College of Economic Administration has five departments: economics, industrial administration, planning and statistics, finances and insurance, and finance and accounting. Like Heida it envisages having new colleges of arts, science and engineering, foreign languages, and political economy by 1990.[40]

Both institutions are rapidly developing lively foreign linkages. By agreement with the University of Southern Illinois, Liaoning University has a number of American professors teaching courses in physics, business managementand law, while their Chinese faculty are teaching programs in a newly created center for research into Chinese culture and economy in Illinois. It also has agreements with two Japanese universities which involve teacher and student exchange. Heilongjiang has special linkages with the University of Alberta as apart of the twinning agreement between the two provinces. It also has links with American, Japanese, and Hong Kong institutions. As the primary higher educational institutions of the provinces, these comprehensive universities will probably figure largely in the programs being developed at the provincial level for sending scholars abroad. They are likely to have a key role in the province both as leaders in curricular transformation and as the filter through which foreign knowledge is passed before its application to provincial development needs.

What channels do provincial universities have for the dissemination of knowledge? Statistics concerning the student body at Liaoning University illustrate the range of people being reached by their programs. In 1985, Liaoning had 4,735 full-time students, of whom 4,100 were on four-year degree programs, 500 on short-cycle programs, and 135 in graduate programs. While the majority of these students were recruited under the provincial plan, 600 were contract students whose expenses were paid by provincial enterprises or bureaus that guaranteed them a job on graduation. In addition to the 4,750 regular students, there were 517 mature students on special short-term leadership training programs. Furthermore, there were 1,802 students in night school programs, and 19,345 in correspondence programs. The net was thus thrown very wide, embracing a total of 26,399 students.[41] This figure could be contrasted with the student body at NEUT, the prestigious metallurgical university in the same city, which had a total of 5,266 undergraduates, 556 graduate students, 256 evening school students, and 292 correspondence students, 6,270 in all, in 1985.[42]

Two Urban Vocational Universities

By 1987 there were reported to be 140 new-style higher institutions, all administered and financed by city governments and intended to meet city-echelon manpower needs.[43] They regard themselves as breaking completely free from the old higher education stereotypes in several ways. Students are locally recruited, they arrange their own living accomodation off campus (usually at home), and they pay modest fees. On graduation they are not assigned posts within the government plans, but they are free to find their own jobs supported by recommendations from their institutions.[44] These universities rely on the financial support of the cities where they are located, and they actively seek support from enterprises through contracts for training needed personnel.

Historically, these institutions made their first appearance in 1980. Some were entirely new creations at that time. Others were developed on the basis of existing part-work, part-study colleges in factories. A third group grew out of the branch colleges established by major national universities in 1978 with the support of city governments. Their teaching programs were largely served by the faculty and library resources of the parent universities, which also approved the conferral of degrees for graduates.

The fact that these are entirely new institutions has given them a freedom of curricular innovation that is the envy of more established institutions. However, those that developed from branch colleges of distinguished universities, such as Shenyang Vocational University, have a concern for academic respectability and ambitions to raise their status that could hinder the full exploitation of this opportunity. In contrast, those that were entirely new creations since 1980, such as Jinling Vocational University in Nanjing, are less likely to be hampered by academic pretensions.

Shenyang Vocational University is closely linked with both Liaoning University and Northeast University of Technology. Its departments of economics and foreign languages had been branch institutions of Liaoda, while its departments of Construction and Electronic Engineering were branches of NEUT. Its first two classes, recruited in 1980, followed full four-year programs and received degrees from the parent institutions in 1984. From 1983, however, when it became a vocational university, all students were recruited for two- to three-year short-cycle programs. In 1985 it succeeded in getting permission from the province to recruit 160 of its 870 new students for new four-year (*benke*) programs, and its leadership is obviously eager to develop this more academic aspect of its work.

In 1985 it had five departments: electronic engineering, construction, economics, foreign languages, and legal and secretarial studies. There is a particular pride in the electronic engineering department, which has the second specialization in robotics to be established in China, in addition to specializations in solar energy, microelectronics, and industrial automation. Economics is also quite a strong department, due to its historical roots in the College of Economics at Liaoning University.

In 1985 there was a student body of 2,200 and teaching was done both by a full-time faculty of 200 and a part-time one of about 100 drawn from other universities. About 20 percent of the full-time faculty were recruited from industry, and close ties with their former units made possible opportunities for student practice. This young, energetic group of teachers was eager to introduce innovative approaches to teaching. Few had graduate degrees, and provision was being made to enable them to raise their standards to the masters level by various study programs. In 1985, twenty of the faculty were following graduate programs at such national universities as People's, Qinghua, Wuhan, Dalian Institute of Technology, and Jilin. A small number will have the opportunity to do masters degrees abroad through participation in the third World Bank educational project.

Since 1983, graduates of Shenyang have been free to seek their own jobs, though in reality the city's demand for them is so great that all who reach acceptable standards are recommended to employing units in accordance with their records. Those with the highest marks are given first choice of the most desirable posts. In addition to the provision for the city's manpower needs, the university has been accepting contracts on a provincewide basis with banks, the oil industry, and other industries that pay in advance for the training of specific numbers of young people for their employment needs.[45]

In contrast to Shenyang, Jinling Vocational University in Nanjing was a new creation in 1980, having no close links with Nanjing's prestigious academic institutions.[46] It has four departments—arts and law, commerce, electrical engineering, and construction. About 90 percent of its programs are paid for in advance by city enterprises and bureaus that wish to ensure a supply of graduates in areas of specific need. Some programs change constantly in response to specific external specifications and others are rooted in the disciplinary and professional knowledge areas of the departments.

In 1987 there was a full-time teaching faculty of 143, with the assistance of another 152 part-time faculty from other institutions, and the total student body was 3,378.[47] As at Shenyang, faculty development is an important concern and is provided through graduate study for young faculty at national institutions and a few places for study abroad.

There is a significant difference in ethos and orientation between these two vocational universities. At Jinling, the commitment to programs that meet practical needs for mid-level manpower is unequivocal. Curricula are expected to change and develop in direct response to the specific demands of employing agencies within the city. This contrasts with Shenyang, which wishes to build up strongly academic programs offering degrees on an equivalent level with other universities, an orientation linked to its historical roots in the four branch colleges set up by Liaoning University and NEUT. The problem of academic drift thus has differing dimensions for different institutions.

What may enable these new institutions to create and maintain a distinctive identity is the strong esprit de corps that exists among their faculty throughout the country. In 1984 they founded a nationwide professional association that had its first meeting in Wuhan that year and its second in Changsha in the autumn of 1985. One of the important concerns of this association is cooperation in formulating teaching plans and course outlines for the new curricular areas being developed in the colleges. With most of the programs being short-cycle, there is no central government direction over this task. The association has six regional branches which coordinate cooperation related to the specific development needs of each region.[48]

Conclusion: A New Ethos for the Chinese University?

In reflecting on the new ethos that is emerging in Chinese higher education, the first point that comes across clearly is the tremendous diversity of types and echelons of institution, a clear contrast to the institutional stereotyping that characterized Soviet patterns of the 1950s. While a diffuse American influence is generally evident, Chinese institutions are not adopting any one model from outside as a pattern for their reform. Instead they are seeking to create their own new model by identifying and building on the strengths that they have and responding to the imperatives of their environment. The new Chinese comprehensive university is likely to have many different forms which may be no closer to the American model than to the Soviet one they are leaving behind. There is a certain exhilaration associated with this quest for a new model, which suggests a resilience in the Chinese scholarly community in the face of foreign domination.

Second, both the structure and organization of knowledge within individual institutions are going through significant changes. In terms of structure, the applied social sciences are no longer isolated in institutions that give them a special authority. They are being reintegrated into virtually all higher institutions as well as being diversified and strengthened. Political science, law, economics, and management now have considerably larger enrollments, and an increasing tendency toward cross-disciplinary studies suggests that all higher students are likely to have some exposure to these areas. Jiaotong University's modular curriculum is the fullest expression of this tendency. All higher students are encouraged to concern themselves in a creative way with those areas of study that will shape China's economic and political future.

Another change in the structure of knowledge evident in all higher institutions is the emphasis on integrating theory and practical application, a dichotomy which the Chinese inherited from the European and Soviet models of the university. Comprehensive universities such as Fudan at the national level and Heida and Liaoda at the provincial level are introducing more practical and technological programs. These will benefit from the theoretical strength already present in disciplines such as economics and mathematics, while responding to national and provincial development needs. In contrast, polytechnical, metallurgical, and agricultural universities are establishing departments in the basic sciences essential for excellence in foundational theory. This balanced and integrated emphasis on theory and practice should make for a lively intellectual atmosphere. The theoretical strength to undertake a creative reinterpretation of foreign-derived theories and their integration into Chinese scholarship is complemented by the social and productive linkages that make possible the dissemination and application of new knowledge to practical needs.

In terms of the organization of knowledge, specializations are now much more broadly defined than before, and both classification and framing have been considerably weakened. The Jiaotong example of twenty-seven specializations being redefined into twelve is the most striking. Furthermore, the full or partial use of the credit system makes possible some interdisciplinary study. Also, outstanding students may participate in double-degree programs that combine natural and social sciences. A general reduction in the number of hours of classroom study from an average of 3,000-3,600 over four years to 2,400-2,600 over the same period, and an increase in opportunities for productive and commercial practice, should make possible a more open and critical learning process.

New conditions for horizontal interaction among scholars within each institution are being created. Newly established schools and colleges integrate the work of departments and research institutes in related fields. At the basic level, teaching and research groups that used to regiment the life of faculty are being replaced in some instances by freely organized academic discipine groups (*xuekezu*).

Third, in place of a centralized regimentation that encouraged little spontaneous interaction among institutions, networks of cooperation are now becoming evident. They are largely limited to the administrative sectors that divide higher institutions—universities under the State Education Commission, technical universities under production ministries, vocational universities under local urban administration—yet in their collective participation in curricular reform and struggle to improve the position of their institutions within the overall system, a group ethos is likely to emerge that has a wide geographical base.

On the other side, however, there are continuing constraints. Vertical divisions among economic sectors remain firmly in place, and horizontal divisions among the national, provincial, and local echelons are probably being increased in the present situation. The lack of cooperation in the development of management theory among institutions under the leadership of different sectors is one example of this problem. The fact that a large number of higher institutions are still possessed by production ministries means that a real transformation of knowledge away from narrow product-definition will be difficult.

The distinction in prestige among national, provincial, and local institutions and the monopoly held by national-echelon institutions over international educational interaction is another serious problem. In these institutions, one of the most commonly used indicators of academic success is the proportion of graduates who pass entrance examinations for graduate school, and the height of prestige comes with being accepted within the even more rigorous competition for graduate study abroad.[49]

The problems of inbreeding in national-echelon institutions are more serious than at a lower level, since most regard their own graduates as superior and see the retention of the best as the only way of ensuring academic quality. The less successful graduates of these institutions are welcomed within lower-echelon institutions, where horizons will be broadened as a result of their presence. However, the inner circle who remain in the top echelon face the temptation of becoming a narrow, self-serving elite whose position of preeminence can best be maintained by close alliances with the political faction in power at present and direct service to current economic trends at the national and international levels.

National-echelon institutions under the State Education Commission are important channels for the influx of foreign knowledge and centers of a constantly growing group of Western and Japanese-educated intellectuals. Their role as shapers of China's internal knowledge system and interpreters of foreign-derived knowledge is of crucial importance. On the internal front, they have the task of reconstituting the social sciences in a way that will promote democratization and so help to resolve the contradiction between traditional knowledge for political control and transformed knowledge for economic development. A rigid scientistic interpretation of the newly burgeoning social sciences could once again serve the purposes of political control and exacerbate this contradiction.

On the external front, they bear the prime responsibility for the selection and reinterpretation of foreign-derived social science materials in the areas of law, economics, management, and international relations. A creative reinterpretation of these fields, grounded in the progressive aspects of Chinese scholarly tradition and of Chinese socialist thought, could result in a modern Chinese scholarship that makes a fresh contribution to the international community and supports a transformative role for China in the global order. In contrast, a servile copying of the advanced social theory of the West in such sensitive areas could make the Chinese intellectual community pawns not only of internal political forces but of the economic and political interests of OECD countries.

Fudan and Jiaotong universities are interesting exemplars of both the opportunity and the danger of the present situation. Fudan's cautious academicism and determination to strengthen both pure and applied knowledge disciplines hold out promise of a vigorous academic environment in which foreign-derived knowledge is reinterpreted and integrated within Chinese intellectual canons in a creative and flexible way. However, the commitment to a strongly academic orientation could result in the adaptation of establishment social science theories from the capitalist world to the service of China's present political leadership. Economics and management, rather than being open, participatory fields characterized by free debate and broad access, could become tools of political control. Fudan's proclivity for associating with dominant power factions was evident in its linkage with the Gang of Four during the Cultural Revolution, and the line between an academic freedom that serves vigorous scholarship and an intellectual authority that allies closely with central political authority is easily blurred in the Chinese context.

For Jiaotong University, the danger is somewhat different. Jiaotong's leadership in university-enterprise linkages and initiative in international economic relations could lead to a genuine invigoration of both management and engineering fields through lively opportunities for practice. Yet it could also encourage a trend already evident in the treatment of knowledge as a commodity. The creative advancement of knowledge in pure or applied fields could be prostituted to the service of national or international economic interests, substituting material for intellectual wealth in the university's own development. A comment by Li Peng after a visit to both Fudan and Jiaotong in early 1986 focused on this danger in the Jiaotong model. He warned that "the university should not engage in business, making money in the name of doing practical research projects. It must concentrate on scientific study and focus its attention on training qualified personnel."[50]

—— 4 ——

CHINA'S UNIVERSITIES
IN THE WORLD COMMUNITY:
CONFORMITY OR TRANSFORMATION?

In this chapter I turn to China's external knowledge relations and the ways in which they have served its reintegration into the world community since 1978. First three distinctive approaches to international relations are delineated: the Maoist view of global order, which continues to inform Chinese foreign policy in the post-Mao era,[1] the functionalist view of equilibrium theorists which underpins American foreign policy thinking, and finally the view put forward by theorists of the World Order Models Project.[2] Central to my analysis are the concepts of this third approach, yet a consideration of the first and second approaches is also important. They reveal the underlying assumptions and expectations of Chinese and Western policy makers who are creating the conditions for China's increasingly rapid integration into the world community.

In sketching out these approaches to an understanding of international power relations, I give special consideration to the place of knowledge in each conception. I then proceed to construct two opposite ideal types of China's potential role in the global community. These types draw upon the historical analysis of an internal contradiction developed in chapters 1 to 3, working out the logical implications of its intensification or resolution. They also make use of World Order Models theory, contrasting the possibilities of a conformist as against a transformative role for China within the world community. By linking together the internal and external aspects of the overall analysis, these two types provide an evaluative framework for looking at both internal higher education developments and the participation of China's universities in international knowledge relations.

The Maoist Image of World Order

Central to the Maoist image of world order are the values of independence, the dignity of statehood, and a self-reliance that does not spurn foreign economic assistance but keeps it in a subsidiary role.[3] These values are seen as an important anchor in face of a global order that is in a continual state of flux and is characterized by an ongoing struggle by superpower nations of the first world to dominate and carry out their will over those of the second and third worlds. Mao was more concerned about this domineering aspect of imperialism and the threat that it held for the sovereignty of other states than its economic roots in capitalism and its perpetuation of an international division of labor.[4]

The single thread uniting what might seem to be erratic shifts in Chinese foreign policy in the decades since Liberation has been the identification of the superpower posing the greatest threat and the creation of a united front against it. In the 1950s, the United States appeared to fit this category, justifying a Chinese alliance with the Soviet Union. When the United States and the USSR reached certain agreements in the Strategic Arms Limitation talks of 1963, the Chinese saw this rapprochement of the two superpowers as a serious threat and actively sought to strengthen their relations both with European nations of the second world and with third world nations. With Soviet success in Czechoslovakia and subsequent hegemonic activities, contrasting to American defeat in Vietnam, the Chinese gradually came to see the Soviet Union as the more dangerous of the superpowers, a perception that seems to be the basis of the rapprochement with the United States initiated by Mao in 1971-72. Since 1982, China has been moving to a more balanced position between the two superpowers.[5]

The Chinese regard the changing roles of the superpowers in the global order as a series of contradictions. In each period it is the task of the leadership to identify the primary contradiction and to unite against it.[6] Thus Chinese foreign policy is not based either on immutable moral principles or on a functionalist sense of the evolution of a complex organism, but on a carefully estimated reaction to the shifting sands of superpower dominance in each era.[7] It is inspired by outrage against the psychological damage caused by superpower action in imposing their will on the world. Self-reliance thus goes even deeper than an economic strategy based on a conviction that China's backwardness is its own responsibility, to a deep belief in the dignity of modern statehood. This concept of self-reliance provided inspiration for the legislation and program of action of the New International Economic Order in 1975 in a situation of mutual legitimation between China and this new international lobby for countries of the South.[8]

If international power relations are seen to be in a state of continued radical flux, to which the leadership must respond in a creative way in each era, how do the Chinese view international knowledge relations? Mao himself viewed knowledge as something constantly being created out of the social and productive practice of the people, rather that as an absolute entity that could be preserved and transmitted.[9] Nevertheless, linkages with the Soviet Union in the fifties included a very important component of the transfer of knowledge in the industrial and technological sciences as well as political theory. When this was seen to stifle Chinese creativity and lead to a cringing spirit of passivity in face of superior foreign know-how, this psychological dependency came under attack. Self-reliant knowledge creation was one of the themes of the Great Leap Forward in 1958.

In the Cultural Revolution period, the Chinese approach to international knowledge flows was deeply rooted in an often noted cultural pride and centricity. While channels of foreign knowledge and technology in specific areas, notably space research and the military, were protected, universities became totally isolated from the foreign academic community, Soviet as well as Western. As centers of revolution, universities disseminated the new knowledge gained through revolutionary practice to a stream of foreign visitors who took back glowing accounts of a society that had achieved true egalitarianism in its social relations.[10] Both Maoist thought and reports of Maoist-inspired practices constituted an alternative body of knowledge in universities of the Western world and Japan which called into question academic and social power relations at a fundamental level.[11]

China saw itself as having a kind of symbolic mission to disseminate throughout the world the exemplar of a society whose progressive social relations held promise for a new kind of economic development, a role that should enhance its national dignity and the status of its socialist culture. While the rhetoric may sometimes have appeared extreme, the fact that the principles of self-reliance developed over this period were adopted as policy in the NIEO legislation by a majority of countries in the South suggests that it was not entirely hollow.[12]

In the post-Mao period, China's foreign relations have some parallels with the fifties, except that Chinese universities are now eclectically linked to institutions in a wide range of countries in both the capitalist world and the Eastern bloc in comparison to a narrow relation to the Soviet Union and a few Eastern European countries in the fifties. A shared political ideology, having the authority of science, and direct party to party ties provided the context within which knowledge transfer took place in the fifties. Now the intention is to preserve the spiritual and moral characteristics of Chinese socialist civilization while introducing advanced scientific knowledge from outside,[13] including, most recently, the science of management. This is seen less as a cultural artifact of advanced capitalist societies than as a value-free set of technologies essential to the effective application of the new knowledge to production. Thus the present determination rapidly to transform the knowledge system by the selective introduction of foreign scientific and technological know-how does not necessarily contravene the spirit of self-reliance expressed in the principles of equality and mutual benefit fundamental to all China's foreign relations.[14]

The key issue for the Chinese thus appears to be more a psychological than a moral one—recognition of the dignity of the Chinese state and a form of knowledge transfer that stimulates the creative thinking of Chinese scholars and specialists rather than reducing them to passive copying of superior foreign know-how. The cultural domestication of foreign knowledge will be a very important part of this creative response.

The Functionalist Image of World Order

The functionalist image of world order emerged in the 1960s when international politics, particularly in the United States, followed the trend of other social sciences in seeking to adopt a scientific rigor in its methodology. This consisted of a focus on quantitative methods involving sophisticated measurement techniques and an attempt to be predictive and forward looking rather than reflective and historical in orientation.[15] The underlying value assumptions of functionalist theory are rooted in a biological metaphor going back to Aristotle, in which global society is viewed as an organism going through a growth process that involves a constant return to the state of equilibrium from the changes or transformations that take place during growth.[16] Whereas for Aristotle and many later thinkers this was a self-conscious use of metaphor, with American positivism of the sixties it was seen as a testable scientific understanding of social processes, bolstered by the collection of social facts and their manipulation by quantitative means of analysis. Thinkers in the field of international relations saw this development as a significant breakthrough moving their discipline forward from a preoperational to an operational stage. It had important consequences for the way in which world order was conceptualized by scholars and by the policy makers whom they influenced.

The central value was equilibrium, defined as a situation in which the contending interests of nations in interaction are satisfied without the outbreak of violent conflict. The essential rules of the system state the behavior necessary to maintain equilibrium. In addition, transformation rules were discovered which dealt with potential destabilizing inputs and actor classificatory variables specifying the structural characteristics of actors. A veritable technology of international relations was created, which purported to explain the phenomenon of equilibrium in international relations not as a value central to a particular ideology, but as a social fact that could be observed, studied, understood, and manipulated.[17]

International relations changed from a field that was concerned with judgment, value conflicts, and a deep sociohistorical understanding to one that claimed scientific objectivity and predictive power. The down-playing of value-related issues comes across in the following typical statement of the period: "More and more value conflicts will be translated into the more tractable form of predictive conflicts, thus bridging the gap between fact and value and liberating our predictions from our prejudices."[18]

The classical view of peace and world order defined as the absence of violent conflict had now acquired a technology that offered the possibility of manipulating international systems toward the preservation of equilibrium. It was depoliticized in the sense that it was regarded as a natural process rather than a value choice. This technology was accompanied by an historical amnesia that saw the equilibrium state of the post-World War II world order not as an artifact created by certain powerful nations in their interests and preserved by patterns of dominance, but as the natural outcome of an evolutionary process in world history. Foreign policy makers were rather like high-level technicians, whose task was to solve the technical problems or dysfunctions hindering equilibrium.

What role does knowledge play in this functionalist image of world order? The focus is likely to be on scientific and technological knowledge, including management technology, which should be transferred to the developing world to contribute to the solution of the technical problems that may hinder their movement along a linear continuum called modernization.[19] Modernization is seen as a natural global process, with the advanced capitalist world at the farthest point of the continuum exemplifying the direction for all other developing countries. The solution of technical problems through the application of scientific and technological knowledge is expected to eliminate dysfunctions in the world system and facilitate the further integration of developing countries into the global order and their advance along the modernization continuum.[20] The resultant strengthening of equilibrium is not seen as a political or cultural choice but as the confirmation of an ongoing scientific process.

This functionalist image of world order could hardly be more different from the Maoist one delineated above. The latter sees the world as in a state of radical flux, with unity against the primary contradiction of superpower domination as the best political strategy. Maoist temporality contrasts strikingly with the permanence of the incremental linear view of global development central to the functionalist image. In addition, the self-consciously adopted psychology of national self-assertion and self-reliance of the Maoist image contrasts with the supposed scientific neutrality of the dominance position enjoyed by advanced capitalist nations within the functionalist image.[21]

The interesting meeting point between the two images is in the agreement, a temporary and relative position for the Chinese, on the importance of knowledge transfer in the sciences and technology and their application to the solution of technical problems. For the Chinese, this ensures the preservation of Chinese socialist culture and values in the modernization process, while for the Americans it preserves unchallenged the ideology of a value-free scientific development process. When the global order changes in Chinese perception, however, they promise no cultural nor ideological loyalty to the nations that are at present the source of useful scientific and technological knowledge.

The most sensitive knowledge area in the transfer process is that of scientific management. For the Americans, its successful transfer to China would signify Chinese acceptance of a depoliticized notion of administration that is essential to the preservation of the ideology of natural evolutionary growth of the world system. This should serve China's smooth integration into the present capitalist world order. For the Chinese, it is merely a set of scientific techniques to be adapted to the support of economic development within a Chinese socialist framework.

The World Order Models Project

The World Order Models Project (WOMP) represents a cooperative effort of social scientists in different nations to develop an approach to international relations that is consciously value explicit in contrast to the functionalist pretense to value neutrality. Its central concept of center-periphery is a value judgment on the manifest inequality between developing and developed nations. Rejecting both the linear view of nations at various stages along a continuum called modernization and the classical Marxist view of imperialism as the inevitable highest stage of capitalism, it posits a dialectical relationship between the rapid development of industrialized centers on the one hand and the inadequate or distorted development of peripheries on the other.[22] The so-called equilibrium of functionalist thought, defined as the absence of violent conflict, is unmasked as structural violence, the preservation of dominance structures by the center that ensure the continuance of patterns of inequality.[23] These dominance structures gained legal sanction in the arrangements for global order put in place after World War II, particularly in the Bretton Woods Agreement.[24]

The goals that shape the World Order Models Project are peace, economic well-being, social justice, and ecological balance. Its research task includes extrapolating trends from the present realities of the world order and creating relevant utopias to work toward. The dissemination of a relevant utopia combines with the empirical aspect of analyzing ongoing trends to form an action strategy. The social scientist is thus working at the interface of structure and culture in a dialectic between empirical and potential reality. The intention is not prediction based on an assumed value-free natural growth process, nor is it a prescription for revolution and delinking based on a classical Marxist analysis, but an understanding of empirical trends and the working out of action strategies for the achievement of world goals.

One of the leading figures in the World Order Models Project, Johann Galtung, developed a precisely defined theory of imperialism that differs from the classical Leninist one in postulating six types of imperialism: economic, political, military, communications, social, and cultural. No one of these is seen as necessarily prior.[25] Cultural imperialism may at times be unaccompanied by economic imperialism, as in the influence exerted by Western Europe on Eastern Europe, and economic imperialism may not always imply cultural imperialism, as illustrated by Japan's postwar economic relations. Political imperialism, for example what goes on within the Soviet bloc, may not always be accompanied by economic imperialism.[26] Since the focus of this study is on the international knowledge system and its link to international power relations, it is cultural and political imperialism that are of central interest.

Hans Weiler has compellingly developed the linkages between these two types of imperialism in a paper that extends the analysis of power and knowledge relations in the nation state to the level of international relations. He first examines the need of the political leadership within the modern nation state to legitimate its policies through scientific research, on the one hand, and the increasing reliance of the scholarly community on political support in identifying and pursuing research problems, on the other. He then extends this analysis of the symbiotic linkages between knowledge and power to the international level of relations between center and periphery nations:

> The [peripheral] state operates to legitimate an essentially transnational system of knowledge production, while the system of research and knowledge production in turn serves to legitimate the transnational qualities of the dependent state, and thus, the transnational power structures of the international system itself. In other words the "vertical" kinds of linkages that characterize the political and economic relationship between the center and the periphery of the international system are not only reflected and reproduced in the vertical linkages prevailing in knowledge structures but derive a good deal of their legitimacy from these very structures of knowledge production.[27]

In an article on international social science research as structural violence, Galtung delineates these vertical linkages in terms of four mechanisms of imperialism. He sees exploitation of the periphery by the center in the vertical division of labor that frequently takes place when center scholars create the theory and periphery scholars carry out humble tasks of data collection or theory application. Penetration takes place to the degree that explanations or theories produced in the center get under the skin of periphery thinkers and researchers, creating the bridgehead of a local bourgeoisie whose cultural alienation from their own periphery is thereby increased. Fragmentation takes place to the extent that researchers in the periphery are separated from one another. They have close links to one or several centers but no channels of communication among themselves or with other peripheries that would create conditions for academic solidarity. Marginalization takes place to the degree that peripheral researchers remain in a permanent status as second-class scholars, dependent on and subservient to the first-class scholars of the center.[28]

What role does the peripheral university play in this international knowledge system? Mazrui sees it as standing at the pinnacle of the structure of cultural dependency, a cultural corporation with political and economic consequences. He shows how strong cultural linkages between peripheral and center universities have served the economic interests of capitalist penetration within dependent societies by producing manpower initiated into cultural norms of the center yet knowledgeable enough about local culture to be able to promote the exploitation of local raw materials and markets. He also explores the political role of the peripheral university in educating successors for the local political elite who can be expected to support the status quo of international relations in the capitalist world order.[29]

In contrast to both the Chinese and the functionalist images of world order sketched above, with their focus on the transfer of value-free scientific and technological knowledge, this image draws attention to the significant cultural and political implications of knowledge transfer even in the areas of science and technology. It is a highly pessimistic picture of the world order that emerges from the scholarly work of the World Order Models Project. The solution suggested, however, by such dependency theorists as André Gundar Frank of the radical delinking of peripheral nations from the world community is not prescribed.[30] China's own Cultural Revolution experience demonstrated the difficulty of such a measure even in a country of its vast size and unique cultural and economic resources. Rather than advocating isolation from the world community, these scholars look for emerging signs of hope and for action strategies that could promote its peaceful structural transformation toward greater equality.

In the international political arena, Galtung sees some promise in the alliance of the Group of 77 Nations and their use of the United Nations as a forum for legislation and action toward a new international economic order (NIEO).[31] Another member of the World Order Models Project, Samuel Kim, has analyzed in detail the development of the NIEO movement and the important contribution made by China's moral and ideological leadership during the 1970s.[32] In a later book, he depicted North-South politics as a contest between two kinds of power, normative and material, and saw some potential for the restructuring of the global order in the normative victories that have been already achieved.[33]

At the level of the international knowledge and research system, Hans Weiler sees signs of hope in newly formed alliances among scholars of the periphery. In some cases they are gaining structural and financial support through such organizations as the Swedish Agency for Research and Educational Cooperation (SAREC) and the International Development and Research Center (IDRC) in Canada. New approaches to defining the problematic and new forms of analysis are emerging in the social sciences, which have greater relevance to peripheral cultures and in some cases have a strong influence on center theorizing as well.[34] The development of dependency theories by Latin American scholars and their profound influence on international social science is an example of counter-penetration.

Galtung suggests four guiding principles for international knowledge relations that stand opposite to the mechanisms of imperialism described above: equity, autonomy, solidarity, and participation. Equity would suggest interaction patterns that are symmetric and horizontal rather than vertical and imbalanced. Autonomy would envisage a form of scholarly cooperation that stimulates creativity and an independent contribution from peripheral scholars rather than coopting them to work within the established theoretical frameworks of the centers. Solidarity refers to the development of close cooperative relations among peripheral scholars in one country or region or among peripheries. Participation refers to the full conscious involvement of peripheral researchers in the creative as well as the technical aspects of knowledge production, so that all are equally enriched by the experience.[35]

At the level of the peripheral university, Ali Mazrui proposes three strategies that would contribute to a transformation of knowledge structures and in turn influence international power relations. The strategy of domestication calls for the strengthening of subjects within the curriculum of peripheral universities relating to local culture and representing locally relevant knowledge. The strategy of diversification calls for the development of a curriculum with a truly global orientation, in the African case including offerings from Chinese, Arabic, and Latin American culture as well as North American and European content. The strategy of counter-penetration is defined as the creation of a unique ethos of scholarship able to make its own impact on world academic centers.[36] A transformation of knowledge structures within the peripheral university along these lines would have important consequences for both the cultural and political orientation of the graduates produced. Since these young people are likely to take up posts of political and economic leadership within peripheral nations and in the international arena, it can be seen how the transformation of knowledge structures might have consequences for the global political and economic order.

Contrasting Images of China's Universities in the World Community

What has the World Order Models literature to say to China at this historic period of reintegration into the world community? What role does it suggest for the Chinese university in the process? To answer these questions, I sketch out two ideal types that crystallize in a logically coherent way the opposite possibilities lying before Chinese universities.[37] The first ideal type is, in Galtung's terms, a relevant utopia. It presents a vision of how China's universities might develop if their internal curricular reform is related to both economic development and political democratization, and if their participation in the international knowledge system is characterized by horizontal as well as vertical interaction patterns. The second ideal type makes the opposite assumptions: a transformation of curricular knowledge that is cosmetic rather than real due to an unreadiness of the Chinese leadership for genuine political democratization, and an integration into the international knowledge system that is characterized by vertical interaction patterns and follows closely the experience of other third world countries in the periphery of the capitalist world order.

In both Chinese historical experience and that of the third world there is plenty of reason to anticipate developments along the lines of the second image. There have also been, however, remarkably progressive currents of Chinese thought and action in this century that suggest the first is not entirely utopian. China may become an exemplar of interdependent development that has transformative possibilities in the world community.[38]

The key purpose of constructing ideal types is to highlight criteria for evaluating what is going on at present within and among Chinese universities, in cooperative projects with industrialized nations and in the general cultural and educational policy of these nations toward China. These criteria go deeper than the functionalist concern with technical solutions to technical problems of knowledge transfer and draw attention to possible cultural and political outcomes of this transfer. The types are merely abstractions in which important features have been exaggerated for the sake of clarity.[39] They are meant as tools for measuring the complex reality of changes now underway and should not be confused with the changes themselves.

In the construction of both ideal types, I begin on the inside from the micro level of the individual higher institution up to the national level. Then I move from the internal situation to external influences, concluding with the contribution of cooperative educational projects and the general cultural policy of capitalist nations toward knowledge transfer to China.

In the first type curricular change takes place at particular Chinese higher institutions along the lines of a weakening of classification and framing, with a more flexible and open definition of knowledge areas and greater teacher and student control over the pedagogical process. Each institution builds its own scholarly ethos, which provides a unifying ideological link among the various areas of knowledge and contributes more generally to the development of a unique modern Chinese ethos of scholarship. New knowledge appropriate to economic and political development needs is constantly introduced, and its sources are varied: local sources leading to an integration of ordinary life knowledge into academic courses, advanced experience in other parts of the province or nation, and material eclectically borrowed from nations of the developed and developing world. A constant process of cultural domestication ensures that foreign knowledge is reinterpreted to suit the local social and cultural environment.

This gradual transformation of the structure and organization of knowledge within higher institutions is accompanied by a change in power relations within the institutions, with students and younger academic staff having greater opportunity to participate in university governance. Power relations in the wider community also change in two important ways. First, the integration of academic knowledge with ordinary life knowledge is part of a process of the dissemination of knowledge to the local community through various forms of continuing education, which encourages higher political consciousness and greater participation in local political processes. Second, the graduates of higher institutions are possessors not only of narrow specialist knowledge but of a broader critical understanding that enables them to be creative in adapting new knowledge to their field of work and to act as responsible decision makers as well as technical experts.

Among institutions within a city, a province, and the whole nation, strong horizontal linkages are created involving the sharing of staff, dissemination of new teaching materials and other resources, and organization of joint programs. In addition to the particular scholarly ethos created in individual institutions, broader regional and even national forms of a distinctive scholarly culture are developed. Inequalities between urban and rural areas, between highly developed East Coast cities and hinterland areas, are reduced by these horizontal linkages, which involve a dissemination of knowledge valuable to both economic and political development. The democratization of knowledge access promotes an economic development that is widespread and benefits a broad range of people by region and social grouping. It is not merely aggregate economic growth concentrated in certain privileged regions and benefiting only a small proportion of the citizenry.

The rapid economic development and gradual political democratization within a socialist framework that accompany this transformation of knowledge structures result in a considerable enhancement of China's status in the global community. In addition to the normative power of an egalitarian socialist society, already evident in the emulation of Chinese achievement by the Group of 77 nations, China now has also considerable material power in the global community. Its exemplification of a genuine interdependence characterized by mutuality and its economic strength make it a natural leader of the third world in pressing for a restructuring of the global economic order along lines such as those of the NIEO legislation and program of action. Its new ethos of scholarship counter-penetrates universities of the center, adding cultural support to these political demands.

What does the inflow of foreign knowledge contribute to this vision? Projects of educational cooperation on Chinese soil act as major channels for the introduction of new knowledge from various nations of the advanced capitalist world. The organization of these cooperative institutions is characterized by equity, with the Chinese taking a full role in the planning and definition of their work. Autonomy is evident in the creativity of Chinese participants, who do not passively absorb the foreign knowledge, but actively transform it toward a cultural and social orientation suited to the Chinese context. In this process they generate new ideas that constitute a fresh contribution to the global scholarly community. Solidarity is evident in links found between cooperative projects and other local or regional institutions that make possible a rapid dissemination of the new knowledge and a cooperative effort to reinterpret it in Chinese terms. Participation is evident in the active involvement of Chinese teachers and educators in the theoretical as well as practical aspects of knowledge advancement and in an openness of these cooperative projects and their resources to the local community. It is also evident in the involvement of an increasing number of institutions by administrative echelon and by geographical region in international knowledge relations.

The cultural policy of the industrialized nations responsible for various forms of educational cooperation with China has an important though secondary role in this transformation. They present the knowledge they introduce not as a set of value-free techniques but as part of a whole social culture, which must be understood in a holistic way yet assimilated by the Chinese in a selective and critical way. They also assist in the widespread dissemination of this knowledge, so reducing regional inequalities.

This sketch is a utopia based on two assumptions: an internal transformation of knowledge-power relations and China's participation in the global order along lines suggested by WOMP scholarship. China's historical experience has shown the difficulties of achieving internal curricular reforms that contribute to both economic development and political democratization. Equally the experience of other third world nations being integrated into the capitalist world order has demonstrated the strength of the dominance mechanisms that maintain the international status quo. The implications of the opposite ideal type thus have to be taken seriously.

In the second type the reform of the higher curriculum within Chinese higher institutions involves the development of new knowledge areas with an exclusive focus on economic modernization. Its sources are largely curricula from advanced capitalist nations, and the inflow of this knowledge is so rapid that cultural domestication is precluded. The new knowledge is not freely disseminated to other institutions or the local community; rather, it is jealously guarded as a source of prestige and power by the particular institution that is its possessor. The transformation of the structure and organization of knowledge in the higher curriculum is thus more cosmetic than real, with new knowledge placed in persisting patterns of hierarchy and control.

With few horizontal linkages being created among higher institutions for the dissemination of new knowledge, a very explicit pecking order is preserved, in which institutions geographically located in large centers mainly on the East Coast and historically holding positions of leadership and prestige monopolize most of the linkages to universities in the large centers of the capitalist world. Their scholars are much more interested in the strengthening of these vertical linkages than the creation of horizontal linkages among themselves and toward hinterland Chinese institutions of lower prestige. They thus become more and more fragmented in their initiation into the academic culture of capitalist scholarship and more and more alienated from their own people.

The graduates produced by these prestigious institutions are experts in sophisticated forms of knowledge that have never been reinterpreted to suit the Chinese context. They are willing and able to work only in highly developed regions already economically integrated into the capitalist world order. In serving the rapid economic growth of the East Coast toward forms of industrialization that suit present world markets, they become more and more isolated from the mass of their own people. A widening development gap between coast and hinterland, between major urban centers and remote rural areas, leads to manifest and growing inequalities and subsequent social unrest. This calls for increasingly repressive measures by a political regime whose main role is to maintain order so that a form of economic growth dictated by the needs of major capitalist centers can proceed unhindered. Far from being part of a democratization of knowledge access and power relations, university scholars and graduates find themselves allies of an increasingly repressive political regime, which is applying foreign scientific, technological, and management know-how to a rapid yet distorted economic growth process.

Such a reintegration into the global order on China's part supports present international power relations rather than transforming them. The authority of a supposed value-free science of management derived from foreign sources is increasingly invoked by a political regime determined to maintain power in face of growing social unrest. Those scholars and institutions that provide the primary channel for this scientific, technological, and management knowledge act as a mechanism of legitimation for the government in its claim to be following a scientific development model. As in China's historical experience, the contradiction between knowledge transformation for economic modernization and knowledge control for political repression intensifies. Economic growth is seen to be possible only at the cost of political repression, and those forms of knowledge likely to lead to genuine political democratization are suppressed. A revolutionary situation develops having some parallels with that of the fifties, when China was being integrated into the economy of Soviet social imperialism. The issues of the repossession of knowledge by the people and the reassertion of Chinese socialist culture are central to agitation for a new Cultural Revolution.

What role do cooperative educational projects play in such a scenario? Such institutions on Chinese soil are characterized by exploitative relations, in which the Chinese are pressured into forms of organization and curricular content dictated from outside. Rather than developing their own collective and creative adaptation of the new knowledge being introduced, they simply copy foreign exemplars and put all their energy into catching up with world standards. The specialist knowledge built up in these centers is guarded as a source of power and prestige rather than disseminated either locally or more broadly in China. Each project has its own vertical line of interaction to the particular metropolitan country of cooperation and no horizontal linkages with other Chinese institutions or with the local community. Finally, Chinese scholars and researchers associated with these cooperative projects are marginalized individuals, permanently part of a second order of scholars dependent on first-class scholars in world centers for theoretical advances in the field.

The policy of the industrialized countries involved in educational cooperation with China is one that focuses on contributing to the rapid economic growth of East Coast centers in China through the transfer of scientific, technological, and management know-how and takes no responsibility for the widening gaps created between coast and hinterland. For the sake of economic benefit, they go along with repressive measures used by the Chinese government to suppress social discontent. The knowledge they export to China is presented as value-free technical knowledge useful for the solution of technical problems, and little attempt is made to ensure that it is understood in its cultural and social context. The cultural and educational policy of capitalist nations thus exacerbates China's already distorted internal change process. This results in China's full integration into the global capitalist economy on terms dictated by OECD countries, for a time at least.

The features of this second type are as exaggerated as the ideal of mutuality presented earlier. Neither image is intended to represent what is actually happening, but simply the logical opposites of the resolution or intensification of China's internal contradiction, transformation, or conformity in China's external knowledge relations.

Conclusion

In these two models I have tried to link the dilemma of knowledge transformation in its internal dimensions, which was explored in the first three chapters, with the external constraints imposed by China's reintegration into the capitalist world order, which have been the central theme of this chapter. The complex reality of curricular change and political economic development in China lies somewhere between the extremes sketched in these polar types. They provide an evaluative framework for reflecting on the contemporary situation.

It is my conviction that the internal dilemma is primary. China cannot be seen as a cultural blank sheet upon which the capitalist world is printing similar patterns to those imposed on other third world nations. Rather it is a nation whose rich cultural tradition has shaped a particular form of modernization over the past century. This culminated in a socialist regime that is still subject to contradictions arising from the persistence of traditional cultural values. The first three chapters therefore sustained an internal focus on the historical and contemporary manifestations of one contradiction and possibilities for its resolution on both the national level and that of individual institutions.

External influences also impinge upon the internal changes underway. The conception of world order discussed in this chapter and illustrated in two opposite ideal types provides a context for evaluative reflection on distinctive national policies of knowledge transfer, differing practices in educational cooperation, and finally the massive multilateral educational influences introduced to Chinese universities through World Bank projects.

——— 5 ———

CONTRASTING POLICIES OF
KNOWLEDGE TRANSFER TO CHINA

China's cultural relations with foreign nations, including the Soviet bloc and many developing countries, have become increasingly broad and eclectic since 1978. Nevertheless there can be little doubt that knowledge introduced to China from countries of the OECD will have the greatest impact over the coming decade. This chapter therefore focuses on the cultural policy of six nations toward China: Japan, France, West Germany, Britain, the United States, and Canada. This cultural policy is seen as derivative of political-economic policy on the one hand, yet also as shaped by deep-rooted cultural and educational traditions on the other. On the first level, a distinction between the relative emphasis on political as against economic objectives may be significant. On the second level, differences in approach arising from cultural tradition are of interest.

Three broad patterns of cultural interaction characterize China's relations with the six countries. Knowledge transfer from Japan to China takes place within the shared understanding provided by common Confucian values. The success that Japan has had in transforming these values for the service of modernity may be of special interest to China. Knowledge transfer from Europe to China proceeds within the cultural context of a shared understanding between two ancient civilizations undertaking modernization. Parallels in European historical experience may be of significance for China's modernization efforts. In contrast, the transfer of knowledge from North America to China represents the contribution of a pioneer civilization in which cultural tradition has not shaped social change to the degree of European and Japanese experience.[1] This might be seen as valuable in shaking off the stranglehold of the past.

To provide a context for evaluative reflection that moves beyond these historical parallels, let me return the first ideal type presented in chapter 4. It envisages a kind of knowledge transfer that contributes to the resolution of China's internal contradiction and supports a transformative role for China in the global order. The values of equity, autonomy, solidarity, and participation highlight the conditions necessary for knowledge to have transformative effects rather than serving short-term foreign interests and ensuring conformity. How might they be expressed in national policy on foreign cultural relations?

Equity draws attention to the way in which bilateral agreements are reached and the mutuality of the interests served. Autonomy touches on the deeper level of mutual respect and understanding. A policy of knowledge transfer sensitive to autonomy would ensure a balance between the applied techniques that contribute directly to Chinese economic development and the theoretical fields that are essential to the capacity for generating new technological developments. A balance between the natural and human sciences, which form their ideological and cultural context, would also be desirable. Evidence of a well-proportioned emphasis on these different knowledge areas, allowing for a critical assessment and selective assimilation of foreign knowledge, would indicate respect for Chinese autonomy and support for China's long-term political and economic development. Solidarity would be served by forms of knowledge transfer that encourage a collective reinterpretation and absorption of new knowledge and its broad dissemination. Finally, participation would find expression in forms of knowledge transfer that elicit the creative theoretical contributions of the Chinese scholarly community rather than allowing them to become marginalized individuals who passively copy theories and techniques produced elsewhere.

An ideal cultural policy might be envisaged as one that transfers knowledge in the context of a whole social culture, providing for it to be understood against this background yet assimilated in a selective and critical way. It is one that provides for the widespread distribution of the new knowledge introduced by geographical region and by social grouping, so that inequalities are reduced rather than exacerbated. Furthermore, channels of mutual interaction open the way for an active Chinese contribution to the cultural, social, and scientific currents of partner nations.

With this ideal of mutuality in cultural policy in mind, and with the sense of China's cultural and educational history that has been developed in earlier chapters, I now examine the different approaches to knowledge transfer exemplified by six OECD nations. Each section begins with a brief consideration of the relevant knowledge tradition, since this is the aspect of culture salient to policies of knowledge transfer. Then the contemporary political economic context of cultural policy is considered. Next, the main lines of cultural policy and the various forms of knowledge transfer are described. Finally, some evaluative reflections are offered on each case.

Japanese Policies

Modern higher education in Japan has been shaped by the cultural values of group identity, verticality of social relations, and exclusiveness, all drawn from the Confucian tradition, according to one Japanese analysis. These persisting cultural values explain the failure in both the Meiji period and the postwar period to implement American-derived patterns of decentralized administration. They probably also account for the attractiveness of aspects of the French Napoleonic university and the Prussian education system which were introduced in the late nineteenth century.[2]

Japan's imperial universities were established with the express purpose of meeting the needs of the state in promoting the science, technology, and social sciences necessary for modern development within a philosophical perspective acceptable to Japanese culture.[3] By 1918 there were five imperial universities, headed by Tokyo University, growing to seventy-five national universities by 1970.[4] The early private universities, most notably Waseda, were set up by progressive thinkers who challenged this role by their support for more liberal and critical social scientific study.[5] Still, the preeminence of the national universities set up to serve the direct interests of the state has never been successfully challenged. In the postwar period, concern for political and ideological control has given away to a conservative desire for universities to make a more direct contribution to national economic needs and the attempt to impose American-patterned boards of trustees who could represent business interests. While this has been protested in the name of academic freedom, some inroads have already been made, the new Tsukuba University of Technology being one example.[6]

What is remarkable in the Japanese higher education system is the success that has been achieved in promoting mass higher education, reaching nearly half the age cohort, within a highly stratified and diversified system, combining national institutions, prestigious private institutions, and local-level institutions of a variety of types.[7] The contours of Confucianism have been preserved in the hierarchical structure of Japanese society and the transfer of familial relations to broader social groups, yet the knowledge content has been transformed in such a way as to make possible Japan's remarkable economic achievements. There is thus an interesting parallel with the Chinese situation. Chapters 1 and 2 have analyzed the contradiction between the attempt of Chinese leaders to use persisting Confucian patterns for political control while encouraging a rapid expansion of the technological sciences for economic development. There could well be a parallel between the contemporary leadership's attraction to Japanese patterns and that of China's early modern leadership, who looked to the Japanese model between 1895 and 1911.

The political context for the revival of Sino-Japanese cultural interaction can be sketched out quite briefly. Diplomatic relations were normalized in 1972, laying a foundation for the development of cultural and educational ties. The Treaty of Peace and Friendship signed between the two nations in August 1978 expresses the intention of promoting the exchange of scholars and students on the basis of the four principles of peaceful friendship, equality, mutual trust, and long-lasting stability. A further strengthening of the political relationship came in September 1984 with the first session of the Twentieth Century Committee for Chinese-Japanese friendship, proposed by the foreign ministers of the two governments in November 1983.[8] Its brief is to explore new possibilities in Japanese-Chinese relations, transcend the differences in social system, seek ways that enable bilateral relations to develop on a long-term, stable basis, and submit proposals to the respective governments. It is to look to the future with penetrating insight and put forward long-term proposals.[9]

Even more important than these well-developed political ties are economic relations between the two countries which have strengthened dramatically between 1978 and 1985. Over that period China's world imports grew from U.S. $9.9 billion to $42.3 billion, while its exports rose from $8.7 billion to $27.4 billion. Japan's share in Chinese imports has varied between 21 and 35 percent over the period, jumping from $8.7 to $15.1 billion between 1984 and 1985. In 1985, 35.8 percent of China's imports came from Japan and China's trade with Japan registered a deficit of over $9 billion.[10] Added to this have been Chinese complaints over the low level of Japanese investment in China, only 10 percent of all foreign investment in 1984 in spite of the Japanese monopoly of Chinese imports.[11] Japanese policy on the export of technology to China has also been seen as rather conservative, and there have been complaints about the quality of some technological imports.

The combination of these economic complaints with fears of a revival of Japanese militarism, provoked by the visit of the Japanese prime minister to the shrine of those killed in the Second World War, sparked a series of student movements in the autumn of 1985 in China. Preparation for the commemoration of the fiftieth anniversary of the December 9th Movement of 1935[12] gave Chinese university students the excuse for a prolonged period of activism. Students openly denounced what they called Japanese economic imperialism. They then linked this with the bureaucratic capitalism of Communist Party officials who use their special privileges as a way of protecting entrepreneurial activities, a situation the students saw as having parallels with the bureaucratic capitalism of the late nineteenth-century Westernization movement. They further criticized the pro-Japanese faction in the present leadership for offering excessive flattery to Japan. Finally they directed criticism at the sons of leading officials now trying to carve out for themselves a secure position within the present power structure, and to secure opportunities for entrepreneurial gain.[13] In their analysis students linked internal tendencies toward a tightening of political control and its abuse with the external danger of economic domination. Their concerns deserve attention, since Japan is the only one of the six industrialized countries that has so far aroused this kind of direct social protest. The orientation toward internal politics of the more extensive student protests of December 1986, discussed in chapter 2, provides an interesting contrast.[14]

These well-developed, yet somewhat vexed, political-economic relations provide the context for cultural and educational relations between Japan and China. The Agreement on Cultural Exchange was first signed in 1979,[15] a Memorandum of Understanding on Scientific Exchange was signed between the Japan Society for the Promotion of Science (JSPS) and the Chinese Academy of Sciences (CAS) in September 1979, an agreement on academic exchange in the social sciences and humanities between JSPS and CASS, also a parallel one with the Chinese Ministry of Education in November 1982.[16] These agreements have led to a dramatic increase in the number of Chinese students and scholars going to Japan, as well as Japanese students and scholars in China. Between 1973 and 1978 only 52 Chinese went to Japan, whereas between 1979 and 1983, it is estimated that 1,716 went on programs sponsored by the Chinese or Japanese governments and 1,098 went under various forms of private sponsorship, often involving Japanese citizens' groups. There has also been an increasing emphasis on accepting Chinese technicians and managers into work-experience programs in Japan and developing educational cooperation outside the Chinese education system under other ministries.

Table 5.1 illustrates the growing number of Chinese studying in Japan under official auspices between 1979 and 1984. An initial focus on undergraduate students and visiting scholars was succeeded by an emphasis on graduate students from 1982. A total of 175 of those in Japan in 1983 were supported by the Japanese government, and another 863 had Chinese government scholarships. In 1984 Japanese government support was provided for 225, with a promise to increase this support to 500 by 1989.[17]

There are no accurate figures available on the knowledge emphasis of these students and scholars, but the majority have been in scientific fields. Of the first group of 379, sent in 1979, 298 were in science and technology, 42 in medical sciences, 13 in agriculture and fishery, and 22 in Japanese language. Since 1979 the Japanese government has assisted the Chinese in providing teachers for language training and cultural orientation given to about 150 students each year, 100 at the Dalian Foreign Languages Institute and another 50 at the Dongbei Normal University. The orientation program included some basic sciences taught in Japanese and courses in politics, economics, and history for those preparing to study the social sciences. The latter group amounted to 30 of the total of 379 students sent between 1979 and 1983. Since 1983 this language orientation program has been changed to accommodate Chinese university graduates preparing to undertake postgraduate study in Japan.[18]

An important distinction between the rather conservative establishment

Table 5.1

Chinese and Japanese Government-Sponsored Students in Japan, 1979–1984

	1979	1980	1981	1982	1983	Total	In Japan, 1984
Undergraduate	—	103	115	117	65	400	364 (17)
Visiting scholar	131	238	224	266	144	1,003	526 (108)
Graduate	—	—	—	148	165	313	148 (50)
Total	131	341	339	531	374	1,716	1,038 (175)

ethos of national universities and the more liberal and critical ethos of prestigious private universities in Japan was noted earlier. Information on the institutional distribution of Chinese scholars and students is of in interest in light of this distinction. Table 5.2 shows that by far the majority have been admitted to Tokyo University and other national universities, with only a small number at private and local institutions.[19]

In addition to this provision for long-term study, the Chinese Ministry of Education and the Academies of Science and Social Science together with the Japan Society for the Promotion of Science provide for shorter-term visits both ways under Chinese and Japanese government support. The CAS specially requested cooperation in the basic sciences, and this has been a focus of their tie with the JSPS. There were also seventy-two university linkages between fifty-three Chinese universities and forty-six Japanese ones in 1985. These linkages enjoy little government financial support,[20] with the exception of the linkage between Tokyo University and the Chinese University of Science and Technology, which is a center of Japanese scientific cooperation with China. It is discussed in detail in chapter 6.

Another quite distinct channel of knowledge transfer from Japan to China is that provided through the Japanese International Cooperation Agency (JICA) which has been active in China since 1978 and has brought a considerable number of Chinese trainees to Japan on work experience programs of six months to a year. Table 5.3 shows the specialist fields of Chinese technical trainees placed in Japanese government agencies.[21]

In addition to the 977 trainees in this government-supported program, other Chinese trainees have been placed in work experience programs in Japanese private industry under the Association for Overseas Technical Scholarships.[22]

Other JICA activities cover a whole range of cooperative projects in China which are rather clearly linked to Japanese economic and trading in-

Table 5.2

Placement of Chinese Government-Sponsored Students in Japan

Type of institution	Undergraduate	Graduate	Total
Tokyo University and other national universities	317	625	942
Osaka Municipal University and other public universities	10	14	24
Waseda University and other private universities	5	31	36
Other institutions	32	4	36
Total	364	674	1,038

Table 5.3

Chinese Trainees in Japan under JICA, 1978–1984

	1978–80	1981	1982	1983	1984	Total
Planning and administration	15	9	17	9	21	71
Public works	86	38	34	41	50	249
Agriculture, foresty, and water	1	37	23	30	18	91
Mining and & construction	26	15	29	30	26	126
Energy	1	4	9	5	4	23
Commerce and tourism	22	19	20	24	31	116
Human resources	—	2	3	27	26	48
Health and medicine	21	33	37	38	44	173
Social welfare	2	6	2	1	—	11
Other	5	8	28	—	41	82
Total						977

terests. They include the modernization of railways and port facilities, mining projects, energy, and telecommunications. There are also a number of educationally and socially oriented projects under JICA. The Friendship Hospital in Beijing, built by JICA, has six Japanese doctors and other Japanese staff, sends twenty Chinese doctors to Japan each year for six-month periods, and is making an important contribution to the fields of orthopedics and neurosurgery.[23] The Japanese Management Training Center in Tianjin, set up in 1983 under the State Economic Commission, focuses on training teachers of management.[24] Other such training institutions under the Ministry of Communications and the Ministry of Railways were in the planning stages in 1985.[25]

These developments indicate that the knowledge transfer in various technological areas outside the education system may be as important as that under educational auspices. These practical technical and social fields are growing in importance within the exchange process and complement the more theoretical academic fields which dominate the experience of Chinese graduate students and scholars in Japan.

When asked what Japanese policy was with regard to the balance of knowledge areas provided for in exchange, a Japanese embassy official claimed that there was no official policy. Japan simply responds to the needs and requests of the Chinese as far as resources allow.[26] The increasing provision for technically oriented work-experience programs indicates a response to the explicit Chinese policy of sending technicians abroad discussed in chapter 2. As for geographical distribution, the Japanese claimed that to have no regional policy but simply to respond to Chinese needs and requests.

The practical aspect of Japan's knowledge transfer to China is openly linked to economic and trade interests, and here the question will be how far it is seen to serve long-term Chinese economic development or merely short-term economic growth. The student protests over Japanese economic imperialism, noted earlier, suggest that there is already some popular unease about the kind of economic contribution Japan is making to China's modernization.

The more theoretical aspect of knowledge transfer, that involving the scholars and students studying in Japan, is characterized by a concentration of the influence of national universities, especially Tokyo University, as against private universities that have a more liberal orientation and local level institutions. This presents an interesting contrast to China's historical experience of educational relations with Japan early in the century. At that time the majority of Chinese students in Japan were in private institutions, and many brought back radical political views.[27] Now the conservative ethos of Japanese national universities may leave its mark on Chinese scholars and students. If so, it could support persisting Confucian patterns in China's knowledge structure rather than contributing to their transformation.

In spite of these areas of potential concern, there are many positive aspects to Sino-Japanese educational relations. Common roots in the Confucian cultural tradition provide an unusual basis for shared understanding. For example, Japan's management science may be more capable of transferal to the Chinese context than Western theory, since the social and cultural conditions for such a transfer are present. Also, Japanese and Chinese literary circles have long provided mutual stimulation to one another, and this is likely to continue under present conditions. Furthermore, Japanese and Chinese science share a set of modern terms developed in the late nineteenth century which could stimulate a distinctively Asian way of looking at basic scientific issues. If economic penetration and political sensitivity are kept at a tolerable level, cultural and educational relations could prove mutually beneficial.

French Policies

Two features of modern French higher education that distinguish it from other nations are the Napoleonic model of the university, set in place in the early nineteenth century, and the *grandes écoles*, which raised the prestige of the applied sciences of engineering and administration above the traditional disciplines and professions taught in the university.[28] Another significant feature of French scholarly culture has been a tendency toward seeing knowledge as a unity, which has stimulated high academic standards and a shared sense of a national intellectual culture, integrating natural and human sciences, pure and applied.[29]

Some aspects of the French intellectual tradition, most notably the integration of scholarly institutions into a modernizing bureaucratic structure, owe at least part of their inspiration to the well-documented French fascination with the Confucian meritocratic system in the seventeenth and eighteenth centuries.[30] It is not surprising, therefore, that French higher education patterns appeared to be an attractive approach to educational modernization in Meiji Japan, and that they were also emulated in the efforts of Chinese scholars in the early Nationalist period to set up a university district system.[31] Equally the example set by the Ecole Polytechnique has undoubtedly influenced China's great polytechnic universities, mediated through the Soviet patterns adopted in 1952.[32] Deep-rooted experiences of cultural and educational interaction thus underlay the political-economic rapprochement between France and China in recent decades.

Although some European nations had given formal recognition to the People's Republic of China in the fifties, Charles De Gaulle's decision to reestablish Sino-French diplomatic relations in 1964 marked an important turning point for Sino-European relations. This French expression of independence from American foreign policy coincided with a Chinese move away from the Soviet Union toward rapprochement with second world powers.[33] The French had an active embassy in Beijing from 1964 and saw themselves as playing a mediating role in assisting China's diplomatic and political reentry into the world capitalist community.[34] For the fifteen years between 1964 and 1979, when U.S.-China relations were normalized, they operated as a kind of bridge between China and Western nations.

Of all the Europeans, French politicians most like to dwell on the theme of the parallel between two ancient civilizations facing modernization which was evoked by European scholars giving advice on Chinese educational reform in the 1930s.[35] Both sides like to resurrect the statement made by a nineteenth-century traveler that France is in essence the China of Europe, as China is in a sense the France of the Far East. Both sides like to remember also that a number of China's distinguished Communist leaders—Zhou Enlai, Deng Xiaoping, Li Fuchun, Li Lisan, and others—spent many years in France as part of the worker-student movement of the twenties.[36] Finally, it may be significant that Maoist ideas disseminated during the Cultural Revolution had a greater impact on France than on other Western countries, an interesting parallel with French openness to Confucian values introduced during the seventeenth and eighteenth centuries.[37]

In contrast to the strength of these political ties and this cultural empathy, Sino-French economic and commercial relations remained at 15-20 percent of the total trade between the European Economic Community and China between 1978 and 1983. The signing, however, of a long-term agreement on the development of economic relations and cooperation in April 1985 was regarded as a breakthrough in Sino-French economic relations.[38] The two governments agreed to expand their cooperation in energy, telecommunications and information, transport, ports and airports, mining, agriculture, and the metallurgical, chemical, machine-building, and textile industries. In addition, under two loan agreements the French government undertook to provide China with development loans and loans for microwave and telephone exchange projects. The clear intention behind this economic support from the French government is a rapid growth in trade between the two countries,[39] as well as a higher level of trade between China and the European Economic community as a whole.[40] The French contributed 31 percent of the total U.S. $1.08 billion investment made by the EEC in China, which in turn represented 7.3 percent of total foreign investment between 1980 and 1985.[41]

Both friendly political relations and growing economic interests thus lie behind French cultural policy toward China and the provision being made for knowledge transfer to China. Most academic and educational interaction takes place under the auspices of a cultural accord first negotiated in 1965, suspended from 1967 to 1973, and renegotiated in detail every two years since 1979. In the 1984-85 program the Chinese undertook to send 120-150 doctoral students and about 60 visiting scholars to France each year.[42] The French government promised scholarships for 30-35 doctoral students, a figure that was raised to 50 in the autumn of 1985, and financial assistance for a considerable number of visiting scholars, totally about 100 fellowships in all. In return the Chinese provide scholarships for 65 French students and scholars in China. By the summer of 1984 there were reported to be 740 Chinese in France: 110 undergraduates in a program already being phased

Table 5.4

Chinese Scholars and Students in France, 1983

Level	Pure sciences	Applied sciences	Social sciences	Arts	Total
Undergraduate	67	75	3	5	150
Graduate	64	80	9	7	160
Visiting scholar	130	87	6	37	260
Total	261	242	18	49	570

out, 400 graduate students, and 230 visiting scholars. About 80 percent were estimated to be in fields of the pure and applied sciences.[43] By 1987 the total number of students and scholars had grown to 1,500.[44] The only breakdown available by level and study area is one reported for the summer of 1983 and given in table 5.4.[45]

The relative emphasis on the basic sciences is an interesting characteristic of the French program. Also, the accord makes specific provision for a certain number in linguistics, literary studies, and social sciences. Most pursue their studies within French universities, but a certain number succeeded in passing the rigorous entrance examinations for study within the *grandes écoles*.

There were about fifty agreements between Chinese and French universities in 1984, but most got very little government funding and were unable to undertake substantial cooperative activities. The development of regional ties between France and China, however, coinciding with a move toward the decentralization of higher education administration in both countries, may open the way for greater support in the future. The French government has focused on one main linkage, that between Wuhan University and the French Ministry of Foreign Affairs, which makes Wuhan University a center of French scholarly culture in China. The conception behind this provision of an integrated exemplar of French intellectual culture in China is discussed more fully in chapter 6. Another significant development on the level of institutional cooperation is the new interest of a few private *grandes écoles*, especially in the fields of management and commerce, in having linkages with Chinese institutions. Some are offering scholarships to Chinese students from their own resources.

French officials claim to have no regional policy in knowledge transfer to China, but simply to be responding to Chinese needs and seeking to concentrate their limited resources in a few regions, with Wuhan as the center point. As for disciplinary emphasis, this has been worked out in cooperation with the Chinese in an attempt to identify priority fields that express both French excellence and areas of importance for China's needs. The following areas have been agreed on jointly: medicine, biotechnology, aeronautics, space, agriculture, economics, law, and mathematics. French scholarships favor students in these areas, and they also give preference to applicants from universities that have institutional agreements with French ones.

Another aspect of French support for educational interaction with China is in the provision of French language teachers for China. About thirty are sent from France each year, six to work in foreign languages institutes preparing students for study in France and the others in the foreign languages departments of various universities. The French have expressed a wish in the accord that some should be placed in technological universities not directly administered by the State Education Commission, in support of attempts now being made to develop the social sciences and foreign languages in these institutions.[46]

In addition to the cultural accord that provides the main framework for academic interaction, an agreement for cooperation in science and technology was signed in 1978 and renegotiated in 1984.[47] Between 1981 and 1984 projects of scientific cooperation grew from 59 to 133.[48] While some of these projects are under governmental auspices from the French side, others involve direct linkages between Chinese ministries and private French corporations. Cooperation in space technology is an interesting example of both government and private linkages. On November 6, 1984, the Chinese Academy of Space Technology under the Ministry of Astronautics Industry signed a protocol for cooperation in space technology with the Matra Corporation.[49] In February 1985 another protocol was signed for cooperation in this field between the French Ministry of Research and Technology and the Chinese Vice-Ministry of Astronautics Industry.[50] Finally, in June 1985 a third agreement was signed between the Chinese and the French National Space Study Center.[51]

Most practical technological training is taking place under the auspices of commercial relations. For example, the Matra Corporation has undertaken to train twelve Chinese engineers for a six-month period. The French government, however, also supports a small program in which French International Agency for Technical Cooperation organizes work experience for technological and industrial trainees under an agreement with the Chinese Enterprise Management Association (CEMA). A six-month French language program is given in the Beijing Institute of International Relations, followed by nine months in France combining work experience in industry with time in a management school, then follow-up activities after return to China. By 1985 ten Chinese trainees had been enrolled in this program.[52]

The French are also strongly involved in a center for management education set up by the European Economic Community and the State Economic Commission in Beijing to train Chinese managers and scholars of management at a fairly high level. The dean of this center is a French professor from the Ecole de Commerce, and there is a clear effort to provide an alternative to the American-initiated management program at Dalian.[53] This project is discussed in greater detail in chapter 6.

As in the case of Sino-Japanese relations, two rather different sets of values and practices are shaping the transfer of knowledge from France to China. The first is associated with the university community and mediated under the terms of the national cultural agreement. The second is related to industrial and commercial cooperation and increasingly attracting the interest of some of the *grandes écoles*.

There are a number of interesting features in the university-mediated exchanges. First, there has been a conscious attempt on the French side to give the Chinese an exemplar of the interconnectedness of knowledge areas within French intellectual culture. The long-term French presence at Wuhan University should enable the Chinese to make a critical assessment of the French knowledge tradition and an interpretation of both technological and social sciences against this background.

Second, the attraction of Chinese thinkers to the French university model due to its geographical and administrative rationalization and its high academic standards has been noted earlier. In the Soviet patterns adopted in China in 1952, the Chinese implemented some of these features, which served immediate development needs yet also inhibited the flexible adaptation of knowledge patterns to changing modernization needs. Given this shared legacy, the changes that have taken place in the French university since the violent upheavals of the late 1960s may be suggestive for present Chinese reform efforts: the creation of the university institutes of technology (IUT), the greater autonomy given to universities over their curricula and financing, and the reorganization of departments into smaller and more flexible *unités de recherche et d'enseignement* which are to encourage a more spontaneous interdisciplinary cooperation.[54] The present Jiaotong University experiment of creating informal academic discipline groups, described in chapter 3, may have some resonance with French experience.

The other side of cooperation, Chinese involvement in high-level French technology and the increasing interest of some of the *grandes écoles* in China, holds promise for a different sort of impact. France's constellation of private enterprise, public corporations, and high-level commercial-technological education in both sectors combines central planning with the market sensitivity of a capitalist society. The original idea of the *grandes écoles* as institutions selecting an elite for technological-administrative leadership expressed a transformation of the Confucian meritocratic ideal that was unique to France's modernization experience.[55] The question of what relevance this historical model has for contemporary China and whether it could support a gradual resolution to the contradiction between traditional and transformed knowledge patterns is a fascinating one.

West German Policies

The German knowledge tradition represents a rather different adaptation to modernity than the French. German universities gained a predominant position as centers of teaching and research in the pure disciplines during the nineteenth century and succeeded in maintaining a remarkable level of autonomy in spite of their financial dependence on the state and the position of their professors as state officials. New applied fields of knowledge relevant to industrialization were largely developed in separate institutions, the *Technische Hochschulen*, which led the way for an excellence in technical education reaching down to the secondary school level.

German cultural policy at the turn of the century encouraged the export of technical schools as both an expression of cultural cooperation and a sound basis for long-term economic cooperation.[56] In the period before the First World War a number of German technical schools were created in the eastern part of China, supported by both the German government and German industry. They flourished and received strong Chinese support. One of them, Tongji Medical and Engineering College, survived the war and continued to prosper under the support of German industrialists even when political and diplomatic relations between the two countries had been broken off. Today, more than sixty years later, it is one of China's major polytechnical universities and has become, once again, a pillar of Sino-German cultural and scholarly relations.[57]

Other influences of the German knowledge tradition were introduced to China through the Japanese patterns emulated in the late nineteenth and early twentieth centuries. German medical science and law as well as the general contours of the modern university were introduced through this channel. An even more direct influence from the German university came about through the experience of the Chinese educator and statesman Cai Yuanpei during a lengthy period of study at the universities of Berlin and Leipzig, and his determination to introduce to China the knowledge patterns of the Humboldtian university. This is evident in the legislation he shaped as minister of education for the new republic in 1912 and even more in his leadership of Beijing University from 1917 to 1923. A commitment to the pure disciplines of knowledge, with high-level commercial and technological training provided outside the university, was to make possible conditions where academic freedom could be realized and a scholarship could flourish that gave general moral direction to the nation.[58]

In fact, neither the German university nor the German *Technische*

Hochschule was to play an important role in Chinese higher education patterns of the Nationalist period. Only after Liberation under a Soviet influence that retained features of the German academic tradition did the fundamental dichotomy between pure and applied knowledge become institutionalized in the Chinese higher education system. Given these direct and indirect influences, West Germany's postwar experience of transforming the knowledge base of its universities, both humanistic and technical, may be of interest to China.[59] The creation of a new level of higher technical education in the *Fachhochschule* is also an innovation relevant to China's new vocational universities.

Diplomatic relations between China and West Germany were normalized in 1972. In contrast to Sino-French relations, few words have been lost in extolling the cultural and political empathy that exists between the two nations. Rather, the focus has been on economic and trade interests. Between 1978 and 1985 West Germany managed to capture and hold the lion's share of Chinese trade with the European Economic Community (EEC). China's imports from the EEC rose from U.S. $2.1 billion to 6.2 billion over this period, and West Germany's share increased from 26 percent in 1978 to 40 percent in 1985.[60] Nevertheless, direct German investment in China by mid-1985 was lower than that of France and Britain, only 16 percent of the European total. In spite of a trade deficit of $1.7 billion in 1985 and relatively low levels of German investment, there has been no Chinese perception of economic imperialism parallel to that of Japan.[61]

High trade figures have been sustained under conditions of an official economic cooperation agreement signed first in 1979 and implemented under the guidance of a joint committee that meets every year.[62] In addition, the German Ministry of Economic Cooperation has generated good will by channeling considerable funds to various economic and technical development projects in China both directly and through other German agencies. A report on development cooperation activities in China prepared by the United Nations Development Program for 1984 listed twenty-one small-scale projects of technical assistance amounting to about U.S. $29 million.[63]

The first agreement of cultural cooperation between West Germany and China was signed in 1977 and is renegotiated every two years. It is a comprehensive document covering cultural, educational, scientific, and technological activities at the national level, under various foundations and academic bodies, and at the level of agreements between German and Chinese universities. The Deutscher Akademischer Austauschdienst (DAAD) administers scholarships for 40 Chinese graduate students each year with the stipulation that 5 should be in the social sciences, 2 in music, 5 in medicine, and 1 in law. In addition, about 150 scholarships are provided through various foundations with special areas of emphasis: the Alexander von Humboldt Stiftung, focusing on basic sciences; the Hanns Seidel Stiftung, focusing on technological and professional fields; the Friederich Ebert Stiftung, which includes social sciences; and others. The agreement also provides for about twenty teachers of German to teach in Tongji University's preparatory center and in the German language specializations of a number of Chinese universities.[64]

About thirty university-level agreements are listed in the document, and provision is made for scholarships and research cooperation among these institutions, covering three-month to one-year visits of Chinese scholars, longer periods for Chinese graduate students, and provision for German scholars to visit China.[65] Also a protocol for cooperation in the basic sciences between the Max Planckt Gesellschaft and the Chinese Academy of Sciences is provided for under the agreement.[66]

The areas of intellectual cooperation covered by this important cultural agreement embrace Wissenschaft in its broadest conception, seen more as cultural consumption than as economic investment and linked to the values of the traditional German university. The generosity of financial provision made by official agencies of various types has meant that Germany hosts the largest number of Chinese scholars of any European country, approximately 1,400 in 1985,[67] a number reported to have surpassed 2,000 by 1987. The focus of emphasis has shifted since 1982 from visiting scholars and undergraduates to a present concentration on Chinese graduate students following doctoral programs. There are no accurate data on the distribution of knowledge areas, except for the figures provided in table 5.5, which represent the situation in 1982.[68]

The relatively small emphasis on pure sciences and human sciences in comparison with France is of interest and may reflect Chinese perspectives on the fields of knowledge most important to them in Germany and the German willingness to respond to a strong Chinese preference for the applied sciences. The DAAD, however, does make some effort to ensure that the human sciences are represented in programs it funds.

Like France's link with Wuhan University, Germany has created a center of intellectual cooperation in China at Tongji University. Up till recently this was confined to the technological sciences, with a parallel support for medical sciences at Wuhan Medical College, the successor of the former Tongji Medical College. In 1985, however, a national center for German studies was established at Tongji with support from both governments and a mandate to extend Tongji's cooperation with West Germany to include the social sciences, particularly economics and education.[69] This project is discussed in more detail in chapter 6. A further development took place in 1987 when China agreed to Germany establishing a Goethe Institute in Beijing, the first foreign cultural institution of this type on Chinese soil.[70]

Aspects of economic cooperation have increasingly dominated Sino-German cultural relations, affecting education as well as other areas. The

Table 5.5

Chinese Scholars and Students in Germany, 1982

Level	Pure sciences	Engin. sciences	Other applied sciences	Social sciences	Arts	Total
Undergraduate	67	114	27	—	—	208
Visiting scholars	108	152	20	11	11	302
Total	175	266	47	11	11	510

German Ministry of Economic Cooperation supports a program for sending Chinese technicians into German industry for work experience, and by 1987 the Carl Duisberg Gesellschaft, which administers the program, reported that 1,800 Chinese technicians and management personnel had had training in Germany since 1979.[71] Another economically oriented project of cooperation is the German Management Training Center, located at the Baoshan Steel Complex outside of Shanghai and supported by the German Ministry of Economic Cooperation and the Chinese State Economic Commission.[72] Further such projects are taking shape through linkages between German Länder and Chinese regional or national authorities in particular sectors. These also gain some support from the German government. For example, the state of Baden-Wurtenburg has set up the Beijing Electrical Appliance Mould Technology Training Center in cooperation with the Chinese Ministry of Machine Building.[73] Technical training is also going on through commercial and industrial linkages with such German industrial firms as Ziemens and Volkswagon.[74]

Broader educational interests are also being served under the aegis of economic cooperation. For example, the German Ministry of Economic Cooperation supports a center for Shanghai primary school teachers that is intended to disseminate new curricular and pedagogical ideas. Direct support is organized through the Hanns Seidel Stiftung. It also supports the teaching of German as the first second language in four Chinese secondary schools in Shanghai, Nanjing, Beijing, and Wuhan, with some provision for Chinese teachers of German to be trained in Germany. The most exciting educational project under discussion in 1985 was the creation of a model *Fachhochschule* with federal German support. There was considerable rivalry among German Länder and Chinese cities, which linked up to gain the prize of this project. The outcome was expected to be a model Fachhochschule in Hangzhou with linkages to Chinese vocational universities in Ningbo, Nanjing, and Hefei for the dissemination of materials and ideas.[75]

Special interest also exists in the area of law. The German government has agreed to support the establishment of an international law research institute.[76] Also China's patent law has been influenced by the German exemplar, with German support given for the establishment of the Chinese Patent Office[77] and German specialists sent to lecture in this area.[78]

Another aspect of Sino-German cultural interaction relates to the scientific and technological cooperation agreement signed between the two countries in 1978. The general areas of cooperation are in energy, raw materials, transport, space, aviation, and the peaceful uses of nuclear energy. Between 1978 and 1984 over thirty projects have been signed for cooperation in satellite communication and data transmission, niobium-tantalum ore prospecting, technical transformation and improved management in enterprises, solar energy experiments, space technology and meteorite research vanadium slag processing, iron ore concentration, coal liquidation, and coproduction of remote control milling machines. Clearly these were all closely linked to economic and industrial interests.[79]

The primary motive force of Sino-German cultural relations seems to be an economic one. Tremendous energy has been put into various levels and types of technical training supported by the federal government, various Länder governments, and large private corporations. The strength and enthusiasm of the Länder governments and their growing regional ties[80] with China suggest that German technical training will reach beyond the few major cities that tend to dominate China's foreign educational relations. German cultural officials see the need, however, for centers of concentration if German development aid is to be effective. They see themselves as responding to a Chinese regional emphasis on the rapid development of the East Coast yet trying to contain the burgeoning university-level and regional-level linkages, all of which need financial support from the federal German government.[81]

As for knowledge areas, the focus on the transfer of practical, technological knowledge comes across clearly in the details given above. It represents the coincidence of an historical German orientation toward exporting technical education[82] and a strong hinese interest in these fields. At the same time, the wealth of German provision for scholarly relations through the many foundations as well as the DAAD has made possible a complementary emphasis on basic theoretical sciences and some provision for the social sciences and humanities.

German educational relations with China are probably the strongest numerically within the European community, yet they remain modest in relation to the much larger number in the United States. It is therefore difficult to speculate on the contribution that German cultural and academic values might make to Chinese development. Speaking at Beijing University, the German chancellor depicted Germany as an enlightened part of the North, seeking a strong and independent role for China as part of the developing South. He spoke also of the need for ideological understanding as the background to the transfer of technology and scientific knowledge,[83] and German cultural policy gives evidence of an attempt to provide for some balance in a situation where technology and technical education definitely dominate the scene.

Will the Chinese succeed in understanding some of the spirit that lies behind German technological superiority, in terms of both basic science and sociophilosophical context? That will be the key to the transfer of knowledge from Germany that helps China to take up a transformative role in the global community. Set against this would be a mechanistic transfer of technological know-how that leads to a dependency on German technology.

In the intellectual arena the German university was once responsible for a German mandarinate that had a role resonating with the intellectual authority of the Confucian scholar-official class, yet this has been transformed beyond recognition by both war and economic change.[84] This makes it an interesting exemplar for Chinese universities which are still struggling to break free from Confucian knowledge patterns. Both the success of German higher education and the obstacles that have arisen to the creation of an integrated university combining traditional faculties, normal colleges, and *Fachhochschule*[85] are of significant interest for China in the recent drive toward higher institutions that are more comprehensive in their curricular offerings.

British Policies

Historically, British educational patterns probably exerted less influence in China than those of any of the other nations discussed in this chapter, with the exception of Canada. In spite of Britain's dominant economic interests in China in the nineteenth and early twentieth centuries, there has never been an Oxbridge on Chinese soil, nor any significant parallel to the influence exerted by German, French, Japanese, and American higher education patterns at various times in Chinese history.[86] Interestingly, however, the British ideal of the scholar-gentleman[87] and the British practice of filling many of its civil service posts with Classics graduates from Oxbridge have a strong resonance with Confucian patterns.[88] The adaptation of British universities to industrialization and a high-technology society is therefore of considerable interest to China.

Britain was one of the few European nations that recognized Communist China in 1950, although diplomatic relations were only raised to the ambassadorial level in 1972. While cultural and economic relations began to flourish after 1978, the colony of Hong Kong was somewhat of an obstacle in political and diplomatic relations. The successful end to long and delicate negotiations for its return to China in 1997 has opened the way for what is seen as a new stage in relations between the two countries.[89]

Between 1978 and 1983 British exports to China ranged between 7 and 16 percent of the European total, a situation which aroused concern. In June 1985 a five-year economic cooperation agreement was signed to "encourage . . . diversified and mutually advantageous cooperation in the economic, industrial, agricultural and technical fields," which went into effect January 1, 1986.[90] Furthermore, in October 1985, the British government provided a Ō100 million soft loan facility to encourage British exports to China. The visit of a British trade mission to China in December 1985, led by senior representatives of six British companies, brought about an agreement for six projects using British technology—a thermal power plant, the reequipping of a tractor factory, and four others. Discussions were started for a further twenty projects.[91] This appears to be the beginning of a British attempt to imitate the more aggressive policies for promoting economic links which have been noted in the German case above.

Cultural relations are regulated through an agreement between the two governments signed in November 1979, and scientific and technological relations are governed by a parallel agreement made in November 1978. Every two years a program of activities covering all three areas is renegotiated.[92] The major British institution responsible for the coordination of exchanges is the British Council, whose role might be seen as parallel to that of the German DAAD. It provides twenty-five scholarships a year for Chinese students and scholars in Britain in exchange for an equivalent number of British graduate students in China. It also assists in placing Chinese students in British academic institutions throughout the country.

Since 1983, the British government has made a particular effort to encourage Chinese study in Britain through the provision of 260 tuition-free places each year. General guidelines for curricular areas stipulate that the 60 places provided by the Foreign and Commonwealth Office give priority to the humanities and social sciences, particularly practical areas such as economics, law, management, project planning, international relations, education, English language and literature, library science, and urban planning. The 200 places provided through the Overseas Development Administration focus on such applied sciences as agriculture and fisheries, transport, mining, shipbuilding, offshore oil, computer technology, and electronics.[93] A clear direction is thus given to curricular areas of practical importance where British educational provision may meet Chinese needs. In addition, a small number of scholarships are provided by other agencies, and short-term academic visits under the auspices of agreements between the Chinese Academy of Sciences and the Royal Society, the Chinese Academy of Social Sciences and the British Academy, and the Economic and Social Research Council are given government support through the Academic Links Scheme. Special provision is also made for the support of direct

Table 5.6

Chinese Scholars and Students in Britain, 1983

Level	Pure sciences	Applied sciences	Social sciences	Arts	Total
Undergraduate	14	27	—	7	48
Graduate	37	76	5	6	124
Visiting scholar	93	278	32	27	430
Total	144	381	37	40	602

institutional-level links between British and Chinese higher institutions.[94] The British seem to have the most carefully thought out policy on disciplinary emphasis in the transfer of knowledge to China. The pattern emerging in 1985, as articulated by a British cultural official, was one of 70 percent emphasis on science and technology, 20 percent on the social sciences, and 10 percent on the humanities.[95]

By the autumn of 1985 there were about 300 Chinese scholars and students in Britain under full or partial British financial support, and another 400-500 on Chinese government funding, a total of about 800. By March 1988, this number was reported to be over 2,000. However, figures showing the level of study and knowledge emphases are available only for 1983[96] and are presented in table 5.6. Since that time, the sending of undergraduates has ceased, and there has been considerable increase in the number of graduate students on master's or doctoral programs, with a greater emphasis on the applied social sciences.

Scientific cooperation between China and Britain is coordinated under general agreements between the Royal Society and the Chinese Academy of Sciences[97] and the China Association of Science and Technology.[98] Cooperative research mainly takes place through the presence of Chinese scientists as visiting scholars in British laboratories. Technological cooperation is thus at a rather high level. There is no strong initiative for the support of work-experience for Chinese technicians and managers in British industry. An agreement between the Confederation of British Industry and the Chinese State Economic Commission provides for five Chinese engineers to be placed in British industry, and it is reported that even the placing of such a small number has created problems in Britain's high-unemployment situation.[99]

As for cooperative educational activities within China itself, the British official focus has been on strong support for English language teaching, both through providing teachers and materials for various Chinese university centers that train college-level English teachers for the whole nation and through support for the programming of English language series on the Chinese Television University. While long-term centers for English language teaching gaining this support have so far been placed in major East Coast cities—Nanjing, Beijing, Shanghai, and Guangzhou—the intention is for British support to move to less favored regions and institutions once the necessary infrastructural support has been developed. The vision of a broad dissemination of opportunity for English language learning demonstrates a sensitivity to the fundamental cultural dynamics of knowledge transfer. Language contains the key to an understanding of the cultural and social context of the technology China is importing from Western countries, and this sustained and careful provision for effective teaching of English should have long-term benefits.

A second area of great importance for China's long-term participation in the world community is that of information and its dissemination. Here a British private initiative—the support of the Thomson Foundation—assisted the creation of an English language newspaper, *China Daily*, which has been extremely valuable for the Chinese as a means of projecting their image to the international business and academic communities. It is probably the most open and critical English language newspaper emanating from a Communist country. It has also led to a joint educational venture, the Xinhua News Agency-Thomson Foundation International Journalism Training Center, which was opened in Beijing in April 1985 with a brief to train journalists for Xinhua's English language section and for other third world countries.[100]

Both official and private British efforts for knowledge transfer to China exhibit a breadth of vision and a cultural reflectiveness that may be compared with the more aggressively economistic policies of Japan and West Germany. Given the small scale of Britain's cultural involvement with China, it is difficult to speculate on the implications of knowledge transfer from Britain to China. What might be noted, however, in contrast to other European nations and Japan, is that the dichotomy between technical and academic educational influences is less obvious. Thus two dangers noted in the Japanese case, and present to a lesser degree in German relations with China, are absent in the British case: the danger of a transfer of technical knowledge only motivated by short-term economic goals and the possibility of traditional academic values being transferred that reinforce the Chinese political proclivity for preserving and using Confucian patterns.

The absence of these dangers is evident in the selection of educational models to be emulated. Two models are of greatest interest: the Open University, which has influenced the Chinese Television University, and the polytechnic, which has been a model in the World Bank-supported project for Chinese urban vocational universities.[101] These represent modern British institutions that have transformed features of the British academic tradition to serve political democratization and local economic development.

At the close of this review of cultural relations between three major European countries and China, it may be appropriate to make a few comments on the involvement of the European Economic Community as a whole in knowledge transfer to China. Until recently, trade issues[102] and a Chinese political concern for an independent Europe[103] were the key features of this relationship. In May 1985, however, this cooperation moved to another level with the signing of agreements on economic, technological, and industrial cooperation. A range of new activities in 1985 indicate that knowledge and technology transfer is likely to form an important role in these agreements. In March 1985, a European Management Training Center was opened in Beijing with European support for the formation of Chinese managers and scholars of management at a high level.[104] In October 1985 a high-level Sino-European symposium on the new technological revolution was held in Beijing.[105] And from January 1986 the European Community opened a permanent mission in Beijing. A year-end article in the Chinese press in December 1985 lauded Western Europe's Eureka program as an effective response to American and Japanese high-technology developments.[106] Evidently the Chinese approve this assertion of technological and economic independence and hope for growing opportunities for technological cooperation and knowledge transfer.

American Policies

American knowledge patterns are rooted in the tradition of the colonial college, a fragmented local institution governed by a board of trustees who represented sectarian Protestant concerns as well as the practical interests of the community.[107] This proved a less constrictive tradition to be shaken off in the modernization process than traditional European or Confucian scholarly patterns. New knowledge found its way quickly into institutions that were oriented toward serving the practical needs of the local community, a service ultimately directed toward the agricultural and mechanical arts vital to modernization.[108] By the time the European idea of the university was finally introduced under German influence in the mid-nineteenth century, higher education foundations were in place that ensured that it neither inhibited the introduction of new knowledge in practical or theoretical fields nor hindered the gradual expansion of a diversified system of higher education able to meet mass needs by the 1960s.

These characteristic features of diversity and integration[109] have meant that the export of American educational patterns has not been characterized by the kind of dualism between the academic and the practical most evident in the Japanese and German cases discussed above. This aspect of American higher education has been deeply attractive to Chinese thinkers since early in this century and was successfully exemplified in the sixteen American missionary colleges and universities on Chinese soil before 1949.[110] The historical survey of Chinese curricular development given in chapter 1 illustrates, however, how attempts to encourage these integrated patterns, bringing together pure and applied, natural and social sciences in a problem-solving approach to knowledge, coincided with periods of political anarchy in recent Chinese history.

The question now may be whether China finally has political and economic conditions favorable to the flexible and integrated knowledge patterns characteristic of the American model. If so, contemporary American influences in China could be quite liberating. Chapter 3 has already indicated reforms taking place in a range of higher institutions that represent a cautious move toward such curricular change.

The other side of contemporary American influence, however, is an openly expressed intention on the part of the American government to use educational relations with China for political purposes. Since the normalization of Sino-American relations in 1979, American officials have encouraged access to their educational and scientific institutions in the expectation that this will influence a new generation of Chinese leaders.[111] They have also been more successful that most other Western nations in ensuring maximum access for their scholars to all aspects of Chinese society, so enhancing the already outstanding Sinological scholarship and intelligence about China that exists in the United States.

While political and cultural goals take precedence, American economic interests in China are also considerable. Between 1978 and 1985, the American share in China's imports grew from 9.2 percent to 11.9 percent, from under U.S. $1 billion to 5 billion, resulting in a Chinese trade deficit of $2.7 billion in 1985. Sino-U.S. joint ventures grew from twenty-one in 1983 to sixty-three by the end of 1984, and total U.S. investment by private corporations in China reached $1 billion by the end of 1984,[112] just behind the $1.08 billion of the EEC. There remain, however, difficulties in trade relations arising from U.S. restrictions on the export of some high-technology items to China.

Cultural, educational, and scientific relations between the United States and China are carried out under the terms of a series of agreements negotiated since 1979. The Agreement on Cooperation in Science and Technology signed by Jimmy Carter and Deng Xiaoping in July 1979 provides the basis for twenty-seven protocols of cooperation in scientific fields between government offices on both sides.[113] The Memorandum of Understanding on the Exchange of Students and Scholars, signed in 1978, became incorporated under this agreement and was replaced by a new protocol for cooperation in educational exchange in July 1985. The other important agreement is a cultural agreement signed first in 1979 with a new program jointly negotiated every two years.[114]

The main support officially given to Chinese scholars by the American government is under the Fulbright program of the United States Information Agency (USIA), which provides for about seventeen to twenty-five Chinese scholars to go to the United States for research in the social sciences or humanities and in some cases to teach Chinese. The same number of American professors are sent to China, mostly to teach in centers of American studies within Chinese universities. Funding is also provided on a competitive basis for American-Chinese university linkages, but only a limited number (five in 1985) succeed in getting this support. The emphasis of the Fulbright program on theoretical work in the social sciences and humanities is consciously intended to offset the very strong focus on the sciences of Chinese students and scholars in the United States who are supported on Chinese government funding. This U.S. government initiative indicates the strong support given to promoting an understanding of U.S. scholarship and the American way of life within China.[115] A second area that gains some federal government support is the Management Training Center at Dalian, run under a protocol between the U.S. Department of Commerce and the Chinese State Economic Commission. It is discussed in detail in chapter 6.

The Committee for Scholarly Communication with the People's Republic of China (CSCPRC) was established by the National Academy of Sciences, the Social Sciences Research Council and the American Council of Learned Societies in 1966 for the purpose of furthering scholarly communication with the PRC. In the more open circumstances of the mid-1980s its aims were to strengthen the American research presence in China, to serve as a catalyst for Sino-American scholarly cooperation, to provide liaison between the American academic community and the Chinese and American governments, to monitor policy issues related to Sino-American academic, scientific, and technological cooperation, and to represent the scholarly interests of its three sponsoring organizations. It provides fellowships for American scholars and graduate students to do research in China, as well as a program for distinguished American and Chinese scholars to make short-term research visits to each country. Over the years it has made possible both scientific and social science research in China and sponsored many cooperative research projects and conferences.[116] By 1985 its focus of interest in the sciences was expressed in an integrated program in the two areas of biotechnology and global change.[117]

A whole range of American philanthropic foundations are also committed to support educational cooperation with China. In 1979 the Chinese Delegation at the United Nations made a request to the Ford Foundation for support in the areas of law, economics, and international relations.

There are now three programs in place that arrange for the formation of young Chinese scholars in these fields in the United States, and also provide various forms of support for key centers within Chinese universities, institutes of political science and law, and research institutes of the Chinese Academy of Social Sciences. The programs are administered by Columbia University (law), the CSCPRC (economics), and the Institute of International Education (international relations).[118]

Christian organizations in the United States are also playing a significant role in support of educational exchange activities. After the normalization of Sino-American relations in 1979, the Chinese government made a payment of around U.S. $10 million to the United Board for Christian Higher Education in Asia in recompense for the property of its thirteen former missionary colleges in China which had been taken over by the Chinese government in the early 1950s. In 1980 the United Board signed an agreement with the Chinese Ministry of Education to use these funds in support of higher education development. A special program for Chinese scholars in the social sciences, humanities, and fine arts enabled 230 people to study or do research in the United States between 1981 and 1987.[119] Support has also been given to two hinterland Chinese universities—Sichuan University in Chengdu and Shaanxi Normal University in Xi'an—to enable them to develop library centers that serve the Southwest and Northwest respectively.[120]

Another Christian organization with significant involvement in the exchange of teachers and students is the China Education Exchange of the North American Mennonite Central Committee. The geographical focus of its involvement is Sichuan, Jiangsu, and Liaoning provinces. A basic principle is complete mutuality in the exchange, and this may be the only project in which nearly as many Chinese teachers come to teach in North American colleges as North American teachers go to China. Students are also exchanged on an equal basis.[121]

The strong American emphasis on promoting a Chinese understanding of the humanities and social sciences as pursued in the United States and American research in China is offset by a Chinese emphasis on the basic sciences and technological fields in the large number of students and scholars sent to the United States. Table 5.7 details the disciplinary emphasis of students and scholars sent on official Chinese programs between 1979 and 1984. The strong emphasis on engineering and physical sciences is noteworthy, as is a modest growth in emphasis on management, humanities, and social sciences.

Of the publicly sponsored students and scholars, half to a third received Chinese government support between 1979 and 1983. About 40 percent were supported by American universities and colleges, reflecting both their success in competing for fellowships and the great enthusiasm of American institutions in seeking support for them. University-level agreements be-

Table 5.7

Percentage Distribution of Publicly Sponsored Students and Scholars in the United States by Field of Study, 1979–1984

Field of Study	1979	1980	1981	1982	1983	1984
Agriculture	3	4	2	3	4	5
Business management	1	1	1	1	1	1
Computer science	5	4	4	4	4	4
Education	1	2	2	2	2	2
Engineering	30	31	31	29	27	29
English as second language	—	1	1	1	1	1
Health sciences	9	10	11	11	10	11
Humanities	1	2	2	3	3	3
Law	—	1	1	1	1	1
Life sciences	9	8	9	10	9	9
Mathematics	6	5	4	4	5	4
Physical sciences	29	25	24	24	25	22
Social sciences	4	3	4	4	5	6
Other	—	2	3	3	2	2
Total	100	100	100	100	100	100
N =	(1,000)	(2,174)	(5,565)	(6,971)	(7,740)	(2,277)

Source: David Lampton, *A Relationship Restored: Trend in U.S.-China Educational Exchanges, 1978–1984* (Washington, D. C.: National Academy Press, 1986), p. 39.

tween about a hundred American universities and colleges and Chinese higher institutions are supported mainly through each institution's own resources, private enterprise, or foundations. The long history of cooperative linkages between Chinese and American universities in the pre-Liberation period as well as the relative financial autonomy of American institutions seems to be the reason for a much fuller flowering of this kind of activity in the American than the European or Japanese contexts.

Another unique feature of Sino-American academic relations has been the efforts made by distinguished American scientists to identify promising talent among Chinese university students in the basic sciences and arrange their entry into American Ph.D. programs in some of the best American centers. About 120 in physics, 100 in biology, and 50 in chemistry are recruited every year, and most of their expenses are borne by the American universities where they study in the form of graduate assistantships. The Chinese leadership hold great hope for the contribution of this group of young scientists if and when they return to China and the new postdoctoral centers were established particularly with this group in mind.

An American study drawing upon visa records estimated that nineteen thousand Chinese students and scholars had gone to the United States between 1979 and 1983, and that twelve thousand were still there in 1984. By 1987, the number was thought to be well over twenty thousand.[122] This inflow has required minimal American federal funding and has depended largely on the enthusiasm and financial flexibility of American universities and colleges. Even if a substantial number of the Chinese in the United States do not return, there can be little doubt that American knowledge transfers will have a more significant role in shaping Chinese educational development than any other foreign influence over the next few years.

What is the likely effect of this powerful influence of the American knowledge tradition on China? The historical analysis in chapter 1 suggests that American knowledge patterns have genuine potential for supporting a resolution of the internal contradiction discussed there. The ways in which pure and applied sciences, natural and social sciences have been integrated in addressing problems of science and society are favorable to both economic development and political participation. Historical experience suggests that the difficulty for the Chinese will be in creating effective institutions for the gradual liberalization of access to knowledge and its reorganization consonant with moves toward political democratization. Nevertheless, the profiles of institutional change given in chapter 3 indicate that a process of this kind is already underway.

If American patterns are culturally appropriate to China's needs, educational relations with the United States may be somewhat threatening politically. The United States is the only Western nation that is explicit about its use of education as an arm of foreign policy and its intention of exercising a political influence on a generation of Chinese youth. The other side of this political programmatic, however, is strong official support given to American studies in China and the formation of Chinese social scientists in the United States. This could well encourage a Chinese understanding of the political, social, and cultural context of American science and technology that would strengthen Chinese autonomy.

Canadian Policies

Canadian universities have a history only slightly longer than that of China's modern universities. Like Chinese universities, they have been influenced by a range of knowledge traditions, the British, Scottish, French, and American probably being the most significant. There the parallel ends, however. China's modern university system has emerged from a scholarly culture and a set of traditional institutions going back several thousand years, while Canada's universities are the products of a pioneer society. Over this century Chinese universities have gone through a series of revolutions and radical changes in both national political policy and national educational model, while Canadian ones have evolved gradually with a slow melding of foreign influences.[123]

The Canadian knowledge tradition is difficult to depict in a few broad strokes. Nor can it be said to have had any definitive historical influence on Chinese higher education which might provide clues to the potential of cultural values transmitted through Sino-Canadian academic exchange. Canadian missionary support for Chinese higher education in the pre-Liberation period was largely integrated with American institutions and had a strong focus on medical education and on Sichuan province. The one interesting point of persistence between the Canadian contribution to Chinese education then and now might be seen as an emphasis on practical and applied fields of the natural sciences.

Canadian-Chinese diplomatic relations were normalized in 1970. One of the motivating factors for this move was clearly the desire to increase trade relations which had already become established in the 1960s. Between 1978 and 1985 Canada had considerable success in this, maintaining a share between 4.5 and 6 percent in China's total imports each year, a figure close to that of the West German share in the Chinese market over the same period.

Nonproblematic political relations and a growing Canadian economic interest in China provided conditions between 1970 and 1983 in which a total of 1,650 Chinese scholars and students spent long-term study periods in Canada and another 864 came on short-term academic visits. This movement was centrally administered through an educational exchange agreement between the two nations that provided for a small-scale exchange of students, and through a Memorandum on Educational Cooperation signed in June 1979 in which the Council of Ministers of Education (Canada) undertook to place Chinese scholars in universities around the country for two-year study periods. In addition, quite a number of Chinese came through university-level linkages and direct application to Canadian universities, and others came for upper secondary education under the sponsorship of Canadian-Chinese relatives.

Fields of study for the long-term students and scholars were given the following emphasis: 24 percent in engineering, 21.3 percent in basic sciences, 9.2 percent in medicine, 3 percent in agriculture, 17 percent in language training, 2.2 percent in arts, and 16.8 percent at the secondary level. The Chinese government financed 36 percent of this total, the Canadian government 12 percent, and Canadian universities 10 percent. Another 22 percent were financed by private citizens. A study of Sino-Canadian academic relations, completed in December 1985, gives fascinating details on the geographical and institutional origins of these scholars and students as well as their distribution among Canadian institutions. It also gives information on Canadian students and professors who have studied, researched, or taught in China by field of study.[124]

A significant turning point in Sino-Canadian educational relations came with the signing of an agreement between the Canadian International Development Agency (CIDA) and the Chinese Ministry for Foreign Economic Relations and Trade (MFERT) for official Canadian assistance to Chinese development in October 1983. The rationale behind this move from the Canadian perspective is well summed up in a report commissioned for CIDA in the autumn of 1985.[125] China's move back into the international community from 1978, taking up its seats in the International Monetary Fund and the World Bank, engaging the involvement of UN organizations in development projects and famine relief, and seeking favorable terms for the import of technology from Japan and other industrialized countries culminated in its inclusion in the eligibility list for foreign aid of the Development Assistance Committee of the OECD. This made possible a rapid opening up of the Chinese market, and Canada clearly wanted to maintain and enhance its participation as well as to add to the export of primary products a component of high-technology items. Development aid was seen as vital for strengthening trade. It also provided new financial resources for the educational interaction that was already underway.

The three areas of concentration selected as appropriate both in terms of Canada's expertise and China's needs as an industrialized developing country that had made agricultural and light industry its priorities were natural resources (energy, forestry, agriculture, and mining), infrastructure upgrading (power, transport, and communications), and the social sector (education, health, training, and management). The focus was to be not so much the transfer of goods and services as the multiplication of contacts between people in which both sides had something to learn and something to impart. The focus on human resources development as against hardware transfer was seen as a contribution to ease internal Chinese constraints and contribute to a long-term economic growth that would benefit both sides. China's own concern for the human and managerial aspects of development became explicit in the documents on the reform of the economic system promulgated in the autumn of 1984 and the spring of 1985 which seemed to confirm the Canadian approach. These have been discussed in chapter 2.

The outcome of this approach to development cooperation by the end of 1984 was fifty-eight separate development projects, covering all the sectors identified above and involving a range of Canadian and Chinese institutions.[126] The total budget for the first five years was nearly Canadian $90 million. The issue of the regional distribution of these projects is worked out between CIDA and MFERT, and an attempt has been made to seek a balance between appropriate concentration in areas geographically compatible with Canadian conditions and a fairly broad dissemination of opportunity. Two provinces where there has been a concentration of resources are Heilongjiang in the northeast and Sichuan province in the midwest. A number of other provincial-level bureaus are also actively involved in some of the projects.[127] A more detailed discussion of several representative projects is found in chapter 6.

Already by 1985 the stimulus provided by these projects for greater educational interaction was evident in that applications for study visas in Canada doubled over the previous year, reaching 1,300 by October, almost as many as the total who had gone to Canada for long-term study between 1970 and 1983. Next to the United States and Japan, Canada had become the third most popular country for Chinese students, with many gaining financial support from World Bank projects for study there.[128]

Parallel to the Japanese and German programs for training Chinese technicians in work-experience situations, Canada has a Human Development Program under CIDA which aims "to contribute to the upgrading of the human resource capacities of up to 367 younger Chinese in key development positions with significant human development functions, concentrating on critical areas in China's development program."[129] By the summer of 1985, 145 Chinese trainees had already been placed in Canadian institutions for work experience, 37 in international trade, 18 in management and related areas, 50 in engineering fields related to transportation, energy, and telecommunications, 18 in agriculture-related fields, and the rest in medical and environmental areas.[130]

A few interesting points of comparison with other countries come out in this brief sketch of Canadian policies of knowledge transfer to China. The administration of various forms and channels of educational interaction is a bureaucratic exercise due to a high level of dependence on federal government financing, yet the process itself is decentralized with a great deal of institution-level interaction. It thus falls between the decentralized U.S. approach and the much more centralized organization that prevails in Europe. Perhaps West Germany has the closest parallel in the relations among federal agencies, Land constituencies, and individual institutions participating in exchange. This makes possible a central definition of cultural and educational policy. Canada, however, has not gone beyond the practical emphases identified above in articulating a policy on the knowledge areas that should receive emphasis in educational relations with China. The result is neglect of both basic natural sciences and theoretical social sciences which stands in striking contrast to American policies.

If inadequate attention has been given to the knowledge question, the mode of knowledge transfer and the commitment to a broad geographical participation on the Chinese side may be significant positive features of Canadian policy. Here there are interesting parallels with Canadian missionary history where such hinterland provinces as Sichuan were deliberately chosen and knowledge transfer was seen as "the multiplication of ourselves."[131]

Conclusion

In China's historical experience, foreign cultural values expressed in specific curricular patterns have had outcomes that were often unintended by the policy makers of the nations in question. Both Soviet and European curricular patterns served to strengthen persisting Confucian values while American ones supported progressive aspects of the Chinese scholarly tradition. This had nothing to do with American, Soviet, or European political policy toward China.

It might be worthwhile, therefore, to reflect on the present situation first from the perspective of the unconsciously held cultural values underpinning intellectual interaction. From this perspective, Sino-Japanese educational relations seem most capable of exacerbating the tension between transformed knowledge patterns for economic development and traditional ones for political control, with Chinese scholars mainly concentrated in conservative national universities. In the German and French cases, the possibility of traditional European academic values harmonizing with a persisting Confucian knowledge orientation seems less likely. Both German and French higher institutions have undergone fundamental changes in recent decades which may be of interest for the Chinese as they seek to implement curricular reforms. In the British case, the traditional role of Oxbridge was close to the Confucian ethos, yet the Chinese have shown a vigorous interest in new models such as the Open University and the polytechnics. Culturally both American and Canadian knowledge patterns are also likely to be supportive of contemporary Chinese curricular reform.

If American patterns hold most promise on the unconscious level of cultural values, they may be somewhat threatening on the political level. In contrast to all the other nations, U.S. political goals are explicit and openly articulated. The parallel with the founding of Qinghua School in 1908 to educate a generation of young Chinese leaders who would be favorable to American interests is compelling. Could American positivism in the social sciences become a new orthodoxy for Chinese social scientists and the final reference point of a scientific model of development and scientific management theories and techniques? If so, a situation that has some parallels with the domination of Soviet orthodoxy in the fifties could emerge.

What makes this situation unlikely, however, is the broader cultural eclecticism of the present period and the variety of sources the Chinese have to draw upon in their reconstruction of the social sciences. Also the internal changes underway in the structure and organization of knowledge, discussed in chapters 2 and 3, should make China's internal knowledge system less vulnerable to external domination than it was in the 1950s.

The threat of political domination is virtually absent in the case of European countries and Canada, probably also Japan. The economic interests of these countries, however, are being served through their policies on knowledge transfer to China. The use of technical education to ensure cultural cooperation favorable to industrial interests is a long-standing tradition in Germany and is clearly evident in present policy. Japan and Canada are equally forward about promoting their national economic interests in China through cultural cooperation. Here there may be a danger of a superficial transfer of advanced social and natural technology that skews economic growth in favor of certain regions and so serves foreign interests as to arouse internal protest, something that has already happened in the case of Japan.

These issues of political and economic interaction might be considered in relation to the World Order Models values of equity and autonomy. One thing that seems quite evident in China's cultural relations with OECD nations is the ability to achieve terms favorable to their own chosen interests in the negotiation of agreements, in some cases, indeed, even to contravene what might seem equitable to the partner nation. What is much more problematic in the present period is the fostering of a genuine cultural autonomy. For this to be done, the Chinese will need a thorough critical understanding of the social and cultural contexts of desired scientific, technological, and management knowledge so that it can be adapted effectively to the Chinese context and in turn generate new understandings that would contribute something fresh to the world community. Interestingly, it seems to be France, Britain, and the United States whose policies on educational interaction are doing most to provide such a context, in contrast with the more economistic orientation of Canada, Germany, and Japan.

Turning to issues of solidarity and participation, the specific concern would be the dissemination of knowledge introduced from abroad and its accessibility to different levels and groups. Here Britain and Canada seem to be the only countries with a clear regional policy. The many regional linkages between Chinese provinces and cities and foreign counterparts, however, may broaden participation. It is interesting to note the special commitment of North American Christian organizations to educational support for hinterland regions and for groups that might not otherwise have an opportunity to be involved. Generally there can be little doubt that the long-term economic interests of OECD countries are more likely to be served by a transfer of technology that contributes to a balanced interregional development in China than by one that concentrates on those regions that promise immediate economic returns.

These reflections on the differing approaches to educational relations with China exemplified by six OECD countries are tentative and exploratory. Moreover, the gap between policies delineated in national and regional agreements and what actually happens in the knowledge transfer process must be taken into account. Chapter 6 therefore moves to the level of the practice of educational cooperation. A series of cooperative projects are reviewed, leading to another level of evaluative reflection.

——— 6 ———

THE PRACTICE OF KNOWLEDGE TRANSFER
THROUGH EDUCATIONAL COOPERATION

The creation of cooperative educational institutions on Chinese soil, involving foreign and indigenous participation, represents a collective form of knowledge transfer that may touch China in a deeper way than the individual contributions of scholars and students returning there under the various bilateral agreements discussed in chapter 5. Such institutions have significant precedents in China's historical experience, and it is possible to look back and see how they became absorbed over time into China's own modernizing higher education system. They may also be judged from the perspective of world order models scholarship.

WOMP values for nonimperialistic interaction between center and periphery nations can be specifically related to projects of educational cooperation. Equity suggests project aims and forms of organization that are reached through full mutual agreement. Autonomy suggests a respect for the theoretical perspectives rooted in peripheral culture that would require center participants to gain a thorough knowledge of this culture. Solidarity suggests forms of organization that encourage maximum interaction among peripheral participants and growing links between them and their fellow researchers. Participation intimates an approach to knowledge that does not stratify in a hierarchical way but assumes the possibility of a creative peripheral contribution from the very beginning.

In the even more concrete form of a project of cooperation in China, an ideal of mutuality might take the following form. Aims and patterns of organization are set by joint agreement from both sides. Foreign participants gain a deep and genuine understanding of Chinese scholarly culture and participate in intelligent dialogue over the differences between it and their own theoretical perspectives. Networks of interaction among Chinese participants in the project and between them and their fellows in other institutions ensure a critical reinterpretation of the new theory and techniques being introduced. Chinese discoveries and contributions in the field are in turn integrated into the dominant paradigm, modifying its direction. A good library is built up, representing a balanced collection of foreign and Chinese materials with a translation policy that facilitates the transfer of ideas both ways, and the creation of some kind of synthesis.

This chapter begins with a consideration of China's historical experience of educational cooperation. The different cultural dynamics that arose out of particular foreign influences are highlighted, as is the contribution made by certain historical projects to China's political and economic development. Then a comparative framework is suggested for considering contemporary projects of educational cooperation representing four different knowledge areas: integrated academic knowledge, basic sciences and technology, management science, and human sciences. The special problems facing knowledge transfer in each of these areas are discussed as a background to the overview of cooperative projects that forms the main body of the chapter.

Historical Reflections on Educational Cooperation in China

The most notable form of educational cooperation in Chinese history was the educational activity of missionaries on Chinese soil. This might be seen as an expression of cultural penetration in its commitment to Christian proselytizing. The outcomes of missionary projects, however, differed in ways that reflected the cultural patterns they embodied and so are of great interest as an aid to interpreting contemporary cultural dynamics. Educational projects expressing intergovernmental cooperation have also been important in China's historical experience. The relative strength of the political or economic motivation behind them is significant, as well as the cultural dynamics represented. The six projects considered here—two French, two American, one German, and one Soviet—represent a range of different influences.

Brief references have already been made in chapters 1 and 2 to Zhendan University (L'Aurore), which was founded by French Jesuits in 1903 in cooperation with a Chinese scholar and ex-Jesuit, Ma Xiangbo. He envisaged a "new style university that would keep pace with Western universities" and integrate the best of Western learning into a modernizing Chinese framework of knowledge. In contrast, the Jesuit fathers' intention was to demonstrate that the Catholic faith was compatible with the highest intellectual endeavor and so make sure that Protestant higher institutions in China did not outshine them. Within two years conflicts between Ma and the Jesuits over the imposition of the French language, French curricular patterns, and French administrative styles resulted in Ma's withdrawal and the creation of a new institution, Fudan University,[1] whose progressive contribution to Chinese development has been noted in chapters 1 and 3. Under firm Jesuit control, Zhendan's high standards in the fields of medicine, engineering, and law ensured graduates whose professional knowledge was highly valuable to a Nationalist government seeking to promote economic modernization. This knowledge was also useful for the consolidation of political control in the pre-Liberation period. Jesuit authoritarianism and the Confucian values that Nationalist leaders increasingly invoked combined, however, to channel Zhendan's developmental possibilities toward a political dead-end. After the Revolution of 1949 it was disbanded, with its medical school used as the basis for Shanghai No. 2 Medical School and its other faculties combined with other institutions.

In interesting contrast, Yanjing University, the foremost American missionary college, stressed the liberal arts, developed new areas of knowledge such as journalism and rural sociology, and supported fine standards of traditional and modern Chinese scholarship. Liberal Protestant Christianity allowed for a sympathetic support of revolutionary activism that contrasted strongly with Zhendan's suppression of all student participation in political activism.[2] The stimulus that American knowledge patterns gave to political democratization contradicted growing American political support for the repressive activities of the Nationalist regime. While Yanjing was closed, along with all other missionary colleges, in the anti-Americanism of the Korean War period, its campus was taken over by Beijing University, and aspects of its scholarly achievements probably enhanced Beida's scholarship, in spite of the limitations imposed by narrow Soviet patterns.

If missionary projects were characterized by an integrated attempt to convey a clear ideological perspective through knowledge transfer, intergovernmental projects in the pre-Liberation period had a cohesiveness that was not rooted in religious ideology. The creation of Qinghua preparatory school in 1908 with American Boxer Indemnity funds had a clear purpose from the American side of educating a new generation of Chinese leaders who would be politically sympathetic to the United States, a goal not too different from contemporary American policy. A national university by 1926, its curricular offerings developed from a broad liberal provision of knowledge areas to a strong focus on the engineering sciences and a commitment to scientific method in the social sciences. Pragmatic, problem-solving science was the ideology that Qinghua offered to the Nationalist government.[3]

In the postrevolution period China's Communist leaders removed all the social science and humanities departments from Qinghua and built upon its excellence in the engineering sciences. In a new Soviet-oriented higher education system, Qinghua was made China's foremost polytechnical university. In sloughing off what was interpreted as American political penetration they destroyed an academic tradition drawn from American experience that had real promise for both the political and economic aspects of socialist construction. This is evident in present attempts to restore the curricular patterns of the pre-Liberation period at Qinghua.

In contrast to Qinghua, the German involvement in Tongji University was a kind of economically motivated penetration. A hospital started by German doctors in 1907 developed into a medical school and an attached engineering school by 1913. Seeing the value of having well-trained Chinese engineers and technicians who were familiar with German technology in China's newly developing modern industries, German industrialists helped to support what was a prime example of the German *Technische Hochschule* on Chinese soil.[4] It served the Nationalist concern for economic modernization without seriously challenging the increasing political repression of this regime. After Liberation, Tongji was integrated into the new socialist higher education system in a similar role to that of Qinghua. The German economic interests that had supported it slid into oblivion, to be revived only in China's rapprochement with West Germany after 1978.

Missionary penetration must be understood primarily in terms of religious and cultural intentions, although the political and economic interests of the missionizing nation were sometimes furthered. Intergovernmental projects are almost inconceivable apart from political or economic motivation. What is likely to be the fate of a cooperative project with neither religious nor political-economic motivation as its guiding force? Here Chinese history has a fascinating exemplar in the Université Franco-chinoise (Zhongfa Daxue).

Zhongfa University was created through cooperation between French radicals and Chinese progressives in 1921. In curricular emphasis the project embraced an admirable range of knowledge areas: biology linked with agriculture and medicine in Lamarck College, physics and chemistry linked with pharmacology and radiology in Curie College, the social sciences in Comte College, and studies in Chinese and French literature and history in Voltaire College.[5] The gentle socialism that formed the ideological basis of the project could not easily be labeled penetration. Precisely because there was little political or economic benefit for France in this cooperative project, French government support remained minimal. While several hundred Chinese young people were enabled to follow graduate programs in France, the university itself made little impact on the Chinese education system or on Chinese society. Its reputation never came near that of a Zhendan or a Yanjing, let alone a Qinghua or a Tongji. After Liberation it was disbanded and forgotten.

China's educational cooperation with the Soviet Union in the 1950s had interesting parallels with earlier Sino-American cooperation. The political motivation for Soviet support to China was clear and unequivocal. The role of People's University as the primary channel of Soviet penetration has been discussed earlier. It might be seen as an exceptionally large-scale and successful cooperative project, which made possible a massive transfer of social and scientific knowledge and technology from the Soviet Union to China.

The intellectual rationale and social technology for a socialist system were effectively transferred and contributed to China's rapid industrialization. While the Cultural Revolution saw an intense revulsion against the external political domination represented by the university, the patterns and forms of social organization transmitted had taken deep root and were gradually revived in the 1970s. A well-developed social technology containing an explicit ideology was successfully transferred and has been subsequently adapted to the new conditions of interdependence with Western capitalist nations arising since 1978.

Something in the strength of Chinese culture, also the fundamental independence and dynamic awareness of the Chinese psyche, has made it possible for these massive transfers of knowledge and technology to be turned to different ends than those intended by the donor countries. In the Chinese context they produced a development that was turbulent and problematic in many ways, yet one that did not lock China into lasting dependence on the United States, the Soviet Union, or Europe.

If penetration was not successful, however, neither was there a developed mutuality in these projects. This may have been because no satisfactory synthesis of Chinese and foreign thought was achieved or because China had not reached the level of economic strength necessary for effective counterpenetration. It was in the Cultural Revolution period, when the Soviet organizational technology channeled through People's University was repudiated and Qinghua and Tongji had been reconstituted as models of a revolutionary university, that a counterpenetration of Maoist educational thought took place. Its impact in Western countries was dramatic, yet short-lived.[6]

China's historical experience raises several questions of interest with regard to contemporary projects of educational cooperation. First, distinctions can be made among forms of cooperation that are economically or politically motivated. Second, the cultural differences among different knowledge traditions can make a real difference, quite apart from the political intentions of the partner nation. Third, linkages created between particular cooperative projects and the rest of the Chinese educational or social system are important. The Soviet influence of the 1950s differed from all earlier ones in the directive power exercised by People's University over the rest of the higher education system. Rather than encouraging the kind of solidarity necessary for a creative Chinese reinterpretation of the social theory introduced, it came to be seen as an instrument of control and repression.

Some kind of synthesis between Chinese and foreign thought is the essential basis for mutuality, and this was no more apparent in the period of Sino-Soviet rapprochement than in earlier periods. The present thus offers the challenge of creating, for the first time, forms of educational cooperation that make possible genuine mutuality. In the depiction of representative projects that follows, the reader may judge how far this challenge is being met.

Cooperative Education Projects: Parameters of Comparison

There can be little doubt that contemporary cooperative educational projects are expressions of political or economic penetration on the part of OECD countries. However, differences in the cultural tradition and educational patterns of each country find expression in certain differences in the practice of educational cooperation. Given the focus of this study on knowledge, the distinction of greatest interest is the curricular component of each cooperative project. Four distinctive knowledge emphases form the organizing principle for this chapter.

The first and least common form of cooperative project is one that attempts a balanced and integrated range of knowledge areas, including natural and human sciences, pure and applied. Although this approach was characteristic of missionary and intergovernmental projects in the pre-Liberation period, it is a rarity in the present situation. It assumes not the transfer of specific, value-free technology, but the presentation of a whole intellectual culture, which must be understood critically if the technology it spawns is to be successfully transferred. It is a form of cooperation that probably requires the breadth of a university to encompass it. Only one cooperative project in the present period fits this category—the French center at Wuhan University.

The second type of cooperative project is one that focuses on the natural sciences and related technology. Here the challenge is twofold: first, the transfer of technological knowledge that can be integrated with and serve to upgrade the present state of the art in China in specific technological areas, and second, the creation of channels of interaction in basic scientific theory that make possible Chinese cognizance of and contribution to world scientific currents. The transfer of technological knowledge unaccompanied by a theoretical integration into basic scientific debates would create dependency and a crude service to economic penetration, in contrast to knowledge transfers that strengthen China's own scientific base and ability to generate new technological knowledge.

The third and probably most popular type of cooperative project is in the field of management science. This might be defined as an applied social science. However, it is no longer just one of the social sciences in Western countries, but has pretensions to becoming the science of sciences, taking over the position progressively abandoned by theology, philosophy, and natural science in the Western intellectual tradition. It brings together approaches derived from such hard sciences as engineering—systems theory and operations research—with softer approaches derived from the psychology and sociology of human and organizational behavior. While claiming to be value-free, a set of technologies capable of increasing efficiency in all aspects of an economic system, socialist or capitalist, it is actually permeated with fundamental values of capitalism. Its transfer as pure technology could imply China's reintegration into the capitalist economic system on the terms of OECD countries. Its reinterpretation within the terms of Chinese socialism could provide Chinese industrialists and managers with tools for building a new socialist model that exemplifies an alternative pattern relevant to other third world countries.[7]

Finally, projects of cooperation in the human sciences are the rarest of all. The understanding they may provide of the social and cultural conditions that form the context for science, technology, and management in Japan and Western countries is of fundamental importance. In the human sciences, unlike the natural sciences and even management technology, the mastery of language is the essential key. Technology may well be transferred even if one does not have a thorough knowledge of English, Japanese, German, or French, but the cultural and social currents of the society that produced it will remain inaccessible. The sensitive teaching of language skills opens up a whole world of cultural and social meanings. Thus projects whose primary aim is language teaching are closely linked to cooperation in the human sciences. Fortunately, they open less rare.

Integrated Cooperation: The French at Wuhan University

Created as a teachers college early in this century, Wuhan University became comprehensive in 1913 and developed into a major national university embracing a wide range of knowledge areas along the lines of the American model. After Liberation, it remained a comprehensive university within the Soviet definition of an institution devoted to pure disciplines in the arts and sciences. Since 1978 such features of its pre-Liberation tradition as the use of the credit system for curricular organization and the provision of a greater breadth of knowledge areas, applied as well as pure, have been revived.[8]

Its openness for innovation can be seen in the way in which the opportunity for a special project of cooperation with France was seized upon in 1979. A French educational delegation visiting Beijing in 1979 suggested the selection of one Chinese university as a focal point for Sino-French intellectual cooperation. Wuhan University's vice-president happened to be in Beijing and expressed the university's willingness to take up this role.[9] Subsequent negotiations resulted in a two-year agreement of cooperation between Wuhan University and the French Ministry of Foreign Affairs in May 1980 and a second, three-year agreement signed in November 1981. The completion of five years of cooperation was celebrated in May 1985 when a third agreement was signed for 1985-87. Subsidiary agreements provide for particular linkages with French universities in Paris, Lyons, and Grenoble.[10]

Administratively, the project is fully integrated within Wuhan University, involving a newly established department of French, a special Sino-French mathematics program in the department of Mathematics, and a research center on French civilization, which involves the cooperative work of professors from the departments of history, philosophy, economics, and literature. About twelve French professors teach on long-term French government contracts within these programs.

The language policy clearly intends the development of a center combining excellence in French language teaching with broad opportunities for intellectual interaction with French scholars and French universities. The department of French has specializations in French language and literature and scientific French. The Sino-French mathematics program provides an initial year for all its students to learn French, then uses French as the main medium of instruction in all courses in the subsequent four years. In addition to the 280 students involved in these two programs, a few other students select French as their first foreign language instead of English, and about 30 percent of the whole student body study French as their second foreign language. The agreement provides for ten Wuhan staff to go to France as visiting scholars on exchange each year. There is thus a small but growing Chinese intellectual community with some shared understanding of and access to French scholarly circles.

The curricular emphasis of this project embraces mathematics, French literature, scientific French, and an interdisciplinary study of French civilization in a research center that has three sections: language and literature, politics and history, economics and management. This center recently gained French approval for a program preparing students up to the level of the Diplome d'Etudes Approfondies, the course preparation for a French doctorate.

Future plans include the development of a program in management science and another one in construction engineering. These applied sciences are to be introduced within the intellectual and linguistic milieu already established. Also a national center of Sino-French mathematics is located at Wuhan University.

This contemporary Sino-French project of cooperation is the only one so far that embraces the human sciences, the pure natural sciences, and related applied fields. There can be little hesitation about regarding it as a form of cultural penetration. Yet this penetration is characterized by conditions in which Chinese scholars may gain a critical understanding of French scholarly culture and may be able to interpret and adapt such technologies as those derived from French management science against this understanding.

Geographically located very close to the center of China, at the axis between north and south, coastal regions and hinterland, Wuhan has the conditions to reach out and create linkages with other Chinese institutions that could be drawn into the task of reinterpreting and disseminating the knowledge transferred from France. Its success in doing this may determine the level of mutuality that can be reached, whether it remains primarily a channel for introducing French-derived knowledge and technology or whether it can gather together a Chinese response of adequate credibility and strength to initiate a counterpenetration of French academic circles.

Cooperation in Science and Technology: German and Japanese Efforts

Two of the most extensive projects of cooperation in science and technology involve distinguished Chinese polytechnical universities and their linkages with West Germany and Japan. Tongji University in Shanghai revived its long-interrupted relationship with Germany in 1978. The Chinese University of Science and Technology was adopted by the Japanese government in a special project of cooperation with the Engineering Department of Tokyo University in 1982.[11]

Tongji's pre-Liberation roots in medical and industrial cooperation between Germany and China were noted earlier in this chapter. After 1949, it was reformed along the lines of the Moscow Civil Construction Institute, narrowing its focus to civil engineering and construction. Since 1978, dramatic curricular changes have taken place, involving the creation of three departments in the basic sciences, the establishment of a school of management with programs in construction management, engineering management, and economic information, and the broadening of engineering programs.[12]

These reforms have coincided with intensive cooperation with Germany undertaken within the terms of the national cultural agreement[13] and partnerships with three German universities. Under this cooperation, over 300 German professors have come to Tongji for shorter or longer periods, and about 150 Tongji faculty have spent time doing research in Germany. Three long-term cooperative research projects have been initiated. One brings together scientific, planning, and management aspects of the study of transportation systems. A second focuses on industrial technology, and a third involves the translation from German of texts and teaching materials relevant to Tongji and the preparation of a journal that will introduce German materials to China. Most recently Tongji has established a research center for German problems which is supported by the Chinese and German governments.[14]

Of Tongji's eight thousand undergraduates, about four thousand have taken German as their first foreign language. A five-year study program allows them an initial period of intensive language study. In the departments of mechanical engineering, electrical engineering, materials science, and chemistry, areas regarded by the Chinese as being advanced in Germany, students follow five-year programs with intensive studies in German spread over the first two years. In the School of Management, an initial year is given entirely to intensive German language studies, and in the subsequent four years at least one course each term is taught in German by a German professor.

In addition the university has a contract with the State Education Commission to provide German language training for Chinese students preparing for university study in Germany. From 1979 to 1981 three groups of secondary school graduates were given a one-year course and sent to undergraduate programs in Germany. Since 1982, classes of about 100-120 Chinese university graduates have been given a one-year linguistic, scientific, and cultural orientation for graduate study. The German government has given financial support to this project by paying the salaries of ten to fifteen German language teachers who teach within the university and preparatory school each year, as well as funding many of the short-term visits and university linkages.[15]

A few distinctive features of this Sino-German cooperation may be noted. The predominant role of the German *Technische Hochschule* is of interest. Tongji University is now seeking to develop into a comprehensive university with a focus on the engineering and management sciences, yet embracing also some natural sciences and humanities. The transformation of the German *Technische Hoschshulen* from institutions with a specific industrial orientation to ones with a much broader curricular provision may be a significant historical exemplar. Second, knowledge is being transferred in a framework that makes possible an understanding of the linkages among scientific theory, technology, and management in the German development experience. If the research in German education and the German economic system planned for in the new research center flourishes, a deeper understanding of the social and cultural milieu of German science and technology should be possible.

Tongji faculty affirm the value of the program, yet they have certain criticisms. One relates to language and the problem of the students and staff in having to master two difficult languages, German and English, in order to keep up with the latest developments in their fields. Another relates to teacher-learner relationships. In the early years of cooperation, German professors who came to give a lecture or report on research results were welcomed enthusiastically, and many learners turned out for their presentations. Recently, however, faculty and students have been less prepared to fill the role of eager learner. Cooperative research is seen as a more valuable form of interaction. The depth and significance of the research problems undertaken may therefore determine whether a real intellectual synthesis between Chinese and German thought results from this cooperation.

The relationship between the Chinese University of Science and Technology (CUST) and Japan is more recent, yet it seems to follow similar contours to the Tongji pattern described above. The creation of CUST in 1958 under the Chinese Academy of Sciences (CAS) marked an assertion of independence by the Chinese against Soviet higher educational patterns which had separated pure and applied sciences, as noted in chapter 3. The combination of science and technology in an institution similar to the American MIT model was intended to provide for the formation of potential scientific researchers for Academy institutes.[16] During the Cultural Revolution the university was moved from Beijing to Hefei, capital of Anhui province, in an effort to take scientific institutions closer to the grass roots of development needs.[17] Since 1978 its reputation for high-level scientific research has been enhanced year by year. However, it was for its democratic leadership and support for student agitation that it gained greatest attention in 1986, as noted in chapter 2.

In the first meeting relating to the China-Japan Cultural Exchange Agreement, held in September 1980, the Chinese requested that Japan cooperate with CAS in developing the educational and research system in engineering. CUST, the sole institution remaining under the jurisdiction of CAS, was suggested as the milieu for intensive cooperation between China and Japan. Members of the university visited Japan in November 1980, and in March 1982 a Japanese delegation, comprising members of the Ministry of Education, Ministry of Foreign Affairs, Japan Society for the Promotion of Science, and Engineering Faculty of the University of Tokyo visited Hefei to discuss the project. In June 1982 an agreement was signed between the two universities with a strong endorsement from both governments.[18]

The main focus of cooperation is on joint research projects in four fields: precision mechanical engineering, materials science and engineering, information engineering, and scientific management. As many as twenty Japanese professors spend several months each year at CUST working on joint research, and Tokyo University sends a certain number of instructors who teach basic subjects in Japanese. Ten Chinese scholars and researchers spend periods of several months each year at Tokyo University under the terms of the agreement.[19]

Like the Tongji project, this Sino-Japanese project seems to provide conditions for the long-term building of mutual understanding within a joint university context and for exploring the links among basic science, engineering science, and management as they have developed in the Japanese context. The absence of complementary research in the human sciences, however, may result in a technocratic orientation in these knowledge transfers rather than conditions for creative reflection on the two societies producing the technology. Also it is not clear how far the basic sciences form an important part of the cooperative research or whether the strengthening of China's independent scientific capacity is a priority.

Cooperation in Management Sciences: American, European, and Canadian Experience

If science and technology were seen by the Chinese as the key knowledge areas for the four modernizations in the late 1970s, management science came to be seen as equally important in the early 1980s. Up to May 1983, the State Economic Commission (SEC) had only five institutes for management training and a total of 100 teachers and 2,000 students. Two years later seventy-six institutes were in place, with a teaching staff of 3,700 and over 10,000 graduates to their credit.[20] Official approval of this new emphasis on management came in the Communist Party's " Decision on the Reform of the Economic Structure," promulgated at the Third Plenum of the Twelfth Central Committee in October 1984. Its call to draw on the world's advanced methods of management, including those of developed capitalist countries, has already been discussed in chapter 2.[21] The dissemination of this document was followed by a series of articles in the intellectual newspaper *Guangming ribao* reflecting on how capitalist management methods could be adapted to China and what a Chinese theory of organizational behavior might look like.[22]

As part of this rapid development of management education, the SEC and the China Enterprise Management Association (CEMA) planned a series of training centers that would be created through economic assistance from OECD countries and located in various Chinese cities.[23] A chain of cooperative projects in management education has thus emerged, with the involvement of the United States, the European Community, Canada, Japan, and West Germany. The American Management Training Center at Dalian was the earliest and in some ways a prototype for those that followed. It is distinguished by its location on the campus of a major technological university, Dalian Institute of Technology (DIT). The Management Training Center recently established in Beijing with support from the European Economic Community has no links with the Chinese education system, yet it does have links to the European academic community. The Canadian Management Training Center in Chengdu has no links with the university community in either China or Canada. Other centers already in place include the Japanese center at Tianjin and the German center located in the Baoshan industrial complex outside of Shanghai, both of which are outside of the higher education system.

Under the overarching U.S.-China Science and Technology Agreement, a protocol was signed in May 1979 concerning the management of science and technology. It resulted in the establishment of the National Center for

Industrial Sciences and Technology Management Development, which opened in mid-August 1980. The center has remained firmly under the control of the SEC and the U.S. Department of Commerce, with only tenuous links to DIT through the cross-appointment of faculty members and informal cooperative activity. Financing is shared by the SEC and the U.S. Department of Commerce, with the latter providing the salaries of American participants and half of their international travel expenses, as well as coordinating the contribution of large American corporations that have donated computer equipment and other technology to the project.

The center aims to train senior managers and professionals for Chinese industry; senior government officials responsible for science, technology, economic planning, and industrial enterprises; directors of China's science, technology, and engineering institutes; and university faculty who will have responsibility for building management education programs throughout China.[24] This order of priority reflects American insistence that the majority of Chinese participants should come from industrial leadership positions. Clearly they would like to see a systematic set of linkages between the center and the Chinese industrial and economic system. The Chinese are more concerned about the formation of teachers and researchers in the field of management for Chinese universities.

About 75 percent of the center's fifty-seven Chinese faculty are drawn from DIT while another 25 percent are drawn from a consortium of eight other universities.[25] The American staff, all part-time but many having a long-term commitment to the program, numbered thirty-six in 1985, twenty-seven university affiliated and nine from the American legal and industrial community.[26] By April 1985, 1,041 Chinese had graduated from the program.

The original or base program consisted of a six-month training for Chinese managers and teachers that covered basic theoretical and practical aspects of American management training. In the summer of 1984, a seven-week senior executive program was started, aimed at high-level managers and modeled after patterns drawn from U.S. historical experience. A third program was initiated in May 1985 which provides three years of instruction in China and the United States and leads to an MBA degree conferred by the Faculty of Management Studies at SUNY Buffalo.[27]

In April 1985, a new protocol was signed for another five-year period. In the evaluative investigation that accompanied this event, graduates reported enthusiastically on the ways in which they had adapted the theory and techniques learned at the center to innovations within their enterprises.[28] One of the important successes of the project seems to have been the horizontal linkages created among managers across different sectors of the Chinese economy and the channels for informal cooperation that have opened up. Alumni groups coordinated by local branches of CEMA have created regional centers where new management literature and theory is discussed and visiting specialists are invited to lecture.[29] Where horizontal linkages seem to have signally failed, however, is in the academic community. The consortium of eight universities that were to participate in the program by sending faculty members apparently takes very little interest, and this cooperation is on the verge of breaking down completely.[30]

The center's greatest weakness, reflected in the speech by SEC Vice-Counselor Zhang Yanning at the anniversary celebration, seems to be the failure to form a strong Chinese faculty with a permanent commitment to its work. Zhang stressed the need for a deepening of course content, and its more specific adaptation to China's changing environment. He also called for a greater variety of training programs. His third point drew direct attention to continuing weakness of the Chinese faculty in size and quality.[31] This is clearly a serious problem if the center is to do more than serve the short-term interests of American economic penetration and American political commitment to China's reintegration into the global capitalist order.

A Chinese commentator gives as the main goal of the project "to use the beneficial portions of the American experience as input in developing China's own body of management theory and practice."[32] This would require a Chinese faculty that cooperates widely with other Chinese academics in theoretical reflection, and a body of literature in which American management theory and practice is reinterpreted and integrated into Chinese management thought. The translation of American literature and case studies has gone ahead at a good speed and provided useful reference materials for management courses throughout the country, but so far there is little evidence of its integration into the Chinese literature. Dalian's plan to start an academic journal apparently intends this development, yet there is very little American support for research and reflection.[33]

Formal relations between China and the European community were first established in 1975, and bilateral trade had grown to U.S. $5.5 billion by 1983. Also thirty joint ventures involving an investment of $900 million had been set up by the end of 1984.[34] Within this context the visit of a delegation of thirty European management experts led to the signing of an agreement early in 1984 for cooperation in establishing a center for high-level management training with a commitment of 3.5 million in Eurocurrency from the European side.[35] This agreement was followed in May 1985 by the signing of a comprehensive China-EEC agreement to enhance cooperation in industry, agriculture, science, technology, energy, communications, transportation, and personnel training.[36]

The new center is a free-standing institution, directly under the SEC and having no affiliation with the Chinese higher education system. Its immediate aims are to train about 100 young Chinese in modern management theory and practice to the level of a European MBA degree. In the long-term, after the first two cohorts have been trained within a five-year period, it is planned for some to take a Ph.D. degree in the field in Europe and return to teach in the center. Most graduates will be expected to move into fairly high-level management positions in Chinese industry.[37]

The first group of thirty-five students were selected in February 1984, all university graduates with a minimum of four years' experience in industry. The training program involves eight intense two-month terms in China over a period of two years, with a prior six months of English language training and a subsequent six months in internships within European enterprises. It is a three-year program leading to an MBA degree, granted by a European committee composed of six European professors of management.

For each of the eight two-month terms, three European professors teach standard European MBA courses. Toward the end of each term students spend one week in a Chinese enterprise applying their skills to research, then present their results. A small library is being developed, but the time pressures of the course leave little opportunity for its use by students. The dean is a French professor of the Ecole de Commerce, one of France's prestigious *grandes écoles*. He is the only European staying for a lengthy period of time and brings some continuity to the program.

The center plans an emphasis on the preparation of high-level teaching material that will have a different theoretical and practical basis than the American-oriented materials produced at Dalian. One small book in Chinese has already been prepared based on lectures of a German professor in the area of planning and control as applied to Chinese industry. The project, however, seems even farther than Dalian from establishing conditions of mutuality that would support the formation of a distinctive Chinese theory of management.

Canadian educational cooperation with China began to blossom with the signing of a general agreement on development cooperation in October 1983.[38] The official involvement of the Canadian International Development Agency (CIDA) coincided with a shift in Chinese perceptions about modernization needs and sudden eagerness to introduce modern management techniques from the West and Japan. It is not surprising, therefore, that a large amount of CIDA support has been directed toward management education. Economic penetration is a clear intention behind these efforts, specifically a desire to maintain and increase trade relations that are favorable to Canada.[39]

The Canada-China Enterprise Management Training Center opened in Chengdu, Sichuan, in June 1984. A free-standing institution, it is responsible to the SEC, the China Enterprise Management Association, and the Sichuan Provincial Economic Commission. The project is under the general supervision of the Ministry of Foreign Economic Relations and Trade. Its objectives are a systematic introduction of theories, methods, and experience of modern Canadian enterprise management, the training of Chinese enterprise managers and directors, development of a Chinese faculty and staff able to undertake teaching, research, and consultancy, and development of a good resource center. Canadian funding provides for training of Chinese faculty in Canada, all expenses of Canadian faculty in China, and computing and library materials.

The involvement of the Association of Community Colleges of Canada (ACCC) in implementing the project from the Canadian side and providing Canadian faculty indicates the strong emphasis on practical management techniques rather than theory. The formation of Chinese faculty has been an important concern from the early planning stages. Unlike Dalian, there was no pool of academic talent in an affiliated educational institution to draw upon. Before the opening of the center, however, four Chinese staff had been given a twenty-month linguistic and management training in Canadian colleges, and there are plans for approximately twenty to have Canadian training, some up to the MBA level. By 1987 there were to be fifty Chinese staff, more than one-third Canadian educated, who would take full responsibility for the future development of the center.

Starting in June 1984 the center received around 120 mid-level management personnel from Chinese industry for six-month programs. Canadian teachers lecture in English with immediate translation into Chinese, and a translation office produces all reading materials and examinations in Chinese. Chinese faculty work along with Canadian teachers and are expected to take full responsibility for teaching within a few years.[40]

In contrast to the practical orientation of the Chengdu center, the Canada-China Management Education Program supports the transfer of management theory through a series of university-level linkages between the two countries. It is coordinated by the State Education Commission (SEdC) on the Chinese side and the Association of Universities and Colleges of Canada on the other. Parallel to the rapid growth of management institutes under SEC, Chinese universities have seen a burst of enthusiasm for the field of management with 164 institutions having set up new undergraduate programs by 1984 and 39 having new graduate programs.[41] This project focuses on eight of China's most distinguished higher institutions, all centrally administered by the SEdC. Three are comprehensive universities with an approach to management rooted in the discipline of economics, and five are polytechnical or engineering universities. Formal agreements were signed between these universities and more than eight Canadian universities, with numerous other Canadian universities participating in a subsidiary way.[42]

Considerable freedom and initiative have been possible for institutions on both sides, and each partnership reflects distinctive approaches to cooperation within the general aims of upgrading Chinese faculty, course content, and resources at each Chinese institution.[43] In some cases a jointly planned MBA program has been developed with Canadian faculty teaching specific parts of the program, while in other cases Canadian faculty have offered courses or lectures intended to fit into Chinese-developed programs. The main idea informing what has been considered a model linkage between Nankai University and York University is that of critical mass—the creation of a Chinese faculty who have had a shared exposure to Canadian management theory and practice and so will be able to work cooperatively in its reinterpretation and adaptation to the Chinese context.[44] One wonders, however, whether the transplanted MBA program that is the characteristic feature of this cooperative linkage will contribute to the formation of a Chinese theory of management or create dependence on the patterns followed in Canadian universities.

The third CIDA-supported management project has links with neither academia nor industry but is located in a land reclamation area of northern Heilongjiang province. It aims to increase the capacity of Liu He Cadre Training College to train competent management personnel for the state farm system of the province, and its $4.5 million budget will enable thirty-three young Chinese teachers to study in Canada at one of three institutions with strong agricultural programs—University of Guelph, University of Alberta, and Olds College. In addition, twenty Canadian faculty will teach at Liu He.

This project is the only center of educational cooperation known to me that is situated in the heart of the Chinese countryside. Originally a May 7th Cadre School highly commended by Mao in the Cultural Revolution, its 280,000 hectares were given by the province to the Land Reclamation Bureau in 1979. They are now used for an experimental farm and forestry plantation which bring in about 800,000 yuan in revenue each year. An additional 1.2 million yuan yearly allocation from the bureau makes possible the support of a modern town with a population of 2,600 staff and their families. Modern housing, a theater seating 800 people, which was built in the Cultural Revolution period, and a large secondary school complement the six-story teaching building, the library, computer center, and hostel facilities. It is a remarkable apparition in a rural area surrounded by fields and peasant cottages with mud walls and thatched roofs.[45]

The college has a department of politics and a department of administration and management. There were about 350 students in 1985, with 120 selected each year by provincewide examinations out of a regional constituency of 100,000 state farm managers. The department of politics provides a two-year program for party secretaries, who gain knowledge in management and agriculture as well as political theory. The department of administration and management provides courses in such fields as economic law, accounting, systems engineering, production management, organizational psychology, and computer applications. In addition to these two-year programs, many short-term programs are provided for factory and farm managers preparing to take state examinations for accreditation, also for English teachers in the region and for technicians who are expecting to be sent abroad by the bureau. A good library is being developed, and faculty have a permanent center at People's University which they visit in rotation in order to keep in contact with recent developments in the field of management throughout the country. Publications and materials emanating from the Dalian center have reached them through this channel.

The transfer of management science and technology to China is thus taking place in differing milieus, the industrial one exemplified in the institutes under the SEC, the agricultural in Liu He Cadre Training College, and the educational in a range of university linkage programs. The economic and agricultural milieus encourage a direct application of new techniques to productive practice and possibilities of a cultural domestication arising out of practice itself.

The academic milieu should make possible a theoretical reinterpretation of Western management philosophy and its integration within the Chinese literature in the field. There are, however, far greater difficulties here than in other fields of knowledge due to the weakness of the indigenous Chinese literature, the historical shifts in China's development orientation, and the fragmentation of management studies among different types of higher institution. Can the Chinese integrate the flow of management theory and technique, eclectically drawn from Europe, North America, and Japan, into their own literature and so develop a Chinese theory of management? If not, they could well become pawns to a Western discourse that might have distorting or exploitative effects in the Chinese context.

Cooperation in the Human Sciences: North American, Japanese, and British Projects

Only one cooperative project that I am aware of focuses entirely on a broad range of human sciences. Significantly, it has been developed through a linkage between Nanjing University and Johns Hopkins University, rather than through intergovernmental cooperation. Nanjing University has been one of the first in China to see the need to move beyond individually oriented exchange relations to project-related cooperation, and this is its most ambitious project of intellectual cooperation.[46]

A general university linkage agreement was first signed between the two universities in 1982, and three detailed agreements relating to the project have been signed subsequently. Both sides felt the need for a center of research that would embrace the areas of history, society and culture, political economy, foreign policy, and international relations. On the American side, the more specific aim has been the professional training of young Americans above the master's level who will work in the fields of international corporate activity, journalism, and education rather than in Sinological scholarship.[47] The Chinese have as their goal not only the training of professionals who will play an active part in Sino-American relations but also the formation of scholars and teachers who can do high level research on American affairs and contribute to the transformation of social science teaching in Chinese universities.[48]

The project is financed more or less equally by the Chinese and American sides, with administration entirely under Chinese control, but teaching and research directed by a joint Chinese-American committee. The Americans are taught in Chinese by Chinese professors and take courses such as the structure of the Chinese economy, Chinese history, the Chinese constitution, the international Communist movement, China's regional policy, Mao thought, and the history of contemporary Chinese thought. Chinese students are taught by American professors and take courses in American culture and society, the American political system and institutions, economics and management, the evolution of the international system, U.S. foreign policy, and comparative politics. A core course for all students on comparative Chinese-Western culture is team taught.

An elaborate modern building has been erected for class, residential, and conference purposes, and its centerpoint is a modern library carrying the most up-to-date American books and journals as well as a good Chinese collection. The Chinese teaching staff consists of Nanjing University professors cross-appointed to teach particular courses, distinguished visiting professors from other Chinese universities, and a core of younger Chinese scholars who are appointed to the center itself. American staff are appointed for one- or two-year periods, and a Chinese and an American director administer all academic activities jointly.

The first group of twenty-three American and forty Chinese master's-level students completed their program in June 1987. The Chinese participants came from national and provincial institutions in many regions. Eleven were enrolled in Chinese master's degree programs and gained recognition for this study as part of their degree requirements. Quite a few others were language teachers, whose social science background was rather weak. The American students tended to be younger than their Chinese counterparts, and both groups needed more language training than the program had initially provided for. In the future greater emphasis will be put on recruiting Chinese participants with a social science background, and applications have gone in to both Johns Hopkins and Nanjing universities for support to develop this into a fully accredited master's degree program. Also efforts will go into developing a strong research facility.[49]

This center for cooperative intellectual endeavor in the human sciences gives hope for a mutuality that stands in contrast to the Dalian center. It could provide conditions for a Chinese reinterpretation of the knowledge and technology being introduced from the United States and so contribute to an independent Chinese scholarship. Yet it could also serve to consolidate the American approach to the social sciences which is being strongly supported through American government-funded programs.

Crucial to intellectual interaction in the human sciences is language mastery. Foreign language teaching is important for China's modernization on two quite distinct levels. First there is the specific task of preparing Chinese students, scholars, or technicians for study abroad. Then there is the more general task of raising the level and quality of foreign language teaching throughout China.

The first level was emphasized from the Chinese side within foreign language institutes and other higher institutions which set up preparatory programs and gained some support from foreign governments in the provision of teachers. The Tongji language school and Japanese language centers at Changchun and Dalian are examples of these. The concept of a language center as a cooperative project, providing language training and cultural orientation for Chinese going abroad, seems to have been pioneered by the Canada-China Language center, which was created to serve the many CIDA-supported projects.[50] Similar cooperative projects are now being developed by the Germans and Italians.

On the second level, the upgrading of foreign language teaching in China through cooperative efforts is exemplified in British and Japanese activities. In 1980 the Japanese government allocated U.S. $4 million to a project for training 600 Chinese college teachers over a period of five years. Each year 120 teachers were selected and given a one-year program in the Beijing Foreign Languages Institute under a staff of nine long-term and fourteen short-term Japanese teachers. At the end of the year they are invited to Japan for a one-month familiarization tour of Japanese society and culture. They are intended to be the mediators of a popular understanding of Japanese life and society, and their role may echo in a small way the influence of Japanese-trained Chinese teachers in the early part of this century.[51]

The British have the most thoughtfully conceived series of cooperative projects in language and linguistics of any foreign country. These projects are funded through the Overseas Development Administration (ODA) and administered by the British Council. The main emphasis is on the provision of over twenty English language teacher-trainers who work in groups of two to three within Chinese higher institutions in Beijing, Shanghai, Nanjing, Hangzhou, and Guangzhou. In some cases their teaching is integrated within the foreign language department of the institution; in other cases it is separate. In all cases students are college teachers selected from throughout the country for a special one-year program. The program involves not only the upgrading of their English competence, but also studies in applied linguistics and teaching methodology that should enhance their teaching skills.

Built into each project is a plan for training three Chinese teachers for each British participant, and it is they who will continue the work after the end of its three-year term. In their first year they work alongside of the British teacher, in the second year they are given the opportunity to do a master's degree in applied linguistics in Britain, and in the third year they return to work as a counterpart to the British teacher. There is thus a multiplier effect which will allow these groups of British teachers to move gradually to other Chinese institutions, possibly in more remote areas. Complementing these more permanent centers are short-term teacher-training programs which are taken constantly to new areas, and considerable British support for curricular development in the Chinese Television University.[52] This sensitive teaching of language and linguistics, aimed at a wide Chinese audience, opens up possibilities for a popular understanding of the Western social and cultural milieu to a wide range of Chinese teachers. Quite different from the French approach described above, it nevertheless shares a long-term vision of what knowledge transfer might contribute to China.

These projects in language teaching draw attention to linguistic study as more than just a tool needed for access to other forms of knowledge and technology. Language forms constitute the cultural and social categories in which a people understand their development. An awareness of this in Chinese participants could have transformative possibilities for specific areas of knowledge and technology that are being transferred to China.

Conclusion: Conformity or Transformation?

A large number of educational projects have been depicted in this chapter, the longest having a history of only five or six years, others barely beginning. All of them mark a stage in China's educational relations with OECD countries that goes beyond individualized student and scholar exchanges to the creation of new cooperative institutions on Chinese soil. All of them clearly combine different elements of cultural, political, or economic penetration. On the other hand, possibilities for mutuality seem more likely in some projects than others. In this brief concluding section, I would like to return to the ideal type of mutuality presented earlier and use the four characteristics of equity, autonomy, solidarity, and participation to reflect comparatively on the possibilities of these projects for a knowledge transfer that stimulates a transformative rather than a conformist role for China in the world community.

Equity was defined in terms of forms of cooperation in which the aims and organizational patterns are jointly agreed on rather than imposed by the center on the periphery. It is difficult to find a single project among all those discussed that has not involved Chinese initiation from the beginning and has not taken shape within mutually created agreements between organizations at a roughly similar level on both sides. The one case of asymmetry is in the rather strange anomaly of a cooperative agreement between the French Ministry of Foreign affairs and one Chinese university. This has not been viewed from the Chinese side as a form of domination; rather, it has increased Wuhan University's access to a broader range of French intellectual resources than would be possible within a university-to-university linkage.

Autonomy was defined in terms of a mutual respect for sociocultural values and theoretical paradigms of the peripheral and center countries taking part in a cooperative project. This is a far more difficult proposition than equity, since it calls for participants from the OECD countries to gain a deep knowledge of the Chinese language, sociocultural institutions, and scientific achievements, and on this basis to participate in intelligent dialogue. In contrast to the missionaries who gained a thorough knowledge of China and built this into their educational cooperation, contemporary foreign participants typically spend no more than one or two months at a time in China and are limited to a very slender understanding of the Chinese social and intellectual universe. The possibilities this provides for theoretical arrogance and exploitation of the intellectual raw data that the Chinese context provides are disturbing.

There are a few groups of participants within the projects described above, however, who may be gaining a deeper understanding of China than is commonly the case. The French project at Wuhan is the only one in which foreign scientists and mathematicians live for a sustained period of time in a Chinese university. The Canadian and European management centers have foreign deans and administrators who live long-term in China. In the American case many professors return year after year and so have built up an understanding of China that is not superficial. British teachers of English language and linguistics often spend several years in China, as is the case with many other language teachers. It will be a long road to reach a level of mutual intellectual understanding that could foster a creative synthesis between Chinese and Western thought, yet a few steps in this direction have been taken.

Solidarity was defined in terms of networks of interaction among Chinese participants that would enable them to unite in the task of critically reinterpreting the new knowledge being introduced and assuring its adaptation to the Chinese context and its broad dissemination. The ideas of critical mass and multiplier effect both relate to this issue. Here the situation so far seems to be mixed. Horizontal linkages within the economic system have been quite successful, involving the joint practical application of eclectically selected foreign management techniques to Chinese enterprise. In academic circles, however, there seems to be less solidarity as Chinese institutions vie for the resources that go with a lucrative university linkage. The sudden influx of foreign funding for Chinese higher institutions has led to a political jockeying that is more likely to hinder than help intellectual solidarity within the scholarly community. The same type of competition exists among Chinese ministries, with economically oriented ministries, for example, unwilling to allow foreign resources at their disposal to fall into the hands of educational authorities.

At the same time, China's socialist infrastructure is capable of promoting a wide range of horizontal linkages. Within the higher education system there are linkages between hinterland and coastal institutions. There is, for example, a national program under the State Education Commission to send young teachers from less favored institutions for upgrading at better endowed ones. At a deeper cultural level, the unity of the Chinese language and the enormous publishing industry within the country provide a milieu for intellectual solidarity that is rare in other third world countries.[53]

Finally, participation was defined as an approach to knowledge that does not stratify in a hierarchical way but assumes the possibility of a creative peripheral contribution from the very beginning. How far are cooperative projects two-way channels that introduce Chinese theories and techniques to the outside world as well as transferring foreign knowledge to China? This presupposes a familiarity on the part of foreign participants with the Chinese literature in the area of cooperation and conditions in which foreign knowledge can be integrated into this Chinese literature in such a way as to elicit an independent Chinese response. In certain fields of the sciences and engineering, it seems clear that this is taking place, and China's scientific achievements are making a genuine contribution to the world scientific community.[54] In management science, however, time pressures and the lack of interest on the foreign side seem to preclude any developed mutuality. In the many interviews I did with Western professors teaching management in China, I did not come across anyone, with the exception of one or two overseas Chinese, who had troubled to find out if there was a Chinese literature in the field or what it might contain. Nor has there been much support for Chinese efforts to develop an independent yet integrated literature in the field. In the human sciences some Chinese literary and social writing has been translated and disseminated in foreign languages, but its scope is limited and its impact is likely to remain small.

——— 7 ———

CHINA'S UNIVERSITIES
AND THE WORLD BANK

The educational activity of the World Bank in China might be viewed as the combined contribution of OECD countries to Chinese educational reform. Its scope is naturally far more extensive than the resources of any one country could make possible, with the result that it touches most echelons of the higher education system, from national to local, and most geographical regions. Up until the mid-1980s, the focus of World Bank support was on higher education, by Chinese choice, and 183 higher institutions, nearly one-fifth of China's total, had received assistance. A consideration of the massive transfer of knowledge and technology made possible through eight higher education projects thus makes a fitting final chapter for this study of China's universities and the open door.

The chapter begins with an overview of World Bank policy for educational lending as it has evolved in recent decades, and some of the criticisms that have emerged in the analysis of the experience of other developing countries. Then the specific conditions of China's involvement with the World Bank and the evolution of its policies toward the use of World Bank funding are discussed. Eight major higher education projects have been undertaken in China, and the analysis illustrates their regional and sectoral distribution in relation to the overall system of higher education. The chapter concludes with evaluative reflections on the ways in which these projects are contributing to changes within the structure and organization of the higher curriculum and more generally in the higher education system as a whole.

World Bank Educational Policy

World Bank educational lending goes back to 1962, and the first educational policy report was published in 1971. In 1974 during the McNamara era a second policy paper was published, which emphasized the four principles of minimum basic education, manpower, efficiency, and equity needs. Lending was to be concentrated at the primary level, and strong support was to be given to the diversification of secondary education, supporting technical streams that would directly serve manpower needs and so promote efficiency. These principles have been largely maintained in the most recent policy paper, published in 1980. In this document the idea of internal efficiency, relating to the effective use of resources within national education systems and the elimination of various forms of waste, was added to that of external efficiency in the 1974 policy paper, which linked education with the labor market. While emphasis on primary education as a human right and a basic need was maintained, caution over the diversification of secondary education was expressed. The greater adaptability, as well as the lower cost, of general secondary education was stressed.[1]

The 1980 paper laid the following five pillars for its policy framework: (1) the provision of basic education to all children and adults; (2) a continued drive to promote equity and productivity by expanding educational opportunity without discrimination based on sex, ethnic background, or socioeconomic status; (3) maximum internal efficiency in the management, allocation, and use of resources; (4) maximum external efficiency by relating education to work and environment and improving the knowledge and skills needed for performing economic, social, and other development functions; and (5) support for developing countries to build and maintain their own institutional capacities to design, analyze, manage, and evaluate programs.[2]

In the paper the goal of equity in the expansion of basic educational opportunities is placed first. The obvious normative appeal of this commitment is reinforced by a strong economic argument for the contribution of basic educational provision to economic development. Internal efficiency is interpreted in terms of qualitative improvement in teaching methods and curricula as well as the fuller and more effective use of material resources. Under the rubric of external efficiency both secondary and higher education are discussed, and a commitment is made to supporting general secondary education in a selective way as well as helping to identify forms of mid-level technical training suited to national economic needs. Support for postsecondary teaching institutions and universities is viewed as "building specific resources that are important for development, such as centers for agricultural and industrial research and professional training programs; developing management capacity through management programs and institutes; establishing basic research capacities through programs and centers in the various disciplines of natural and social sciences; and setting up outreach programs to directly involve universities in national development." To alleviate critical shortages of professional manpower, assistance is promised for increasing "student places in development-oriented disciplines such as agriculture, engineering, medicine, science, economics and management, and in developing alternatives to the university model such as community colleges, polytechnics and the open university."[3]

The publication of this policy paper in 1980 triggered vigorous debates among development educators. From the cultural point of view, the document was seen as somewhat reductionist and mechanistic with human persons subordinated to the fulfillment of economic needs and teachers and the teaching-learning process subsumed under "the internal efficiency of educational systems."[4] From the political point of view, the bank's concern with equity and rural development was seen by one critic as expressing a rather naive adherence to basic tenets of the "development of underdevelopment" thesis in its questionable assumptions about rural development as a basis for economic growth and its advocacy of an educational decentralization that could threaten the political unity and stability of developing nations.[5] Another critic felt that this affirmation of the economic promise of basic education masked some of the real and difficult choices that have to be made in developing countries between policies that accord with social justice and those that promise direct economic returns.[6] A more sophisticated development of the economic argument appeared in a 1985 World Bank publication that used cost-benefit analysis to demonstrate that the social rate of return on investment in primary and secondary education in developing countries is higher than on investment in higher education, which offers high personal rates of return. The pressure for the financial rationalization and even privatization of higher education that this argument leads to is particularly problematic in the context of a socialist country.[7]

From a broader developmental perspective, there have been several radical critiques of the World Bank's involvement in the third world. In these it is interesting to note that educational projects have come under less criticism than projects in other sectors.[8] Agricultural projects have been censured for the support they have often given to large landowners and their encouragement of an export-oriented agribusiness that threatens the food supply of the poorest in some countries. Industrial lending has been criticized for the reluctance with which public sector industrial development is supported and the expansion of heavy industry in such areas as steel is underwritten. Energy policy has been criticized for the way it has sometimes served American oil interests by denying loans to public-sector oil exploration and development. The strongly egalitarian orientation of educational policy since the McNamara era, however, and the provision of an economistic rationale for equity of provision could not easily be faulted even within the neo-Marxist framework of understanding development in the context of imperialism. Convincing arguments of neocolonialism or the use of schools to foster an elite favorable to metropolitan interests could not easily be sustained.[9]

In spite of this, there can be little doubt that World Bank lending is intended to support an increasing interdependence between the developing and the developed world. The conformity of peripheral economies to the world capitalist order is justified on the basis of such classical principles as the theory of comparative advantage. There is a tendency to support private-sector industry and agriculture or forms of collective organization within socialist countries that are autonomous from the state itself.[10] The alliance between the World Bank and the International Monetary Fund gives it tremendous economic leverage in shaping the direction of those national policies which its loans are used to support. A whole generation of national leaders is given training in the bank's Economic Policy Institute for the role of managing national projects and ensuring accountability and information systems that fit into bank patterns. In a small country this can amount to an ideological control of national policy making that threatens national autonomy. Also the cost of administrative and bureaucratic infrastructure for the implementation and monitoring of bank projects can be taxing to governments of developing countries.[11]

These arguments give cause for concern, yet they may assume a certain passivity on the part of developing countries and underestimate their cultural and political resilience under threat of external domination. They also bring into question the legitimate freedom of third world leaders to choose the risky yet potentially worthwhile course of greater economic interdependence with OECD countries.

China and the World Bank

The Chinese case is a particularly fascinating one with regard to the criticisms delineated above. The choice to join the International Monetary Fund and take up a seat in the World Bank in 1979 was made by political leaders who had seen the economic limitations of an isolationist development decade during the Cultural Revolution and were prepared to face the political and cultural risks of initiating a greater interdependence with OECD countries.[12] They come from a position of strength rare in the developing world, in the sense of a well-developed independent industrial base and an agricultural system transformed first by thorough land reform and then by the deregulation and individual initiative of the responsibility system adopted in 1978. Their need for IMF assistance in the temporary financial problems of an overambitious development program between 1978 and 1980 held little threat of developing into a long-term foreign debt problem. Furthermore, they faced squarely from the beginning the implications of being integrated into the World Bank's international accounting and information system.

The ten-volume World Bank study of the Chinese economy, produced by a thirty-member World Bank team in 1980-81, initiated a new era in China scholarship in the detailed statistical information it provided on five priority sectors: human resources (health, education, and population), agriculture, transportation, energy, and industry.[13] For their part, the Chinese demonstrated their determination to exercise a strong intellectual participation in the whole process of reintegration into the world order through the priorities expressed in their first loans. The story of the first World Bank mission visit to China to explore possible projects is well known, yet it bears one more repetition as it illustrates a persisting orientation of Chinese culture. While the first mission included specialists in the areas of agriculture, industry, and energy, there was no educator. Yet the Chinese had already decided on higher education as the first priority in projects to be supported by bank lending! Of the ten initial World Bank China projects, the first, fourth, and ninth were all devoted to aspects of the higher education system: University Development I, touching the top echelon of national priority universities; Agricultural Education I, contributing to higher agricultural education and research; and the Polytechnic/Television Universities Project, addressing the lowest echelon of vocational and television universities.[14] This focus on higher education may have reflected the Chinese determination to engage with World Bank representatives on a level that ensures China's own intellectual autonomy.

By 1985 eight projects in higher education and research were already underway, and another three were under discussion. Table 7.1 illustrates the situation toward the end of 1985.

Chinese success in persuading bank advisers to concentrate so many loans in higher education is rather remarkable given the bank's educational lending policies reviewed earlier. It was justified through figures provided to bank investigators in 1980 and 1981 concerning achievements already attained in basic and secondary education. These compared favorably with other less developed countries. In contrast, Chinese enrollments in the higher education system were far lower than other developing countries due to the radical policies of the Cultural Revolution era.[15]

Ironically, however, the policies pursued since 1978 had already set in motion changes in the education system that brought into question the permanence of earlier achievements and the wisdom of the bank's unusual focus on loans for higher educational development. Table 7.2 was first constructed in 1980, then revised in 1985. It shows how secondary enrollments began to fall below the norm for other less developed countries in 1980, and by 1982 were down from 47 percent to 30 percent of the age cohort. Equally serious, primary education dropped well below the earlier 90-plus percent participation rate and had very high wastage rates. Both phenomena were apparently linked to the agricultural responsibility system and the child labor it encouraged. In contrast to the fall in primary and secondary participation rates, higher education showed a dramatic upsurge between 1980 and 1983 and is expected to continue to rise steadily until the year 2000. This up-

Table 7.1

World Bank Education Projects in China, 1985

Project name	Loan	Credit	Total	Total cost	Years	Ministry
Active:						
University development I	100	100	200	295	1981–86	MOE
Agricultural education/ research I	—	75	75	201	1982–88	MAAF
Polytechnic/TV university	—	85	85	206	1983–89	MOE
Agricultural education II	45	24	69	175	1984–89	MAAF
Rural health and medical education	—	85	85[a]	290	1984–89	MOPH
Agricultural research II	—	25	25	59	1984–89	MAAF
University development II	—	145	145	1,162	1985–90	SEdC
Provincial universities	—	120	120	477	1985–90	SEdC
Future						
Technical education	—	130	130	230	1987–91	SEdC/ MOLP
Instructional materials/ curriculum design, computer education	—	—	60	60	1987–92	SEdC
Innovative graduate curricula	—	—	140	140	1988–92	SEdC

Source: ''World Bank Group Education Projects in China: Project Summaries,'' paper issued by World Bank, Washington, D. C., February 1985. All figures are in $U.S. millions. While loans are funded by the International Bank for Reconstruction and Development at commercial rates, credit refers to International Development Association funding, which is interest-free and has lengthy repayment terms.

a. Of which $43 million was for medical education.

surge has been given strong support by World Bank financing.

By 1985 there was a convergence of views on World Bank investment in education between China's State Planning Commission (SPC) and personnel within the World Bank. The SPC placed a moratorium on new projects to allow for a reorientation of attention away from higher education to other levels and sectors. Likewise bank leaders pressed for the development of some projects in basic and secondary education before any further higher education projects were approved.

The bank view came across clearly in a country economic report, *China: Long-term Development Issues and Options*, which considered all aspects of China's development up to the year 2000, using comparative and Chinese

Figure 7.1. **Enrollment Ratios in Formal Education in China: China (1950–1983 and targets for 2000); Other Developing Countries (1950–1980)**

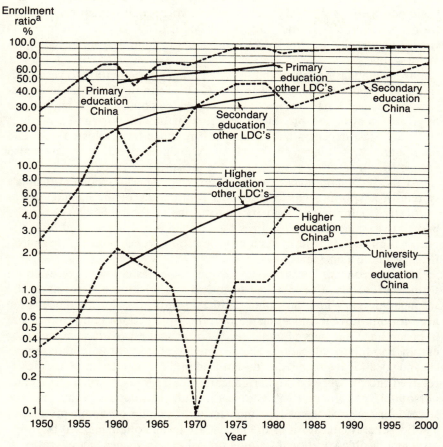

Source: *China: Issues and Prospects in Education*, annex I to *China: Long-Term Development Issues and Options* (Washington, D.C.: World Bank, 1985), p. 56. Appreciation is expressed to Goddard Winterbottom, chief, Editorial and Production Division, The World Bank, for permission to reprint this figure.

[a]The enrollment ratio expresses the number of students enrolled in a level of education as a percentage of the relevant age group.

[b]Targets for nonuniversity higher education in 2000 are not available.

data to estimate necessary means to achieve the economic and production levels desired by China's leadership. The report has six annexes including one on education, which focuses on four aspects of the education system: basic education, secondary technical and vocational education, teacher training, and the cost and financing of education. Higher education is viewed as already moving forward in an appropriate way and needing no major changes.

Strong emphasis is placed on the need for greater attention to basic education to counter the present wastage effects of the rural responsibility system and to meet long-term needs for an educated populace. The importance of greater central and provincial government funding for rural schools is stressed, since decentralization and self-reliance have allowed poor and remote areas to fall increasingly behind. A compulsory education law is also advocated, a measure that was realized in the spring of 1986.[16]

At the secondary level, two issues are given special comment. China's system of keypoint secondary schools is criticized for the inequity of opportunity it supports.[17] Priority institutions at the higher level may be necessary to concentrate resources for excellence of teaching and research, but at the secondary level such a policy contravenes both equity and efficiency, in the bank view.[18]

As for secondary vocational education, some hesitation is expressed on China's rapid move to increase technical and vocational streams at the secondary level. While the Chinese official justification for the move is the need for mid-level technical manpower, the more serious political problem has been huge numbers of upper secondary school graduates competing for entrance to higher education. The channeling of many of these into technical and vocational streams that do not lead into higher education has greatly relieved the pressure on higher education entrance.[19] Nevertheless, bank personnel are reluctant to endorse the Chinese solution to this problem since their research seems to demonstrate the greater economic promise of a solid general education at the secondary level, complemented by short-term and flexible vocational training provision. Finally, teacher education is emphasized in the report, and the greater integration of the present pre-service and in-service training system is advocated.

The World Bank emphasis on educational equality coincides with the concerns of a particular interest group in Chinese educational circles. This group may use World Bank support to legitimize their views in a way that has parallels with the use made of the League of Nations report during the 1930s. One astute Western Sinologist has noted how "these lines draw the profile of a lobby of professional administrators of education who retain part of the egalitarian ideals and social concerns which past educational policies before Mao's death had imposed on them for many years, and who wish to strengthen and widen their hold on educational matters in the face of growing interference from economic quarters and local interests."[20] The reform document of May 1985, whose higher educational implications were discussed in detail in chapter 2, was largely the work of this same group.

No new bank educational projects were approved in 1986, but by 1987 several were under preparation and they reflected the new orientation. The only one approved in 1987 was a basic education project in the remote and impoverished province of Gansu that focuses on teacher training for primary and lower secondary school teachers and is intended to enable people's teachers (*minban jiaoshi*) who are now reliant on local resources to qualify as part of an expanding public teaching force supported by higher government levels. The project also undertakes to give special support to 400 junior secondary schools and students in Gansu's sixteen poorest counties. It is an integrated part of a wider bank project that includes a U.S. $130 million IDA loan for agriculture, a $20 million IBRD loan for industry, and a $20 million IDA loan for education. This kind of intersectoral cooperation is unusual on bank projects and is creating some difficulties in Washington, yet it is regarded as a desirable new approach to educational lending.[21]

Returning to table 7.1, the view of bank educational projects in 1985, it can be seen that this basic education project has been introduced ahead of the projects envisaged for the future at that time. The technical education project that was supposed to begin in 1987 has been delayed due to inadequate research preparation within China[22] and an ongoing debate in the bank over the economic benefits of secondary technical education. However, a project on some form of technical-vocational education at the secondary level is expected to be implemented in 1988, after the sector report on this form of education in China is completed.[23] The instructional materials project has evolved into one that focuses on support for the production of textbooks, enhancing publishing quality and presentation rather than curricular content. While the initial focus is on production processes in Beijing, provincial and local institutions will be given selective support on the dual principle of special provision for the production of primary and secondary texts in less developed regions and the enhancement of quality university texts in the more advanced university presses.[24] Finally, the innovative graduate curricula project is still under discussion. The Chinese favor support for 200 priority fields at the doctoral level, with a focus on scientific research equipment and faculty development.[25]

The World Bank Contribution to Chinese Higher Education

While projects at other levels are still at a preparatory stage, the eight higher education projects listed in table 7.1 are all in operation and some have been completed. It is therefore possible to review their evolution between 1980 and 1987 and to reflect on the impact they are making on China's overall higher education and research system. The geographical location and disciplinary orientation of the 183 universities selected to participate is of special interest, as is their position within the overall higher education system.

At this point, a brief review of the administrative organization of the higher education system may be helpful. Table 7.2 illustrates the three main levels of administration, with a distinction at the national level between the comprehensive, polytechnical, and normal universities administered by the State Education Commission and the specialized institutions administered by various sectoral ministries. Province-level universities expanded most rapidly during the Great Leap Forward of 1958, while local institutions, especially the 140 vocational universities, have mainly emerged since 1980.

The chronological evolution of World Bank higher education projects, depicted in table 7.1, reflects Chinese educational priorities in an interesting way. The first project was designated to upgrade twenty-eight national keypoint universities under the administration of the Ministry of Education (now the State Education Commission) with a special emphasis on science and engineering curricula and the enhancement of research facilities. The next priority was higher agricultural education, and the second, fourth, and sixth projects involved national agricultural universities (under the Ministry of Agriculture, Animal Husbandry, and Fisheries and the Ministry of Forestry), provincial colleges, agricultural research centers, and the agricultural extension system. The third project moved from the national echelon to the local level, the newly emerging short-cycle vocational universities administered by city governments and intended to serve local needs. It also gave support to the nonformal system by providing for the national and provincial television universities. The fourth project moved to another sector at the national echelon, universities under the Ministry of Public Health and the medical extension system. Project seven gave support to a whole range of specialized universities under national ministries as yet unserved by other projects, including Metallurgy, Finance, Telecommunications, Aeronautics, Geology, and Transport. Finally, the eighth project addressed universities under provincial bureaus of higher education which serve each province.

Approximately 183 higher institutions in the formal system out of the 1985 total of 1,016 regular institutions were included in these projects: 30 universities under the Ministry of Education (now the State Education Commission), 34 under a range of other national ministries, 32 under agriculture and forestry (including 13 provincial), 14 under public health, 56 at the provincial level, and 17 short-cycle vocational universities administered by city governments. This indicates a broad sectoral spread of assistance, in which no major sector is neglected. However, there has naturally been fierce competition among institutions in each of these sectors to be included in projects, and some anomalies have resulted. The combination of a very large

Table 7.2

Three-Tiered Administrative Structure of Chinese Higher Education, 1985

1. National level		2. Provincial level	3. Local level
State education commission	Other ministries and commissions	Provincial/municipal higher education bureaus	City higher education bureaus
38 institutions (29 keypoint)	285 institutions (59 keypoint)	510 institutions (8 keypoint)	181 institutions (no keypoint)

Source: Adapted from *Zhongguo jiaoyu nianjian 1982–1984* (Changsha: Hunan Education Press, 1986).

infusion of funds for sophisticated research and teaching equipment, a wealth of opportunities for faculty to study abroad, and a generous Chinese commitment to construction and furniture has meant an inevitable widening gap between institutions included in the projects and those that were less fortunate. On the other hand, the inclusion of 86 institutions from the provincial and local echelons, nearly half of the total, opens up possibilities for international contact that were remote before, as the sketch of Chinese policy on international exchange presented in chapter 2 indicates.

The geographical location of participating institutions is also an important issue. The first project tended to have the strongest bias toward a few privileged centers, while the last has the most equal geographical distribution with all provinces and autonomous regions participating, excepting Tibet. Clearly, sectoral and echelon considerations came first, and it was only when the province-level administration became involved that this degree of geographical equalization could be achieved.

In the first project five of twenty-eight participating universities were in the capital city of Beijing, two in neighboring Tianjin, five in Shanghai, two in the Northeast, and one each in Shandong, Hangzhou, and Hefei. The Southeast had only three participating universities, and the remaining six were in the central or hinterland cities of Wuhan (two), Chongqing, Chengdu, Xi'an, and Lanzhou. In this project, the North was favored over the South and the East Coast over the hinterland. The latter bias was not surprising given the predominance of distinguished universities in great eastern cities and the intention of the project to strengthen centers of excellence already in existence. The relative neglect of the South may have been less excusable.

Inclusion in the project constituted a powerful endorsement of a university's standing and reputation, which meant intense competition among institutions and major regions. In Beijing both medical and agricultural universities were included even though their curricular focus would have made them more suitable to participate in later agricultural and medical projects. Shanghai was not to be outdone and two of its institutions, Tongji University and the Shanghai Institute of Finance and Economics, were added to the project at the last minute. In the case of Tongji the West German government insisted that this center of Sino-German interaction be recognized by inclusion in the project.

The geographical orientation of projects under specialist ministries largely reflects the ministry's priority judgments and the competition among institutions within one jurisdiction or under different jurisdictions. The twenty-nine agricultural universities included in the first two agricultural projects covered a broad geographical spread and included thirteen institutions administered at the provincial level. The medical and health project focused on three provinces and an autonomous region—Sichuan, Heilongjiang, and Ningxia (all hinterland areas) and the coastal province of Shandong. The thirteen key medical universities, however, were spread across major cities, with three in Beijing and two in Guangzhou. Institutions participating in University Development II, the seventh project, are quite widely spread throughout the country, representing the competing interests of ministry-regulated specializations. The seventeen vocational universities of the third project are situated in major cities, and their importance may be linked in some cases to the new status of such cities as Shenyang and Wuxi as municipalities directly administered by Beijing. Finally, as stated earlier, the provincial universities project has the broadest and most equitable geographical spread.

The accompanying map details the geographical dispersion of the Chinese universities and colleges that are participating in World Bank development projects.[26] Both the sectoral and the regional spread are quite remarkable and offset the more scattered and uncoordinated contribution being made to Chinese universities through the bilateral projects discussed in chapter 6. Table 7.3 indicates regional concentration in a descending order, the degree to which provincial capitals have monopolized projects in each region, and the proportion of project institutions to regular and keypoint institutions in the locale.

Table 7.1 gave estimated total budgets for each project, showing a considerable range between U.S. $59 million for the most modest and $1.16 billion for the largest. With the exception of two projects, most of the World Bank funding was in IDA loans which are interest-free with lengthy repayment periods. In all cases World Bank funds were designated for the provision of equipment not available in China and for technical assistance in the form of scholarships for study abroad and the visits of foreign specialists to China. All construction costs, local equipment costs, and local study pro-

Table 7.3

Geographical Distribution of Universities Participating in World Bank Projects DEFGH

Province/City	A	B	C	D	E	F	G	H
Anhui	1	—	1	1	—	—	1	1
Beijing	5	2	2	1	3	6	7	2
Fujian	1	—	—	—	—	—	—	2
Gansu	1	—	—	—	—	—	—	1
Guangdong	2	1	1	—	2	—	—	2
Guangxi	—	—	—	1	—	—	—	2
Guizhou	—	—	—	—	—	—	—	2
Hainan Island	—	—	—	—	—	1	—	—
Hebei	—	—	—	—	—	—	—	2
Heilongjiang	—	—	1	3	—	1	3	3
Henan	—	—	1	1	—	—	—	2
Hubei	2	1	1	1	—	1	1	1
Hunan	—	—	1	1	1	—	2	2
Jiangsu	—	—	2	1	—	—	2	1
Jiangxi	—	—	—	1	—	—	—	2
Jilin	1	—	—	1	1	—	2	3
Liaoning	1	1	1	1	1	—	1	—
Nanjing	2	3	1	1	1	—	2	1
Nei Mongol	—	—	—	1	—	1	—	2
Ningxia	—	—	—	—	—	—	—	1
Qinghai	—	—	—	—	—	—	—	1
Shaanxi	1	1	1	—	1	2	1	2
Shandong	1	—	1	1	1	—	—	1
Shanghai	5	1	1	—	—	—	5	3
Shanxi	—	—	—	—	—	—	—	2
Sichuan	2	1	1	1	1	—	6	3
Tianjin	2	—	1	—	—	—	—	2
Xinjiang	—	—	—	1	—	1	—	2
Yunnan	—	—	—	—	—	—	—	2
Zhejiang	1	—	—	1	—	—	—	2
Total	28	11	17	19	12	13	33	52

A = University Development I
B = Agricultural Education/Research I
C = Vocational/Television Universities Project
D = Agricultural Education II
E = Medical Education
F = Agricultural Research II
G = University Development II
H = Provincial Universities Project

grams were met from the Chinese side, and in many cases the actual Chinese contribution was understated in the budget. The huge Chinese contribution to University Development II (over $1 billion) reflects both the wealth of the national ministries that finance these universities and their commitment to the project, as does the $357 million pledged by provincial governments in the eighth project. These are probably more realistic estimates of Chinese input than those of the earlier projects.

While the general contours of all projects are similar, they differ in the relative importance attached to major budget lines and in curricular emphasis. In the organization and supervision of projects a distinction can also be made between those that are administered directly by the State Education Commission and those under the ministries of Agriculture and Public Health. While these two ministries have selected overseas consultants to assist in their projects directly, the State Education Commission has its four projects under the supervision of an international panel of distinguished scholars and a parallel internal panel of Chinese scholars. The four international panels are located in the cities of Washington, Ottawa, and London. This innovative approach to the oversight of the projects was initiated by a World Bank educator who saw the importance of peer review in the selection of the many foreign consultants who are assisting in these projects.[27]

In the review of the eight projects that follows, I begin with the projects administered by the State Education Commission and monitored by Chinese and international advisory panels, since these cover most sectors and levels of the higher education system. Then the specialized projects under the ministries of agriculture and public health are reviewed. Finally, an attempt is made to anticipate the overall impact of these massive projects on the organization and direction of China's higher education.

University Development I

The first university project had three major aims: increasing enrollments in the fields of science and engineering to meet national manpower needs, improving the quality of teaching and research in these two areas, and enhancing the management effectiveness of all aspects of the higher education system.[28] Of the twenty-eight higher institutions included in the project, the eleven comprehensive and two normal universities had strong departments in the basic sciences but little provision for engineering or applied sciences, an orientation dictated by the Soviet model. The twelve polytechnical universities, also administered directly by the State Education Commission, had a broad range of engineering sciences but weaker basic science departments. The inclusion of the other three institutions, Beijing Agricultural University, Beijing Medical University, and Shanghai University of Finance and Economics, reflected the dominance of Beijing and Shanghai noted earlier.

Table 7.4

Regional Concentration of Higher Institutions Participating in World Bank Projects[a]

Municipality/province/ autonomous region	No. of participating institutions (in capital city)	Total number of universities in 1980 (keypoint)
Beijing	22	50 (22)
Sichuan	16 (10 in Chengdu)	43 (9)
Jiangsu	16 (10 in Nanjing)	42 (9)
Shanghai	16	32 (8)
Hubei	15 (15 in Wuhan)	36 (7)
Heilongjiang	10 (10 in Harbin)	28 (4)
Guangdong	9 (8 in Guangzhou)	30 (4)
Liaoning	8 (6 in Shenyang)	36 (5)
Jilin	8 (6 in Changchun)	25 (3)
Shandong	7 (5 in Jinan)	34 (3)
Shaanxi	7 (7 in Xi'an)	33 (6)
Hunan	7 (5 in Changsha)	22 (3)
Anhui	6 (4 in Hefei)	22 (2)
Tianjin	6	17 (2)
Henan	4 (3 in Zhengzhou)	25
Zhejiang	4 (3 in Hangzhou)	22 (1)
Fujian	3 (2 in Fuzhou)	16 (1)
Guangxi	3 (2 in Nanning)	18
Xinjiang	3 (2 in Urumchi)	12 (1)
Nei Mongol	3 (3 in Hohhot)	14 (1)
Jiangxi	3 (2 in Nanchang)	17 (1)
Guizhou	2 (2 in Guiyang)	15
Yunnan	2 (2 in Kunming)	17 (1)
Gansu	2 (2 in Lanzhou)	12 (1)
Shanxi	2 (2 in Taiyuan)	16 (1)
Hebei	2 (1 in Shijiazhuang)	27 (1)
Qinghai	1 (1 in Xining)	6
Ningxia	1 (1 in Yingchuan)	4
Tibet	0	4
Total	188	675 (96)

a. The discrepancy between the total of 188 institutions in this table and the map and the earlier total of 183 is due to the fact that some institutions participated in more than one project.

The project's budget of $295 million was allocated roughly in the following manner: 21.1 percent to civil works; 68.4 percent to research instrumentation, teaching labs, and computing facilities; 10.5 percent to technical assistance, including study programs for faculty abroad and the invitation of foreign specialists for consultation. The funding was not equally divided among the twenty-eight institutions. Nine were given priority status as leaders in general curricular and research strengthening, and these received relatively higher allocations. Priority scientific areas for development were identified in each institution and equipment selected accordingly. Most institutions developed either a computer center or a center for analysis and testing, in some cases both.

The technical assistance aspect of the project was given great importance, and each university selected foreign specialists in areas they considered vital for curricular development and research. These nominees then had to be approved by the Chinese Review Commission and the International Advisory Panel to the project. The Chinese panel was composed of six distinguished Chinese scholars, a chair and five cochairs, each representing a major disciplinary area: physics, chemistry, biology, engineering, and computer science. The International Advisory Panel was chaired by a distinguished American physicist with five cochairs, including a Australian biologist, a French chemist, a Japanese physicist, a German engineer, and a British computer scientist. The executive direction of the panel was located in the National Academy of Sciences in Washington.

Under this arrangement, which allowed for both local Chinese initiative and high-level academic review to ensure academic standards, 405 specialists were invited to the twenty-eight Chinese institutions, with some having thirty to thirty-five such visits, others as few as two or three. The national origin of the specialists reflects a predisposition to American expertise, with 49 percent American, 17 percent British, 10 percent West German, 9 percent Japanese, 3 percent Canadian, 2 percent French, and 10 percent other. Normally each specialist spent one month in a science or engineering department of one project university, then wrote a detailed assessment and set of recommendations relating to the curriculum, research, faculty quality, and departmental organization. In addition, six groups of management specialists in the fields of library administration, student records, university fiscal administration, computer center management, computer software, and educational statistics held seminars attended by representatives of all the project universities.[29]

The second aspect of the technical assistance component of the budget was designated for programs to allow faculty periods of research and study abroad, and 800 places were originally planned for. This aspect has been so vigorously pursued that 2,471 faculty from the twenty-eight universities had gone abroad for research and study under World Bank funding by the end of

1985, with some universities having sent nearly 100 faculty
esting policy differences emerged in the relative emphasis
gave to sending mature scholars for one- to two-year vis'
grams and younger faculty for master's or doctoral level prog...
emphasis on the latter category reflected a policy of promoting youn...
scholars and giving strong support to creating a new leadership cadre, while
an emphasis on the former reflected the greater weight of the middle-aged
scholar contingent, many of whom had suffered during the Cultural Revolution and were determined now to seize the opportunity for enhancing their
status as well as their research and teaching skills. The overall outcome indicates the victory of the scholars who gained 1,565 places in contrast to 906
given to young faculty going for graduate study.

From an initial bias toward American universities, with over 90 percent
going to the United States in the first year, the assistance of the International Advisory Panel made possible a more balanced exposure to universities
and institutes in a range of OECD countries. Of the total of 2,471 at the end
of 1985, 59 percent had gone to the United States, 14.3 percent to Canada,
8.3 percent to Britain, 7 percent to Japan, 4.3 percent to West Germany, 2.2
percent to France, 1.4 percent to Australia, and others to Sweden, Switzer-
land, Belgium, and New Zealand. The predominance of North American
scholarly influence is clear in this pattern, yet it will not be unchallenged,
and there remains the possibility of an eclectic selection of curricular ideas
and organizational patterns from a variety of sources.

The first university development project was one of the first to be completed, and various forms of evaluation have been carried out. Quantitatively, there can be little doubt about the success of the project, in terms of both
the technical assistance program depicted above and the expansion of science and engineering enrollments which have surpassed the 30-40 percent
target at the undergraduate level (from 106,274 to 157,003) and contributed
to a 400 percent expansion from 5,690 to 23,657 at the graduate level. The
student-faculty ratio has correspondingly increased, and more efficient
utilization of classrooms, laboratories, and libraries can be quantitatively
demonstrated. The general scholarly level of faculty has been enhanced, and
research productivity is evident in 19,000 contributions to journals of the
Academia Sinica per year, 2,100 to recognized foreign scientific journals.

Both undergraduate and graduate course reforms have supported the
general reform developments discussed in chapters 2 and 3, with a greater
emphasis on fundamental theory, more interdisciplinary work, more hands-
on laboratory and computer work, and a reduced number of classroom
hours, leaving more time for self-study. Greater efforts toward the broadening and liberalization of undergraduate programs are still urged in project
reports,[30] suggesting that implementation of national policy is extremely
difficult, even under the comparatively favorable conditions present in these

national priority universities.

In research, there may be more serious problems, relating to the effective maintenance and appropriate use of the sophisticated instrumentation that was purchased, not always with the full participation of the scientists in each university. The cost of maintaining the equipment is such that there is great pressure to use it for industrial service contracts that make little contribution to applied or basic knowledge in the field and can dissipate faculty energy and time.[31] The fragmentation and isolation that resulted from Soviet patterns, as well as the absence of a strong research mission in the university between 1952 and 1978, mean that it has been extremely difficult to create a vigorous research environment in which there is lively interaction across specializations and departments and among institutions.

Vocational and Television University Project

Project three touched the opposite end of the formal higher education system and had a whole different set of opportunities and problems. The first part of the project was to support the development of short-cycle vocational universities, the newly created echelon within the formal higher education system that is administered by city governments. Its specific objective was to increase the output of mid-level technicians needed by urban enterprises through increasing enrollment at seventeen of the newly emerging vocational universities, and also to improve the quality of training and standards of management and to assist in planning for the development of a future vocational university system.

The second part of the project was divided between supporting the central television university of Beijing and nine provincial television universities that have their own transmitters, also providing services for the remaining nineteen television universities. Of the $206 million budget, 37 percent ($76 million) was designated for vocational universities within the formal system, 21 percent ($43.3 million) for the central television university, and 42 percent ($49 million) for provincial television universities. While television universities and other institutions within the informal higher education system are extremely important for Chinese development, it has not been possible within the scope of this book to deal with them in detail. They do not have the breadth of contact with the international community that characterizes the formal system, nor are they likely to be pacesetters in the same way, although their role in the dissemination of knowledge and the broadening of educational opportunity is important.[32]

The seventeen vocational universities participating in the project are located in sixteen major cities (two in Beijing). Two have already been profiled in chapter 3: Jinling in Nanjing and Shenyang in Liaoning province.

The intention of the project is to develop strong programs that are directly linked to major enterprises in these cities to train people who can bring a technological leading edge to bear on urban industrial development. Thus advanced computer systems and instrumentation suited to new technological fields such as robotics are being emphasized. Curricular innovation is in no way hindered by central regulation since the new reform document, discussed in chapter 2, gives full freedom to local initiative in the establishment of new short-cycle specializations. The onus is thus on the faculty to develop solid technological content and a practical orientation for new programs.

In many cases they have been cross-appointed from regular academic universities, since many of the vocational universities grew out of the branch colleges of national universities which were set up in the late 1970s. This strong academic input is further strengthened by the fact that some young, newly appointed faculty are given one- or two-year postgraduate study programs as nondegree candidates at the master's level in major national universities. This results in a strong academic orientation and a tendency to rely on the teaching plans and outlines of parallel specializations in academic institutions, with some adaptation to suit special local conditions.

On the other hand, strong links are being created among the 140 vocational universities in all parts of China, with the 17 World Bank-supported institutions taking the lead as virtual keypoints of the system. A national association of faculty coordinates national and regional committees which are responsible for curricular development. The real challenge for those involved in this development is to break away from traditional academic values and create a new ethos for the vocational university as a locally oriented, technologically innovative institution rather than a second-rate academic institution overshadowed by those above it in the hierarchy.

Support for a new ethos might also come from appropriate linkages with higher institutions in OECD countries. Yet these linkages have proved difficult to create, and the relatively small budget allocation for technical assistance (1.5 percent as against 10.5 percent in University Development I) suggests that international cooperation was not seen to have the importance it had in the first university development project. In contrast to the thirty or forty specialists who visited universities of the first project and gave varying suggestions and comments, each of the seventeen vocational universities has had only one team of visiting specialists who looked at overall management, curricular development, and computing facilities.

The most disturbing finding of the first team, which visited five of the vocational universities participating in the project in the autumn of 1985, was that although the project had already been in operation for two years, not one of the eighty places for faculty study abroad had been taken up. The obstacles seem to have arisen from a number of sources. The institutions themselves have insufficient contact with higher institutions in OECD countries to know how to select appropriate programs for their faculty and arrange applications. The section within the State Education Commission responsible for administering the scholarship funds insists on very high standards in the language tests it administers and has apparently not been helpful in facilitating linkages. Also there do not seem to be clearly defined faculty development plans with reference to study abroad, though there are well-organized programs with as many as thirty faculty at a time doing postgraduate study at major Chinese universities.[33]

It remains to be seen how these institutions will succeed in overcoming the barriers to study abroad for their faculty and whether they will make contact with the sort of institution whose experience will strengthen their efforts to create a strong ethos suited to local urban development needs. Both the British polytechnic and the German *Fachhochschule* are useful exemplars in the technological creativity and high standards of their programs, while the North American community college may be important as the institution that has been most successful in creating an ethos independent of the academic spirit of the university.

University Development II

University Development II has as its aims the expansion of undergraduate enrollments in engineering, economics, finance, and law and related postgraduate programs, at differential ratios, to overcome the present imbalance of the overall enrollment structure. It is to give priority resource allocation to facilities that already have strong implementation and leadership capacity in these two areas, so as to create centers for training personnel for other institutions and related industries. Its qualitative goals relate to curricular transformation toward more broadly defined specializations with greater theoretical strength and potential for innovation, and to improving efficiency in all aspects of university planning and resource allocation and assisting in setting up evaluative procedures for the whole university system.

The sector approach adopted in the planning of this project meant that specific institutions were not supposed to be identified at the beginning; rather, 11 fields of engineering as well as the social science areas of economics, finance, and law were selected, and it was decided that 111 engineering departments, 27 economics and finance departments, and 6 law departments would participate. In reality, political pressures in China ensured that the 34 of the 39 institutions taking part in the project were in the previously neglected sector of the national-echelon institutions administered by ministries other than the State Education Commission.

An interesting aspect of the project is that it represents the first move on a broad scale within the higher education system to draw upon foreign resources in the transformation of such social sciences as economics, finance, and law. Initially People's University was the only institution under the State Education Commission included in the project. Chapters 1 and 2 have depicted the special role played by People's in cooperation with the Soviet Union in the 1950s. It is significant, therefore, that it should again play a leading role in this sensitive area of knowledge. Together with it in the project are a regional institute of political science and law and three of finance and economics, as well as the University of International Business and Economics, formerly the Beijing Institute of Foreign Trade. The relevant social science departments of Fudan, Nankai, and Xiamen were subsequently added to the project, as were centers for the training of technical teachers at Beijing Teachers University and Wuhan University. These five universities had all been participants in University Development I, but only their basic science departments had benefited, which justified their inclusion in this project.

The total budget for the project of $1.16 billion ($145 million from the bank) is far higher than any of the earlier projects, reflecting both a more realistic assessment of Chinese inputs than other projects and the financial strength of the specialist ministries whose higher institutions are included in the project. While the bulk of the financing is for construction (55.8 percent) and equipment (34 percent), $48 million (4.1 percent) has been earmarked for faculty development fellowships, $16 million (1.4 percent) for specialist services, and $45 million (3.9 percent) for exchange programs.[34] It seems likely that the program will provide several thousand places for faculty study abroad as well as a large number of consultant visits and other forms of international exchange and cooperation.

The engineering aspect of the project has developed rapidly along lines fairly similar to University Development I, with sophisticated instrumentation being ordered, specialist visits organized, and programs for faculty development abroad being set up at each institution. In the social sciences, however, things have moved more slowly. Here it is not a question of a large equipment budget nor of departments where the presence of visiting specialists for a month or more investigating all aspects of curriculum and research could be so easily accommodated. After some delay, a series of seminars was finally arranged for the summer of 1987, with specialists from Japan (two), England (one), West Germany (one), the United States (four), Canada (one), and Australia (one) in the fields of economics and finance teamed together with Chinese specialists in eight different project institutions. This culminated in a joint seminar held at Fudan University in the end of the summer to discuss guidelines for national curricula in the fields of economics, finance, and management.[35] The foreign consultants were first asked to give their views on existing Chinese programs they had observed, and then invited to collaborate with Chinese participants in developing three main program profiles, one management-related, with a definition of core areas that should be common to all specializations.[36]

This development of the social sciences in interaction with the outside world may be the most crucial aspect of present reforms. On the one hand, the Chinese are determined to retain control of these sensitive areas, in order that the definition of their economic and political future should be worked out in their own terms. It is also virtually certain, given the nature of Chinese tradition and Chinese socialism, that these fields will continue to be seen as the overall guiding force for all other areas of knowledge. At the same time, there is a growing realization in China of the need for these fields to be transformed if they are to be effective in guiding a modernization process that proceeds in interdependence with the world community.

One of the ideas suggested by a World Bank educator involved in the project was for the establishment of a national social sciences center whose role would be systematic theoretical research on the Chinese economy and Chinese social development. The adaptation of social science theory from the developed capitalist world to the Chinese context would be a prime responsibility of this center, and other institutions seeking to transform their social science departments could look to it for guidance. There are no doubt a number of institutions in China that aspire to such a role, and it will be interesting to see if one such center does emerge. The function carried out by People's University as the prime institution responsible for the adaptation of Soviet social sciences to China in the 1950s indicates the vulnerability such a center might have to dogmatism and the establishment of a new locus of intellectual authority.

The international advisory panel of University Development II is located in the National Academy of Sciences, Washington, D.C., and led by a distinguished American scholar, with a Japanese scholar in economics and a German engineering scholar as the other two members. All aspects of the project's development are monitored by this panel in cooperation with a parallel Chinese advisory panel. Since this project is the first to give weight to the social sciences, the most sensitive aspect of the Chinese knowledge system, its progress will be of special interest. In contrast to the scattered bilateral projects in this field, it could bring a foreign social science influence to the center of Chinese internal policy processes. In light of historical experience, the leading role of such institutions as People's University and Fudan University in the project may be of particular significance.

Provincial Universities Project

The provincial universities project aims to support the government's program to develop higher education at the provincial level through assistance to key provincial universities and provincial higher education authorities. As in other projects, the main objectives are enrollment expansion, educational program improvement, and management reform. The intention, however, is to support the formation of manpower specifically for provincial needs with a particular emphasis on teacher education. This project has included a number of provinces and areas that so far had not participated in World Bank higher education projects. Participating in the project are four regional teachers universities administered by the SEdC, twenty-four provincial teachers universities, eighteen provincial comprehensive universities, and seven technical, five medical, and two agricultural colleges, a total of sixty institutions in all. Special assistance is also given to provincial bureaus of higher education in the task of developing provincial higher education master plans and teacher education plans.

In a total budget of $477 million ($120 million from the bank), expenditures are divided as follows: 38 percent for civil works and furniture, 52 percent for equipment, 7 percent for fellowships, 1 percent for specialist services, and 1 percent for higher education development. The provision for study programs abroad and the invitation of foreign specialists as consultants opens up prospects for lively intellectual interaction between Chinese provincial universities and their foreign counterparts. This is a level of cooperation that received little priority in the national policies for international educational relations depicted in chapter 2.

The executive direction of this project is located in Ottawa, with the chair of the international advisory panel being a distinguished Canadian chemist and former university president, while the cochairs are an American higher education administrator who was formerly chancellor of a state higher education system and a British physicist who is director of an institute of higher education. The fact that all higher education in Canada comes fully under provincial jurisdiction may make it a suitable location for cooperation at this level, and a whole series of specialist visits to departments of Chinese provincial universities are underway, monitored by this panel and its Chinese counterpart.

A total of 8,700 fellowship years abroad were planned within the project with the intention being for each of the 238 departments of the 60 project universities to have 6 graduate degree holders by the end of the project. However this initial commitment to graduate programs for younger faculty soon gave way to the dominance of mid-level faculty going abroad as visiting scholars. Likewise the intended support for scholars in such soft fields as education and psychology has given way to a predominant emphasis on the hard sciences in both the invitation of specialists to China and opportunities for study abroad.[37] These choices may reflect the reluctance of Chinese officials to risk support for younger scholars, who are likely to be critical and innovative and who could also become part of the brain drain that is now feared. This is especially the case in the soft sciences where new ideas are most threatening. Such risks are likely to be even less acceptable at the provincial than the national level.

These four projects cover the three echelons and four majors sectors of the Chinese higher education system. The involvement of both an advisory panel of distinguished Chinese scholars and an international advisory panel in the supervision of each project constitutes a significant expression of the principle of university autonomy, since these panels are to ensure the application of educational and academic criteria in the oversight of the projects. Through the international advisory panel, Chinese institutions are being introduced to a global network of scholarship, which has its own culturally defined dynamics of interaction. While major national universities in China have already been a part of this community for some time, provincial and local institutions are being given an opportunity for participation unparalleled in their history. The benefits they receive and their ability to disseminate these through the various channels of service open to them will demonstrate the extent to which foreign-derived knowledge can contribute to local development needs.

Agricultural Education and Research Projects

Three of the first six higher education projects were devoted to agricultural education and research, indicating a high Chinese priority on this area. These three projects supported institutions under the ministries of Agriculture, Animal Husbandry, and Fisheries (MAAF), Forestry, Water Conservancy, and State Farm and Land Reclamation, as well as the bureaus of Aquatic Products and Meteorology. While other projects focused on the higher education system, these projects included research centers under the Academy of Agricultural Sciences and other bureaus, mid-level technical schools under the MAAF, and universities and colleges under agriculture-related ministries.

Agricultural Education I involved eleven key national-echelon agricultural universities, six agricultural research institutes, and the creation of a national institute for rice research. Its objectives were to improve the quality of teaching and research, expand enrollment and research capacity, and strengthen the organization and management of resources in agricultural education and research. In a total budget of $201.6 million (75 million from the bank), 42 percent was earmarked for equipment, 44.2 percent for civil works, and 13.8 percent for technical assistance. Under the latter, provision was made for 389 faculty fellowships for study abroad, 41 at doctoral level,

147 at the master's level, and 201 visiting scholar places. Foreign specialists were invited for consultancy at the discretion of the MAAF.

Agricultural Education and Research II built upon the first agricultural project with the intention of extending assistance to a wider range of agricultural/geographical regions and placing greater emphasis on the role of the agricultural college as a community and regional resource. Its objectives were (1) to expand pre-service and in-service training at twenty-three key agricultural colleges; (2) to expand the community service role of the agricultural college by establishing regional training and extension support centers functioning within the colleges teaching/research framework which would train staff and provide technical service for the MAAF extension system; (3) to assist the government in defining a strategy for secondary/postsecondary agricultural education by introducing a pilot program to strengthen twelve mid-level technical schools; and (4) to support evaluation, planning, and preparation of future projects.

This project included seven institutions under the MAAF and other agriculture-related ministries, the eleven colleges of the first project, thirteen provincial-level colleges, and twelve mid-level technical schools. The emphasis was on dissemination and community service rather than the high-level theoretical research which was an important focus of the first project. In a total budget of $175 million ($69 million from the bank), 39.8 percent was for civil works, 48.1 percent for equipment, 7.4 percent for fellowships abroad, and 4.7 percent for specialist services. A total of 302 fellowships abroad were planned, 19 at doctoral level, 125 at master's level, and 158 for one-year visiting scholar programs.

Agricultural Research II had a total budget of $59 million ($25 million from the bank) and focused on the enhancement of facilities for agricultural research in 15 agricultural research centers, as well as support for 10 county-level agrotechnical extension stations. The intent was that the research centers be enabled to cooperate more closely with agricultural universities and gain support for a small graduate study program. These 15 centers are identified on the map yet not included in the total count of 183 higher institutions.

These three projects in agricultural education and research express both the high Chinese priority on agricultural development and the determination of the Chinese MAAF to retain strong Chinese control over higher education in this area. The idea of an international advisory panel was rejected in favor of close monitoring of projects by the MAAF with the help of foreign consultants whom they selected, largely from the American Chinese community. Officials within the MAAF considered that overinvolvement of foreign academics could lead to the waste of resources and unacceptable interference by foreign specialists who do not have an adequate understanding of Chinese development needs.

At present the Chinese agricultural education system has a strong practical orientation and good community linkages through the extension system, and the emphasis is on preserving and enhancing this service aspect of its role. While the American Land Grant model has been recommended to the Chinese, as discussed in chapter 3, it was a considered Chinese decision not to adopt this model but rather to move forward on the basis they have already laid. They are also strongly interested in French agricultural education at the higher level and have had considerable assistance from French agricultural research and education institutions. Because of the *grande école* ethos in France, the prestige of specialist agricultural schools is higher than that of departments of agricultural science within universities. The Chinese see this as a more practical model for them to emulate than the American Land Grant university.[38]

Rural Health and Medical Education Project

Like the agricultural project, the rural health and medical education project involved higher education yet had as its key target the whole medical system. Its principle objectives were (1) to improve the health status in forty-six counties of three provinces (Heilongjiang, Shandong, and Sichuan) and one autonomous region (Ningxia); (2) to enhance the quality of education, training, and related research in thirteen core medical colleges[39] and universities and increase the capacity of those colleges to provide continuing education and training materials to practitioners of one hundred province-level medical colleges; and (3) to help improve management and evaluation of the health sector by strengthening two newly created national institutions—the National Center for Preventive Medicine and the Research Center for Health Planning—and to support applied research at the Sichuan Institute for Materia Medica.

In a total budget of $322.8 million ($85 million from the bank), 24.8 percent was designated for rural health, 43.6 percent for medical education, and 32.6 percent for strengthening management, evaluation, and research. In the medical education budget about 7 percent was earmarked for training, including substantial provision for study abroad, and 4.8 percent for technical assistance and personnel recruitment. The project oversight has been entirely in the hands of the Ministry of Public Health, and it has been advised by bank officers in the selection of foreign specialists for consultancy work on the project. Through a special emphasis on epidemiology and preventive medicine, the bank advisers hoped to confer prestige on these areas of great importance and to assist the Chinese in bringing their considerable past achievements into line with the new profile of disease within China, which is closer to that of middle-income countries than of poor developing countries. A higher incidence of heart disease and cancer contrasts with the former focus on infectious diseases. What has been called the second health care revolution thus has new challenges to meet.[40]

While it was recognized that the thirteen medical universities involved in the project would wish to obtain sophisticated instrumentation for research and teaching, the intention was for 20 percent of the funding to go toward areas that involve concepts and ideas. First, the universities were to be encouraged to take a leading role in the development of a whole new set of strategies for preventive medicine which address the new disease profile resulting from Chinese success in the first health care revolution. Second, universities were expected to take a lead in transforming management practices within the health sector in terms of planning, resource utilization, and health policy formulation and implementation. Third, universities were responsible for continuing education, particularly the upgrading of the large contingent of doctors educated during the Cultural Revolution period. Finally, universities were to lead in the area of clinical epidemiology, the design, measurement, and evaluation of research projects related to preventive medicine. This leadership role required a multidisciplinary approach with the planned participation of different departments within each institution. The technical assistance aspect of the program related specifically to these four needs and aimed to support Chinese institutions in taking up leadership in these areas.[41]

Issues Arising for World Bank Higher Education Projects

This review of the eight World Bank projects now operating within the Chinese higher education system indicates that their orientation is very much in line with the policy statement on higher education in the 1980 World Bank policy sector report. Development-oriented disciplines have been stressed, and efforts have been made to adjust enrollment ratios to the needs of the economic system. Higher agricultural education, the basis for continued prosperity, has been appropriately emphasized, as has medicine and health. In the pure and applied sciences, there has been an attempt to balance support for basic research facilities and for the development of technologically innovative areas suited to changing industrial needs. Some attempts have also been made to support the growth and improvement of social science programs, though foreign involvement in this sensitive area is likely to be more difficult than in any other. Finally, teacher education is being strongly supported over twenty-eight provinces, municipalities, and autonomous regions, a move that should contribute to the new policy of providing nine years of compulsory education for all. Both the disciplinary spread and the involvement of local, provincial, and national-echelon institutions seem to be appropriate to present Chinese development needs.

One still may ask, however, whether the departure from the usual World Bank focus on basic education was justified, and whether the enormous expenditure on the Chinese higher education system is defensible in a situation where rural education at the basic and secondary levels is given little central government support and has regressed over recent years.[42] The transition rates from primary to lower secondary school fell from 79.9 percent in 1978-79 to 67.6 percent in 1984-85, and from lower to upper secondary they fell from 44.4 percent to 27.1 percent over the same period. In cities and towns the transition from primary to lower secondary has risen from 87.5 percent to over 100 percent, probably reflecting the absorption of some rural graduates in county towns, while in rural areas it has dropped from 76.4 percent to 58 percent. The transition from lower to upper secondary has dropped from 83 percent to 55.5 percent in cities and towns, and from 33.5 percent to 11.9 percent in rural areas. As these figures only deal with graduates, they mask the even more serious problem of the dropout rate in rural education.[43]

This is an issue of the development model favored. The Chinese have good reason, based on their Cultural Revolution experience, to turn away from rural-oriented self-reliance and put their efforts into a modernization policy that combines incentives for agricultural development with a continued emphasis on the application of science to industrial development and a conscious effort to bring high technology into selected economic sectors, as well as to move gradually toward greater economic integration with the capitalist world. This requires considerable sophistication in the research and intellectual formation carried out in the higher education system and that has obviously been given first priority at present. The technical assistance components of all World Bank projects open doors to lively interaction between China and OECD countries through a large Chinese scholarly presence in universities within the OECD and many specialist visits to Chinese institutions. This both complements and strengthens the contacts going on through the bilateral relations discussed in chapters 5 and 6.

One aspect of World Bank projects that gives cause for concern, however, is the huge expenditure on highly sophisticated scientific instrumentation requiring expensive facilities and very high-cost maintenance. How vital is it to the kinds of scientific research being done at project institutions? There have been debates over the relative value of concentrating this equipment in analysis centers open to all departments and industrial users or placing it in relevant departments, and over the relative value of mainframe computers as against systems of micro- and minicomputers. These debates are overshadowed by the larger question of how far this exponential leap in the instrumentation available to university scholars will contribute to the quality of the scientific work going on. There is evidence of its creative use in some cases. Yet there are also serious pressures to raise funds for its maintenance through soliciting industrial research contracts that make no contribution to applied or basic knowledge in scientific fields. If the scientific instrumentation ends up as a weight that suppresses rather than stimulates scientific creativity, it would be most unfortunate.

Most World Bank projects have included modest funding for library development. Yet this aspect gains little attention and has not been fully implemented.[44] If one imagined a flood of books and journals pouring into Chinese university libraries in equivalent weight to scientific instrumentation, the possibilities for stimulus to creative thought, and for satisfaction to the curiosity and thirst for knowledge that is so evident a characteristic of Chinese students, are tremendous. There would be no maintenance problems, yet the contribution to a qualitative improvement in university programs could be striking.

Finally, the two models adopted for the supervision of project implementation and the oversight of the foreign contribution deserve some comment. The agricultural and medical projects involve Chinese institutions that are already closely linked to extension systems in these areas, and the projects encourage the strengthening of these linkages so that innovations can be appropriately disseminated. In this kind of situation, the supervision of the appropriate Chinese authorities, in consultation with bank specialists, may have been the wisest choice and represents a common pattern in other developing countries participating in World Bank projects.

In contrast, the establishment of a Chinese and an international advisory panel to supervise the other four projects represents an interesting innovation in bank policy, possibly one that was stimulated by the exclusive focus on higher education which is unusual for bank projects. The two panels ensure a rigorous academic review process over the foreign specialists invited to participate in Chinese university reforms, and an eclecticism in the cultural contributions made, with attempts to ensure participation from a wide range of OECD countries. The panels have also been able to exercise some restraint and guidance in the matter of equipment purchase, especially in the later projects. Their role as a kind of buffer between Chinese universities, Chinese and foreign governments and the international business community should create conditions where scholars from China and OECD countries can interact in an exchange process that brings into play the initiative of persons and institutions, yet is subject to strict academic review.

The value of the panels for assuring high standards of research and teaching that will enable Chinese institutions to participate in a fuller and more equal way in the international scholarly community is without question. What may be more problematic is whether distinguished foreign scholars, and indeed high-level Chinese scholars, will be as successful in supporting the service and dissemination aspects of the role of Chinese institutions. This aspect of work is just as significant in comprehensive, engineering, and teachers universities as in the agricultural and medical institutions, yet it may not be as well integrated into local and regional networks for knowledge dissemination.

Conclusion: Prospects for Resolution and Transformation

In conclusion I would like to reflect broadly upon the impact of World Bank projects in Chinese higher education by returning to two aspects of the evaluative framework developed earlier. The first focused on an internal contradiction within Chinese higher education over the whole twentieth century—the tension between a hierarchical knowledge structure and an organization of knowledge characterized by strong classification and framing, on the one hand, and the recurring efforts to transform these knowledge patterns for the service of economic development, on the other. The second aspect pointed to the role of China's universities in the world community and used the values of equity, autonomy, solidarity, and participation to assess the extent to which relations of mutuality were being created. At this point it may be valuable to reflect on the ways in which World Bank projects have assisted Chinese universities in facing these two challenges.

If one considers first the organization of knowledge within Chinese higher institutions, it seems clear that bank projects are having a considerable effect in the direction of a weakening of classification and framing. The redefinition of disciplines and specializations in a more open way, with a stronger theoretical basis and broader practical application, is being supported through the presence of foreign specialists in Chinese departments and the exposure of a large contingent of faculty to study and research in universities abroad. The greater openness among different knowledge areas, the encouragement of multidisciplinary and elective studies, and the reduction in lecture hours in favor of experimentation and self-study have all been given impetus by bank projects. Probably the strongest internal dynamic for this transformation comes from the new emphasis on research as an important function of university departments, and World Bank projects have made an important contribution to the strengthening of the research function.

The structure of knowledge in the higher curriculum may be more resistant to change. Of all the eight projects, only one involves the social sciences in a substantive way. While the inflow of expertise and the opportunities for research abroad should contribute to the diversification of these sensitive areas of knowledge, they could also confer a new authority on these disciplines as pursued in prestigious national institutions creating a parallel situation to their association with the Soviet Union in the 1950s. The caution with which this aspect of University Development II is progressing, in contrast to the engineering aspects of the project, indicates the tensions associated with a genuine transformation of knowledge structure.

Understandably, the Chinese are determined to maintain control over the terms in which their political and economic development is discussed and defined. Yet will they allow a broad internal participation in debates in this area? How far will the genuine intellectual freedom expressed in the slogan of "letting a hundred flowers bloom" be possible? The strengthening of social science enrollments across a broad range of institutions is significant evidence of some movement in this direction. Yet there is a continuing tendency to maintain tight control and reaffirm their unity and position of supremacy in what may be both an intuitive Confucian reflex for the preservation of political order and a necessity of the Leninist state. Universities such as People's University and Fudan University could use World Bank support to affirm their leadership in this role, becoming new centers of intellectual authority and establishing a new orthodoxy by drawing on selected foreign theory. However, the wide range of other institutions that are also developing programs in this area and the eclectic involvement of many OECD countries in these fields makes this kind of intellectual domination less possible than in the past.

A second aspect of the transformation of knowledge structure is less problematic. The strengthening of short-cycle programs so that they reach half of higher education enrollments is receiving support through the third World Bank project. This should confer some prestige on a sector of the higher education system that has been deprived since 1952, except during the Cultural Revolution period. It should bring together the goals of knowledge for practical economic development and local political participation and make possible a more balanced structure of expertise within the overall scientific-technical work force.

Perhaps the most striking line of change within the overall structure of the higher education system is a remarkable diversification of institutions, by level, by program orientation, and by administrative sector. Higher institutions have been given greater autonomy over their programs, and those participating in World Bank projects have also received considerable resources to pursue the vision and developmental plans they have for their institutions. Chapter 3 illustrated the increasing diversity that is likely to characterize institutions of different echelons and in differing geographical regions. This should enrich the overall higher education system and make possible a gradual widening of local political participation along with improved service to the economic development needs of particular areas. Scholars within higher institutions face an essential tension between developing a level of intellectual sophistication that makes possible a fruitful use of international contacts and strengthening the local linkages that enable them to disseminate knowledge and ensure its application to local development needs.

In reflecting on this needed balance between an appropriate contribution to internal development and fruitful relations with the world academic community, I would like to return to the ideal type of mutuality sketched out in chapter 4. The values of equity, autonomy, solidarity, and participation there informed a vision of China's universities contributing in a balanced way to national development and also making their own distinctive contribution to the world academic community. How far will World Bank projects help to realize this vision?

Let me begin with the value of participation. The most striking point that has become evident in this chapter is the broad geographical spread of higher institutions taking part in bank projects and the fact that local and provincial echelon institution have made up 86 of the total of 183 institutions. While regional imbalances are still obvious, notably the relative strength of the North over the South and the predominance of a few major cities, this geographical breadth could not have been achieved through bilateral cooperation. Also the echelon spread from national to local would not likely have been reached through SEdC efforts at sending scholars abroad, nor through bilateral projects, both of which have tended to focus on national-level institutions. Through bank support, provincial-echelon institutions are now developing their own lively programs with foreign counterparts. Local institutions have had greater difficulties in establishing satisfactory interaction with similar institutions in OECD countries, but this situation is improving.

The geographical and the echelon spread of participation is remarkable and bodes well for the development of a broadly based ethos of Chinese scholarship that can contribute in a creative way to the world scholarly community. Inevitably, however, there are a large number of institutions, over 700, that have not participated in World Bank projects and are almost certain to fall farther behind in both material and intellectual resources. An important test for the 183 project institutions may be the degree to which their participation is seen to strengthen their support for other institutions. If massive foreign and Chinese funding is perceived only to raise their prestige and status, not to make a practical contribution to their constituencies, there would be little hope of them playing a transformative role either within China or in a world context.

This leads one to the value of solidarity and the ties of communication that are built among intellectuals at the local, regional, and national levels, as well as with intellectual communities in other developing nations. If China is to create a strong and independently based ethos of scholarship that has something new to contribute to the global community, networks of internal cooperation will be its essential basis. The fragmentation that has often characterized scholarly communities in other developing countries must be avoided.

The conditions of both Chinese culture and Chinese socialism make this less problematic for China than most other developing nations. China has the advantage of a unified written language, rooted in a highly developed scholarly culture, and a huge and growing publishing industry. The number and circulation of scholarly journals since 1978 have grown tremendously, making for a lively shared intellectual community to which foreign language publications remain peripheral. Furthermore, Chinese socialism has ensured a system of higher education in which considerable cooperation exists, both within and among differing sectors and echelons. Sectoral cooperation can be seen in the close links among institutions under particular ministries at the national level and in the integration at the provincial level that comes from planning for the needs of the province as a whole. Interechelon cooperation is coordinated by the State Education Commission and evident in such programs as the provision of postgraduate study in major national universities for faculty of new vocational universities and of provincial-echelon institutions.

The other side to this solidarity, however, is a tendency for the center in China to hold in place a hierarchy that monopolizes most international contacts for national-echelon institutions and gives them the role of passing knowledge down through the system to the lower echelons. This is being modified by the new freedoms given to individual higher institutions over their programs and their international contacts. World Bank projects are giving some substance to this freedom in making possible broad international linkages for provincial and local-echelon institutions. Yet these institutions must also support one another in forming a distinctive regional orientation and an ethos of local service. Linkages with the outside world through the bank or through bilateral connections convey both tremendous prestige and considerable material improvement on an institution, making for intense competition among institutions and a new role for their leaders as lobbyists to gain these advantages. This could mitigate against solidarity and lead to fragmentation within local intellectual networks.

Solidarity is in turn the essential basis for autonomy. An autonomous, internally generated Chinese technology must be rooted in both strength and creativity in the basic sciences. This is essential for the adaptation of advanced foreign technology to Chinese conditions in such a way that it is effectively used and stimulates further technological developments. World Bank projects have made possible greater Chinese intellectual interaction with the world scientific community than in any of the bilateral projects, and here lies the hope for a stimulus that could make for a strong independent Chinese scientific community. The role of the international advisory panel in four of the projects may be particularly important in relation to this issue.

In the social sciences, autonomy is both more crucial and more difficult. A Soviet-derived Marxist-Leninist social science was successful in the 1950s in steering a rapid industrialization program, yet its doctrinaire rigidity and its mechanisms of control through the intellectual center established at People's University produced a strongly antagonistic reaction. The Cultural Revolution decade represented true Chinese autonomy in the social sciences, with the absolute ascendance of Mao Thought. This experience showed both the symbolic importance of autonomy to the Chinese and the need for that autonomy to be built upon an acceptable synthesis between Chinese and foreign thought. Maoism in its extreme form proved to be no more than a return to Chinese feudalism, one which did not have the sophistication necessary to guide China along a pathway toward modernization. The creation of a new synthesis in terms of a Chinese theory of management that is compatible with Marxism-Leninism and Mao Zedong Thought yet also selectively integrates aspects of Western social and economic theory is probably the greatest challenge of this period. It must be capable both of guiding China's internal modernization and negotiating a genuine interdependence for China in the world capitalist community.

The only World Bank project contributing to this area is University Development II, and it is focusing on national institutions that have a tendency toward intellectual authority deeply rooted in Confucian tradition. It remains to be seen whether they will foster a Chinese approach to the social sciences that is built up through participatory scholarly debates at all levels and allows for some intellectual freedom.

As for equity, there can be little doubt about full and equal Chinese participation in negotiations over the agreements that underlay each World Bank project. In fact, the Chinese have had remarkable success in ensuring strong emphasis on higher education so far, in direct contravention of usual bank educational policy. The next decade of China's development experience will demonstrate whether or not this has been a wise use of educational resources and what China has been able to achieve in terms of both national and international development through these projects in higher education.

POSTSCRIPT

This book has been infused with a considerable measure of idealism and hope, inspired both by the visionary programmatic of world order models thinking and by the author's personal appreciation for Chinese culture and its traditional and modern achievements. However, the decision to create a model that highlights the most positive and hopeful tendencies in recent educational development has been offset by the introduction of a second model that uses both the development experience of other third world nations and China's own historical experience to crystallize some of the negative possibilities in the present transition from isolation to integration within a world community dominated by the capitalist nations of the OECD. The intention in the formulation of these models was to devise instruments of measurement that go deeper than technical issues of efficiency and effectiveness in evaluating the general cultural, political, and economic outcomes of this historic process. It is still far too early to reach any definitive conclusions, yet I hope the framework these models provide will be useful both to policy makers and to scholars who are involved in shaping or evaluating cultural and educational relations between OECD nations and China.

My conviction throughout this study has been that China's educational development and the ways in which the Chinese leadership deals with educational reform are of primary importance to the success of the open door. While there are importance choices to be made by those responsible for the cultural and educational policy of OECD nations toward China, it will ultimately be the internal situation that determines how well the knowledge and technology introduced from abroad serves China's modernization. In identifying what I see as a central contradiction in Chinese higher education development—the tension between traditional knowledge patterns for political control and transformed ones for economic development—I have tried to provide an internal evaluative perspective on the change process.

My conclusions on the curricular transformation underway at the level of both national policy and individual institutions may be somewhat optimistic, however. What I was not able to do in this study was to observe actual interaction within the classroom or university department. Reports from both Chinese scholars abroad and Western scholars who have been invited to investigate specific fields indicate that the kind of transformation suggested by policy documents and enthusiastically discussed by such university leaders as the heads of academic affairs offices are far from being fully implemented.

My analysis suggests that the difficulties in realizing curricular reform are not merely technical, but are rooted in both the power concerns of China's Marxist-Leninist state and a tradition of rule through the regimentation of knowledge that goes back for millennia. The implications of genuine curricular change for the democratization of Chinese society are immense, and it is this that the political leadership must face in the coming decade.

The student demonstrations of December 1986 were a good test of official response to this issue, and it is unfortunate that most of the educational policies that have followed indicate a return to the old techniques of repression rather than a creative tapping of student initiative for change. Thus military training has been introduced on many university campuses,[1] and there are reports of its specific use to discipline students who are regarded as unruly or insubordinate. Both short-term social practice activities[2] and a policy of sending all university graduates to work at the grass roots in the first years after graduation[3] are perceived less as a healthy exposure to the real-life conditions of production than as a measure of retaliation against students for their outspoken involvement in local and national political issues. Finally, the threat of new controls over study abroad, with specific quotas limiting access to the one country—the United States—that offers most opportunity and financial support, has led to further student activism in early 1988. The most disturbing feature of these putative restrictions is that everyone knows a quota system will favor those able to use the back door, and the flow abroad could again be dominated by those best able to curry political favor and least likely to make profitable use of such study or research opportunities.

On the other side of the picture, however, both the Thirteenth Party Congress in October 1987 and the subsequent National People's Congress of March 1988 reaffirmed the open-door policy and strengthened the hands of a young group of party leaders associated with the former premier and now party general secretary, Zhao Ziyang. Given this situation, it is not difficult to predict continuing tensions in the higher education system over the coming decades.

The worst scenario would see the economic pressures of the forced subordination of the university system to market demands[4] reinforcing political pressures for conformity, a process that could well be exacerbated by the economistic purposes of several OECD nations in their knowledge interactions with China. There might be short-term economic benefits for both China and OECD nations in such developments, but in the longer term the goose that produced these golden eggs—the university system—would be destroyed.

The most hopeful scenario would be one in which the political leadership made a genuine commitment to the creation of democratic institutions that could absorb and utilize the positive energy of a Chinese youth educated in more open and critical ways. The university community would be strengthened in its commitment to the advancement as well as the dissemination of knowledge through its ties with universities around the world. Balanced economic development and gradual political democratization would complement one another in this scenario, with the university achieving a transformation of curricular patterns that served both effectively.

NOTES

Introduction

1. See, for example, Samuel Kim, ed., *China and the World* (Boulder: Westview Press, 1984); Samuel Ho and Ralph Huenneman, *China's Open Door Policy: The Quest for Foreign Technology and Capital* (Vancouver: University of British Columbia Press, 1984).

2. See, for example, Jan Ingvar Lofstedt, *Chinese Educational Policy* (Stockholm: Almqvist and Wiksell, 1980), and Theodore Chen Hsi-en, *Chinese Education: Academic and Revolutionary Models* (New York: Praeger, 1981).

3. Susan Shirk, *Competitive Comrades: Career Incentives and Student Strategies in China* (Berkeley: University of California Press, 1982); Robert Taylor, *China's Intellectual Dilemma: Politics and University Enrolment 1949-1978* (Vancouver: University of British Columbia Press, 1983); Jonathan Unger, *Education under Mao: Class and Competition in Canton Schools* (New York: Columbia University Press, 1983).

4. Joseph Ben-David, *American Higher Education: Directions Old and New* (New York: McGraw Hill, 1972); J. Ben-David, *Centers of Learning* (New York: McGraw Hill, 1977).

5. Joseph Ben-David, *Fundamental Research and the Universities* (Paris: OECD, 1968).

6. Basil Bernstein, *Class, Codes and Control: Towards a Theory of Educational Transmission*, 3 vols. (London: Routledge and Kegan Paul, 1974-77); Michael Young, ed., *Knowledge and Control* (London: Collier Macmillan, 1971); M. Young and G. Whitty, eds., *Explorations in the Politics of School Knowledge* (England: Nafferton Books, 1976).

7. K. J. Holsti, *The Dividing Discipline: Hegemony and Diversity in International Theory* (Boston: Allen and Unwin, 1985), documents the remarkable academic hegemony held by this classical approach into the 1970s. The major challenges of the seventies have been the new academic legitimacy attained by dependency/world capitalist-system theories and world/global society models.

8. Martin Carnoy, *Education as Cultural Imperialism* (New York: David MacKay, 1974), is perhaps the most striking application of the work of Lenin (*Imperialism the Highest Stage of Capitalism*) and dependency theorists such as André Gundar Frank and Fernando Cardoso to international education relations.

9. Frances Moulder has used the macrohistorical approach of Immanuel Wallerstein, *The Capitalist World System*, vol. 2 (New York: Academic Press, 1980), to explore the economic underdevelopment of China in *Japan, China and the Modern World Economy: Towards a Reinterpretation of East Asian Development ca 1600 to ca 1918* (Cambridge: Cambridge University Press, 1979).

10. The group has been responsible for the journal *Alternatives* since the early seventies, edited in India by Rajni Kothari. Major writings include Samuel Kim,

Toward a Just World Order (Boulder: Westview Press, 1984); Rajni Kothari, *Footsteps into the Future: Diagnosis of the Present World and Design for an Alternative* (New York: Free Press, 1974); and Johann Galtung, *The True Worlds: A Transnational Perspective* (New York: The Free Press, 1980).

Chapter 1

1. Joseph Ben-David, *Fundamental Research and the Universities.*

2. Michael Young, "An Approach to the Study of Curriculum as Socially Organized Knowledge," in *Knowledge and Control*, ed. M. Young. See also Young, "The Schooling of Science," in *Explorations in the Politics of School Knowledge*, ed. M. Young and G. Whitty.

3. Fritz Ringer, *The Decline of the German Mandarinate* (Cambridge: Harvard University Press, 1969), p. 111.

4. Pascale Gruson, *L'Etat Enseignant* (Paris: Mouton, 1978), p. 91.

5. Basil Bernstein, "On the Classification and Framing of Educational Knowledge," in *Knowledge and Control*, ed. M. Young, pp. 47-69.

6. Joseph Needham, *A Shorter Science and Civilization in China*, ed. Colin Ronan (Cambridge: Cambridge University Press, 1978).

7. Ichisada Miyazaki, *China's Examination Hell: The Civil Service Examinations of Imperial China* (New York: Weatherhill, 1977).

8. Kenneth Folsom, *Friends, Guests and Colleagues: The Mu-fu System in the Late Ch'ing Period* (Berkeley: University of California Press, 1968).

9. *The Mencius*, vol. 2 of *The Confucian Classics*, trans. James Legge (London: Trubner, 1875), pp. 207-208.

10. Wolfgang Franke, *The Reform and Abolition of the Traditional Chinese Examination System* (Cambridge: Harvard University Press, 1960), p. 13.

11. Actually, lower-echelon civil service posts were sometimes filled by *juren* (scholars who had passed the second degree), but the more prestigious posts were reserved for *jinshi* (scholars with the third and highest degree).

12. Joanna Menzel, ed. *The Chinese Civil Service: Career Open to Talent?* (Boston: D. C. Heath, 1963).

13. Adam Liu Yuen-ching, *The Hanlin Academy: Training Ground for the Ambitious 1644-1850* (Connecticut: Archon Books, 1981).

14. Quoted from a book published in 1838 by the English writer, C. T. Downey, in Teng Ssu-yu,"Chinese Influence on the Western Examination System," *Harvard Journal of Asiatic Studies* 7, 4 (1942): 290.

15. John Meskill, *Academies in Ming China* (Tuscon: University of Arizona Press, 1982).

16. Shu Xincheng, ed., *Zhongguo jindai jiaoyushi ziliao* (Documents of Recent Chinese Educational History), vol. 2 (Beijing: Renmin Jiaoyu Chubanshe, 1979), pp. 671-72.

17. Xiao Chaoran et al., *Beijing daxue xiaoshi* (A history of Beijing University) (Shanghai: Shanghai Jiaoyu Chubanshe, 1981); William Duiker, Ts'ai Yüan-p'ei: Educator of Modern China (University Park: Pennsylvania State University Press, 1977).

18. Zhou Yutong, *Zhongguo xiandai jiaoyu shi* (Contemporary Chinese educational history) (Shanghai: Liangyou Tushu Yinshua Gongsi, 1934), pp. 30-33, 200-20.

19. Donald Jordan, *The Northern Expedition: China's National Revolution of 1926-28* (Honolulu: University Press of Hawaii, 1976).

20. *Qinghua daxue xiaoshi gao* (A draft history of Qinghua University) (Beijing: Zhonghua Shuju, 1981).

21. Jessie Lutz, *China and the Christian Colleges* (Ithaca: Cornell University Press, 1971).

22. Fudan University is typical of these. See R. Hayhoe, "Yige daxue xin chuantong de kaichuang: Fudan de zhaonian" (The forging of a new university tradition: Fudan's early years), *Fudan xuebao* 2 (March 1982): 100-105. See also Anthony Li, *The History of Privately Controlled Higher Education in the Republic of China* (Westport, Ct.: Greenwood Press, 1977).

23. Francoise Kreissler, "L'action culturelle Allemande en Chine de la fin du XIXè siècle à le seconde Guerre Mondiale" (Doctorat du 3ème cycle, Ecole des Haute Etudes en Sciences Sociales, 1983), chap. 2.

24. R. Hayhoe, "Towards the Forging of a Chinese University Ethos: Zhendan and Fudan 1903-1919," *China Quarterly* 94 (June 1983): 324-41.

25. Contemporary discussions of educational reform by American-returned Chinese educators show the strong connection in their minds between educational reform and political democratization. See, for example, Chuang Chai-hsuan, *Tendencies Towards a Democratic System of Education in China* (Shanghai: Commercial Press, 1922); Djung Lu-dzai, *A History of Democratic Education in Modern China* (Shanghai: Commercial Press, 1934); and Yin Chiling, *Reconstruction of Modern Educational Organization in China* (Shanghai: Commercial Press, 1924). See also Barry Keenan, The Dewey Experiment in China (Cambridge: Harvard University Press, 1977), and Hubert Brown, "American Progressivism in Chinese Education: The Case of Tao Xingzhi," in *China's Education and the Industrialized World: Studies in Cultural Transfer*, ed. R. Hayhoe and M. Bastid (New York: M. E. Sharpe, 1987).

26. *Jiaoyu faling* (Educational regulations) (Shanghai: Zhonghua Shuju 1947), pp. 141-44.

27. For a good contemporary picture of the higher education system in the early Nationalist period, see Zhou Yutong, *Zhongguo xiandai jiaoyushi* (Shanghai: Liangyou Tushu Yinshua Gongsi, 1934), pp. 184-234.

28. *Zhongguo jiaoyu nianjian* (China education yearbook) (Shanghai:, Commercial Press, 1948), p. 530. Between 1930 and 1937 the number of students enrolled in arts dropped from 6,706 to 4,130, in political science and law from 15,899 to 7,125. By contrast, science enrollments grew from 2,872 to 5,768, engineering from 3,734 to 5,768.

29. John Israel, *Student Nationalism in China: 1927-1937* (Stanford, Hoover Institute for War, Revolution and Peace, Stanford University Press, 1966), pp. 23-24.

30. C. H. Becker et al., *The Reorganization of Education in China* (Paris: League of Nations Institute of Educational Cooperation, 1932); Ernst Neugebauer, *Anfänge pädagogische Entwicklungshilfe unter dem Völkerbund in Chine 1931 bis 1935* (Hamburg: Mitteilungen des Instituts für Asienkunde, 1971).

31. *Zhongguo jiaoyu nianjian*, pp. 490-530; *Jiaoyu faling*, pp. 143-82.

32. Brian Crozier, *The Man Who Lost China* (London: Angus and Robertson,

1977); Robert Payne, *Chiang Kai Shek* (New York: Weybright and Talley, 1969), pp. 160-65.

33. John Israel, *Student Nationalism in China*, deals well with these intellectual currents.

34. Ruth Hayhoe, "Catholics and Socialists: The Paradox of Sino-French Educational Interaction," in *China's Education and the Industrialized World*, ed. Hayhoe and Bastid.

35. F. Kreissler, "Technical Education as the Key to Cultural Cooperation: The Sino-German Experience," in *China's Education and The Industrialized World*, ed. Hayhoe and Bastid.

36. Philip West, *Yenching University and Sino-Western Relations 1916-1952* (Cambridge: Harvard University Press, 1977).

37. There are several excellent studies of Communist educational experience in Yan'an and in the prerevolution period generally. See Michael Lindsay, *Notes on Educational Problems in Communist China 1941-1947* (New York: Institute of Pacific Relations, 1950); Mark Selden, *The Yenan Way in Revolutionary China* (Cambridge: Harvard University Press, 1971); Peter Seybolt, "Yenan Education and the Chinese Revolution 1937-1945" (Ph.D. dissertation, Harvard University, 1969); Wang Hsueh-wen, *Chinese Communist Education: The Yenan Period* (Taiwan: Institute of International Relation, 1975).

38. "Resolutions of the First National Conference on Higher Education," in *Chinese Communist Education: Records of the First Decade*, ed. S. Fraser (New York: John Wiley and Sons, 1965), pp. 92-98.

39. Between 1947 and 1962, arts and social science enrollments fell from 46.6 percent of the total enrollment to 7.6 percent. See *Zhongguo jiaoyu nianjian 1949-1981* (China education yearbook, 1949-1981) (Beijing: Zhongguo Dabaike Quanshu Chubanshe, 1982), pp. 239-40.

40. Chung Shih, *Higher Education in Communist China* (Hong Kong: Union Research Institute, 1953). An interesting contemporary Chinese perspective on this reform is given in *Tianjin shiyuan xuebao* 2 (1982): 19-25.

41. Cheng Chi-yuan, *Scientific and Engineering Manpower in Communist China 1949-1963* (Washington, D.C.: GPO, 1962). This book details the remarkable success of the early Communist regime in training scientific and technical manpower to serve rapid economic modernization.

42. *Renmin ribao*, September 26, 1953; Qian Duansheng, "Higher Education Takes a New Road," *China Reconstructs* (September-October 1953): 4.

43. Interestingly, this terminological distinction is very similar to the one made in the early republican period and in the early Nationalist period. Actually the word *daxue* simply means higher school in China, and it is popularly used to cover all types of higher institution. In the more open conditions of the post-1978 period, when American patterns are once more being emulated, there is a parallel with the early twenties when the distinction between *daxue* and *xueyuan* lost any importance. Now, in fact, many *xueyuan* are renaming themselves *daxue*. In writing of higher institutions in the contemporary period, I have therefore not maintained the distinction in my English usage.

44. Leo A. Orleans, *Professional Manpower and Education in Communist China*

(Washington, D.C.: GPO, 1960), gives a clear picture of the system put in place in 1952.

45. Richard Suttmeier, *Research and Revolution* (Lexington, Mass.: D. C. Heath, 1974), pp. 68ff.

46. This perception of the problem of the higher education system informed a whole series of aritcles in the Chinese press and journals in the early eighties. See, for example, *Jiaoyu yanjiu* 6 (1981): 40-45 and *Guangming ribao*, December 2, 1980. Naturally the links with political order are not drawn in the way that I have done.

47. See Liu Shaoqi's speech at the inauguration ceremony of People's University in 1950 in *The Collected Works of Liu Shaoqi*, vol. 2: *1945-1957* (Hong Kong: Union Research Institute, 1969), pp. 235-54.

48. C. T. Hu, "Chinese People's University: A Bastion of Marxism-Leninism," in *Universities Facing the Future*, ed. W. R. Niblett and R. F. Butts, World Yearbook of Education 1972-73 (London: Evans Bros., 1972). For a Chinese view of the special role of People's University in the social sciences, see *Gaojiao zhanxian* 5 (1982): 11-12 and *Jiefang ribao*, October 4, 1980.

49. The extreme antagonism aroused by this role is evident in such a statement from the Hundred Flowers Period as "A Great Beehive of Doctrinairism," in *The Hundred Flowers Campaign and the Chinese Intellectuals*, ed. R. MacFarquar (New York: Octagon Books, 1974), pp. 86-87.

50. Julia Kwong, *Chinese Education in Transition* (Montreal: McGill University Press, 1979), gives a clear picture of the educational reforms of the Great Leap period, their link to concepts of economic development, and their subsequent demise in the retrenchment of the early sixties. Stewart Fraser, ed. *Chinese Communist Education: Records of the First Decade* (New York: John Wiley and Sons, 1965), pp. 268-410, gives translations of the major educational documents of the period. These reforms are now being given quite a positive evaluation in China as an attempt to assert Chinese control and direction over higher education patterns that had been shaped along Soviet lines. See *Jiaoyu kexue yanjiu* (Wuhan) 1 (1984): 1-19.

51. Jan Löfstedt, *Chinese Educational Policy* (Stockholm: Almqvist and Wiksell, 1980); Theodore Chen Hsi-En, *Chinese Education since 1949: Academic and Revolutionary Models* (New York: Pergamon, 1981).

52. S. Shirk, *Competitive Comrades: Career Incentives and Student Strategies in China* (Berkeley: University of California Press, 1982); R. Taylor, *China's Intellectual Dilemma* (Vancouver: University of British Columbia Press, 1982); J. Unger, *Education under Mao: Class and Competition in Canton Schools* (New York: Columbia University Press, 1983).

53. Irving Epstein, "The Politics of Curricular Change," in *Education and Social Change in the People's Republic of China*, ed. John Hawkins (New York: Praeger, 1982), provides a sensitive analysis of curricular change in post-1949 China. However, the characteristics of the Chinese knowledge tradition are not fully developed nor integrated within the interesting use of Bernstein's notions of framing and ritual.

54. The document that best expresses the educational principles of the time is the "Chronology of the Two-Road Struggle in the Educational Front in the Past Seventeen Years," *Chinese Education* 1, 1 (1968): 3-58.

55. Mao Zedong, "On Practice," in *Selected Works of Mao Tse-tung*, vol. 1 (Bei-

jing: Foreign Languages Press, 1975), pp. 295-309.

56. "A Great Beehive of Doctrinairism." See MacFarquar, *The Hundred Flowers Campaign*, pp. 86-87.

57. Evidence for this is found in the brief history of People's University in *Zhongguo gaodeng xuexiao jianjie*, pp. 5-7. Enrollment figures are given on page 2.

58. Don-chean Chu, *Chairman Mao: Education of the Proletariat* (New York: Philosophical Library, 1977). This book provides a detailed view of Mao's approach to knowledge, teaching, and the curriculum. Major educational documents of the Cultural Revolution period are found in Hu Shiming and E. Seifman, *Towards a New World Outlook* (New York: Ams Press, 1976).

59. Chen Hsi-En, *The Maoist Educational Revolution* (New York: Praeger, 1974), gives a clear portrayal of the overall educational reforms of the Cultural Revolution period.

60. Quoted by Zhang Liuquan in *Zhongguo shuyuan shihua* (Beijing: Jiaoyu Kexue Chubanshe, 1981), p. 135.

61. Sheng Langxi, *Zhongguo shuyuan zhidu* (The Chinese shuyuan system) (Shanghai: Zhonghua Shuju, 1934), pp. 47, 76. This writer draws a parallel between the teaching and learning style of the *shuyuan* and Dewey's five stages of reflective thinking and problem solving.

62. Evidently some Chinese saw this connection. Zhou Rongxin, the newly appointed Minister of Education in 1975, attacked Dewey's precepts of learning by doing because they denied talented young people access to higher intellectual knowledge in the context of the Cultural Revolution reforms. See J. Gardner, "Chou Jung-hsin and Chinese Education," *Current Scene* 15, 11-12 (1977): 1-14.

63. William Hinton, *Hundred Day War: The Cultural Revolution at Qinghua University* (New York: Monthly Review Press, 1972).

64. *Strive to Build a Socialist University of Science and Engineering* (Beijing: Foreign Languages Press, 1972). Also in Peter Seybolt, *Revolutionary Education in China: Documents and Commentary* (White Plains, N.Y.: International Arts and Sciences Press, 1973).

65. R. Hayhoe, "A Comparative Approach to the Cultural Dynamics of Sino-Western Educational Cooperation," *China Quarterly* 104 (December 1985); J. Israel, ed., "Draft History of Qinghua University," in *Chinese Education* 15, 3-4 (Fall-Winter 1982-1983).

66. "Liberal Arts Should Take the Whole Society as a Factory," in P. Seybolt, *Revolutionary Education in China*, pp. 313-33.

67. Ibid., pp. 322-23. The ideological consensus that Bernstein thought might be necessary to the integrated code of curriculum is evident here.

68. Ibid., pp. 319-20.

69. *Xuexi yu pipan* 1 (1973).

70. For an analysis of the journal's political role, see Ting Wang, "Propaganda and Political Struggle: A Preliminary Case Study of Hsüeh-hsi yu P'i-p'an," *Issues and Studies* 13, 6 (June 1977): 1-24; and John Gardner, "Study and Criticism: The Voice of Shanghai Radicalism," in *Shanghai: Revolution and Development in an Asian Metropolis*, ed. C. Howe (Cambridge: Cambridge University Press, 1981), pp. 326-47.

71. Hayhoe, "Yige daxue xin chuantong de kaichuang."

72. The contradiction between the progressive nature of American knowledge patterns and the reactionary nature of American political interference can be seen also in Japan, where radical teachers embraced American educational patterns while attacking American political policy. See the statement made by the Japanese Teachers Union in *Learning to be Japanese*, ed. E. Beauchamp (Connecticut: Linnet Books, 1978). See also M. Carnoy and H. Levin, *Schooling and Work in a Democratic State* (Stanford: Stanford University Press, 1985), for an attempt to take into account the progressive aspects of American school culture within an analysis still fundamentally Marxist.

75. "Resolutions on Certain Questions in the History of our Party since the Founding of the PRC," *Beijing Review* 27, 6 (July 1981).

76. This approach to the Cultural Revolution is interestingly developed in Jack Gray and Gordon White, *China's New Development Strategy* (London: Academic Press, 1982).

Chapter 2

1. *Achievement of Education in China: Statistics 1949-1983* (Beijing: People's Education Press, 1984).

2. Ibid., p. 53.

3. Ibid., p. 63.

4. *Zhongguo jiaoyu nianjian 1949-1981*, p. 236. The rich and detailed information given in this publication on all aspects of higher education development in China since 1949 has been the indispensable main source of data for this chapter.

5. Ibid., pp. 237-39; Theodore Chen Hsi-En, *Chinese Education Since 1949*, pp. 182-85.

6. Ibid., p. 266.

7. *Achievement of Education in China*, p. 62.

8. *Zhongguo jiaoyu nianjian*, pp. 265-66.

9. Ibid., p. 267. People's University is described as the *muji*, mother aircraft or launching aircraft, of political legal education, and this directive function was maintained by its graduate programs and the fact that it accepted professors from other institutes of law and politics for short-term refresher courses.

10. Ibid., pp. 422-24. Variations in the courses over time and among different types of institution are described in detail in this section on higher political education. The special role of People's University in training political educators for higher institutions is made explicit on p. 424.

11. Ibid., pp. 270-71; *Achievement of Education in China*, p. 51.

12. Throughout the two sections of the yearbook describing the evolution of political science and law, finance and economics as fields of study after 1949, People's University is the constant reference point.

13. Ibid., p. 261. A very clear and explicit definition of the teaching plan (*jiaoxue jihua*) is given here, appropriately in the section on normal higher institutions.

14. Ibid., p. 264.

15. Ibid., pp. 332-42, 348-52.

16. Ibid., pp. 54-55.

17. Ibid., p. 53.

18. Ibid., pp. 82-87.

19. *Zhongguo jiaoyu nianjian*, p. 268.

20. *Achievement of Education in China*, pp. 52-53. This record does not attempt to establish the number of specializations between 1965 and 1977.

21. One of the most balanced studies of the period is Chen Hsi-En, *The Maoist Educational Revolution*.

22. *Achievement of Education in China*, pp. 54-55.

23. *Beijing Review*, no. 27, July 6, 1981, pp. 6-39.

24. *Xinhua* (London) (hereafter *XH*), December 6, 1982.

25. Valuable ongoing discussion of these legal developments can be found in the journal *Chinese Law and Government*.

26. Andrew Nathan, *Chinese Democracy* (New York: Alfred A. Knopf, 1985).

27. David Goodman, *Beijing Street Voices: The Poetry and Politics of China's Democracy Movement* (London: Marian Boyas, 1981).

28. William L. Parish, ed., *Chinese Rural Development: The Great Transformation* (New York: M.E. Sharpe, 1985).

29. *XH* special issue, October 22, 1984.

30. Ibid., p. 7.

31. Samuel Ho and Ralph Huenemann, *China's Open Door Policy*, chap. 2.

32. See *XH*, August 12 and 13, 1985, for interesting discussions by Xue Muqiao and Fei Xiaotong on economic cooperation between the coastal regions and the hinterland. See also *Renmin ribao*, December 9, 1985, in FBIS, no. 241, December 16, 1985, pp. K8-K12.

33. Deng Xiaoping, "Speech at the National Education Work Conference April 22, 1978," *Beijing Review*, no. 18, May 5, 1978, p. 7.

34. *Zhongguo jiaoyu nianjian*, p. 237.

35. *Achievement of China in Education*, p. 53.

36. In 1980 a useful chart was issued by the Chinese Educational Assocation for International Exchanges which made clear the three major administrative groups of the then 675 higher institutions in the system. This has been widely reproduced in Western sources. See, for example, the section on China in R. Cowen and M. McLean, *International Handbook of Educational Systems*, vol. 3 (London: John Wiley and Sons, 1984), p. 120.

37. *Zhongguo jiaoyu nianjian*, p. 239.

38. "Decision of the CPC Central Committee on the Reform of the Education System" [May 27, 1985], FBIS, no. 104, May 30, 1985, p. K7.

39. "Revamping China's Research System--Excerpts from Premier Zhao Ziyang's March 6 Speech at the National Science Conference," *Beijing Review*, no. 14, April 8, 1985, pp. 15-21.

40. "Decision of the CPC Central Committee on the Reform of the Education System," p. K8.

41. Ibid.

42. Ibid., p. K9.

43. *Achievement of Education in China: Statistics 1980 to 1985* (Beijing: People's Education Press, 1985), pp. 20-21.

44. Ibid. pp. 22, 21, 29-30.

45. *Beijing Zhongguo xinwenshe* in Chinese, June 13, 1985, in FBIS, no. 115, June 1985; Beijing *Xinhua* in Chinese, June 18, 1985, in FBIS, no. 118, June 1985; *XH*, June 27, 1985.

46. In fact this point is not made explicit in the reform document, and apparently there were intense debates over it during the preparation of the document. But I was informed by officials of the first and second departments of higher education within the State Education Commission and officials of provincial higher education bureaus that final decision-making power over the establishment of *zhuanke* specializations had been given to the provinces.

47. *Zhongguo jiaoyu bao*, June 7, 1986; *Renmin ribao*, June 4, 1986, in JPRS-CPS-86-059, July 17, 1986, pp. 41-43.

48. *XH*, July 15, 1985; *Renmin ribao*, March 26, 1986, in FBIS, no. 61, March 31, 1986, pp. K23-K24.

49. *China Daily*, July 23, 1986, p. 1.

50. *Wenzhai bao*, no. 365, November 16, 1986, in FBIS, no. 227, November 25, 1986, p. K16.

51. For the new approach to economics, see the famous "Ma Ding" article and the subsequent debates: *Gongren ribao*, November 2, 1985, in FBIS, no. 99, May 22, 1986, pp. K3-K9; *China News Analysis*, no. 1317, September 1, 1986. For the new approach to political science, see the interview with Yan Jiaqi, head of the Political Research Institute, Chinese Academy of Social Sciences, in Beijing *Xinhuashe* in English, June 14, 1986, FBIS, no. 117, June 18, 1986, pp. K5-K7.

52. Wan Li, "Changing Educational Theory and Methods," *Beijing Review*, no. 24, June 17, 1985, pp. 19-21.

53. Su Shuanbi, "Some Questions Concerning the Promotion of the Contest of One Hundred Schools of Thought," *Guangming ribao*, April 30, 1986, FBIS, no. 96, May 19, 1986, pp. K4-K12.

54. Feng Lanrui, "Academic World Cannot Flourish Without Freedom and Democracy," *Shijie jingji daobao* (Shanghai), May 26, 1986, in FBIS, no. 112, June 11, 1986, p. K6.

55. Du Feijun, "Talking about the 'Double Hundred Policy' and Its Guarantee by the Legal System," *Renmin ribao* (Overseas Edition), June 15, 1982, in FBIS, no. 122, June 25, 1986.

56. Wang Huning, "Heading for Efficient and Democratic Political Structure," *Shijie jingji daobao*, July 21, 1986, in FBIS, no. 151, August 6, 1986, p. K5.

57. Bao Xinjian, "An Inquiry into the General Goals of the Reform of China's Political System," *Guangming ribao*, July 1, 1986, in FBIS, no. 141, July 23, 1986, pp. K4-K7.

58. "Wang Hanbin Explains NPC Electoral Revision," Beijing *Xinhua*, November 5, 1986, in FBIS, no. 225, November 21, 1986, pp. K6-K10.

59. Beijing *Xinhua* Hong Kong service, July 20, 1986, in FBIS, no. 139, July 21, 1986, pp. K5-K7; Ma Zhenggang, "On the Role Played by Political Restructuring in Promoting the Development of Spiritual Civilization," *Guangming ribao*, June 16, 1986, in FBIS, July 14, 1986, pp. K29-K33; Zhang Qiong, "A Brief Talk on Reform of the Political Structure," *Zhongguo fazhi bao*, August 11, 1986, in FBIS, no. 165, August 26, 1986, pp. K27-28.

60. Feng Xianggang and Cheng Jianping, "A Review of the Symposium on Higher Education Administration," in *Jiaoyu yanjiu*, no. 5 (May 1986), translation in JPRS-CPS-86-076, October 1986, pp. 19-24; *Guangming ribao*, September 17, 1986, in JPRS-CPS-86-083, November 16, 1986, pp. 50-51.

61. *Renmin ribao*, October 22, 26, 31, November 4, 14, 1986.

62. *Shijie jingji daobao*, November 24, 1986; *Beijing Review*, no. 50 (December 15, 1986), pp. 16-17.

63. An internal document of the World Bank (May 1986) based on a study of the twenty-six universities in the First University Development Project suggested clear guidelines for the financial rationalization of Chinese higher institutions. In spirit this document fits with the general Bank view that higher education students should pay more of the cost of their education, since the social rewards are so high. However, the particular hardship this causes in a socialist society is not taken into account.

64. Beijing *Xinhua* in English, July 11, 1986, JPRS-CPS-86-063, August 1986.

65. *China News Analysis*, no. 1328, February 1, 1987.

66. *Renmin ribao*, December 4, 1986.

67. *China Daily*, January 6, 1987.

68. *China Daily*, January 15 and 20, 1987.

69. *China Daily*, January 16, 1987.

70. Interview with Li Jiabin, deputy director, First Department of Higher Education, State Education Commission, September 7, 1985.

71. Interview with Zhu Chuanli, deputy director, Second Department of Higher Education, State Education Commission, June 25, 1987.

72. The conflict between this figure and that given earlier of 368 engineering specializations probably reflects the slow progress in implementing these changes.

73. For discussions of engineering curricular reform, see the articles by Zhang Guangdao in *Renmin ribao*, August 8, 1982, and *Hongqi* 23 (1984). See also *Zhongguo jiaoyu bao* 5, May 8, 1984.

74. Interview with officials responsible for the Engineering and Agricultural-Forestry sections of the Second Department of Higher Education, State Education Commission, September 7, 1985, and June 25, 1987.

75. Interview with Li Jiabin, deputy division chief, First Department of Higher Education, September 7, 1985; also with Zhu Chuanli, First Department of Higher Education, June 25, 1987. For discussions on curricular developments in these areas, see *Gaojiao zhanxian* 1 (1986), pp. 20-23 (economic management); *Liaoning shangzhuan xuebao* 2 (1984), pp. 75-78 (accounting); *Gaojiao zhanxian* 2 (1984), pp. 2-4 (law); *Renmin ribao*, August 21, 1983 (law); *Zhonguo jiaoyu bao*, May 19, 1983 (finance and economics).

76. *Gaojiao zhanxian* 12 (1982) pp. 16-18; 7 (1984), pp. 46-48; 2 (1986), pp. 7-9.

77. Interview with Mr. Li Jiabin, deputy division chief, First Department of Higher Education, State Education Commission, September 7, 1985.

78. Interview with Professor Liang Zhiwen, vice-director, Jilin Province Educational Commission, September 29, 1985.

79. Interview with Mr. Kang Yongxiang, vice-director, Liaoning Province Higher Education Bureau, September 23, 1985.

80. In the education reform document, explicit suggestions are given for the uni-

versalization of the credit system for curricular organization. All of the twenty-five or so higher institutions I visited in September-October 1985 either already had or were at that time starting some form of credit system. For a discussion of the credit system, see *Gaojiao zhanxian* 9 (1984), pp. 6-8.

81. In all of the twenty-five institutions I visited, a reduction in curricular hours from over 3,000 in a four-year period to a range between 2,400 and 2,600 was reported, though it is hard to discover how well these reforms are being implemented. Resistance from faculty defending the importance of their courses is endemic!

82. A new direction for political education in higher institutions was put foward at a national meeting in November 1984. The document that emerged was published in *Zhongguo jiaoyu bao*, November 12, 1984. A thorough discussion of its implications is found in *Jiaoxue yu yanjiu* (People's University) 6 (1984), pp. 1-26; 1 (1985), pp. 21-35. These articles in themselves suggest that People's may be taking up once again its watchdog role over the political and ideological health of the higher education system.

83. My comments here are drawn from an illuminating discussion of the subject at Heilongjiang University, October 4, 1985. For press discussions relating to course reform, see *Zhongguo jiaoyu bao* 7, September 24, 1985; *Jiaoyu yanjiu* 12 (1985), pp. 1-7; *Jiaoxue yu yanjiu* 2 (1983), pp. 1-5; 2 (1984), pp. 25-28; *Gaojiao zhanxian* 3 (1986), pp. 21-24.

84. See *Shanxi daxue xuebao: shekeban*, no. 1 (1985), pp. 144-46; *Heilongjiang gaojiao yanjiu*, 1 (1985), pp. 11-17; *Zhongguo jiaoyu bao*, March 5, 1985; *Guangming ribao*, March 25, 1985.

85. See *Wuhan shifan xueyuan xuebao* 4 (1983), pp. 7-14, for a representative article on the importance of a psychological understanding of youth for effective political education.

86. This information was gathered in interviews at Beijing University of Iron and Steel Technology, Qinghua University, and Dongbei Teachers University. The document of November 1984 and its implications for training a new contingent of political instructors are discussed in *Gaojiao zhanxian* 3 (1985), p. 11.

87. *Zhongguo jiaoyu bao*, May 16, 1987.

88. *Beijing Review*, no. 22, May 30, 1983, p. xi.

89. *XH*, July 9, 1985. This official figure probably underestimates considerably the number who have gone under private auspices.

90. Interview with Mr. Zhang Baoqing, Foreign Affairs Office, State Education Commission, September 14, 1985.

91. Interview with Mr. Zhang Yanling, deputy director, Bureau of Education, and Mr. Zhang Xingren, Foreign Affairs Office, CAS, September 9, 1985.

92. Interview with Mr. Wang Shirong, division chief, Foreign Affairs Bureau, CASS, September 18, 1985.

93. Interviews with Mr. Zhao Andong and Mr. Gan Cheng, Shanghai Higher Education Research Society, October 17, 1985.

94. Interview with Ms. Wang Jinluan, Foreign Affairs Office, Jiangsu Provincial Bureau of Higher Education, October 11, 1985.

95. Interview with officials in the provincial bureaus of higher education, September 23 and 29, 1985. Figures provided by Huang Shiqi give evidence of greater provincial activity than my interviews suggested. See "Contemporary Educational Relations

with the Industrialized World: A Chinese View," in *China's Education and the Industrialized World*, ed. Hayhoe and Bastid. For a press account of Fujian province's activity, see *Zhongguo jiaoyu bao*, May 21, 1985.

96. Interview with Mr. Zhang Baoqing, September 14, 1985.

97. These changes are reflected in the official reports of conferences on study abroad held in 1980, 1984, and 1986. See *Xinhua* (Beijing), January 4, 1980, in FBIS, January 9, 1980; *Xinhua* (Beijing), November 29, 1984, in FBIS, November 30, 1984; *Zhongguo jiaoyu bao*, May 17, 1986.

98. See *Zhongguo jiaoyu bao*, July 20 and December 28, 1985, January 4, 1986; *Wenhui bao*, July 13, 1985; *XH*, July 20 and November 25, 1985. See also *Shenzhou xueren*, no. 6 (March 1988), p. 21, for an account of the work of the postdoctoral centers.

99. *Beijing Review*, no. 22 (May 30, 1983), p. xi.

100. Leo A. Orleans, "Chinese Students and Technology Transfer," *Journal of Northeast Asian Studies* 4, 4 (Winter 1985), pp. 3-25.

101. Huang Shiqi, "Contemporary Educational Relations with the Industrialized World: A Chinese View," in *China's Education and the World*, ed. Hayhoe and Bastid.

102. *Jiefang ribao*, June 12, 1987, translated in *Chinese Education* 21, 1 (Spring 1988).

103. *New York Times*, March 24, 1988, p. 7.

104. *Renmin ribao* (Overseas Edition), April 6, 1988.

105. For a detailed study of Chinese students in the American context, see Leo A. Orleans, *Chinese Students in America: Policy, Issues and Numbers* (Washington, D.C.: National Academy Press, forthcoming).

106. Major comparative education journals include *Waiguo jiaoyu* (put out by the Central Institute for Educational Research), *Waiguo jiaoyu dongtai* (put out by Beijing Teachers University), and *Waiguo jiaoyu ziliao* (put out by East China Teachers University). Also, articles on education in foreign countries appear regularly in *Zhongguo jiaoyu bao* and in various educational journals.

107. Interview with Zhang Baoqing, September 14, 1985.

108. *China Daily*, January 16, 1986, p. 4.

Chapter 3

1. For an interesting retrospect on this reform, see Wang Gongan, "Jianguo yilai woguo gaodeng jiaoyu de gaige" (Reforms in our country's higher education since Liberation), *Jiaoyu kexue yanjiu* (Wuhan) 1 (1984), pp. 1-19, in *Daxue jiaoyu* G4, no. 9 (1984), pp. 15-33.

2. The first volume of a new history of Fudan giving intensive coverage of the period from 1905 to 1949 has recently come out: *Fudan Daxue zhi* (Shanghai: Fudan Daxue Chubanshe, 1985). See also Hayhoe, "Towards the Forging of a Chinese University Ethos."

3. R. Hayhoe, "Yige daxue xin chuantong de kaichuang: Fudan de zhaonian," *Fudan xuebao* 2 (March 1982), p. 102.

4. *Chen Wangdao wenji* (Selected essays of Chen Wangdao), vol. 1 (Shanghai: Renmin Chubanshe, 1979), pp. 273-79.

5. This comes from remarks made by Xie Xide at Fudan's eightieth anniversary, May 1985. Like many other universities, Fudan's enthusiasm for educational reform

has led to the publication of a new internal journal, *Fudan Education*, which has been issued regularly since the fall of 1984. See *Fudan jiaoyu* 2, pp. 1-2, for Xie's speech. A more detailed account of how she conceives the university's development and future role is found in the first issue, pp. 3-9.

6. Interview with Qiang Lianqing, head of the Academic Affairs Department, Fudan University, October 15, 1985. See also articles by Qiang in *Gaojiao zhanxian* 4 (1983), pp. 10-12; 12 (1985), pp. 30-32.

7. Fudan's reforms have often been featured both in the Shanghai press and in the national press. See, for example, *Wenhui bao*, January 23, August 25, September 20, 1984, and *Zhongguo jiaoyu bao*, October 6, 1984, January 8, June 18, 1985.

8. *Wenhui bao*, May 4, 1984.

9. Ling Hongxun, "National Jiaotong University," in *Zhonghua minguo daxue zhi* (A record of universities in the Chinese Republic), ed. Zhang Qiyun (Taibei: Zhonghua Wenhua Chuban Shiye Weiyuanhui, 1954), pp. 108-13.

10. Mary Rankin, *Early Chinese Revolutionaries: Radical Intellectuals in Shanghai and Chekiang 1902-1911* (Cambridge: Harvard University Press, 1977), pp. 61-64.

11. *North China Herald and Supreme Court and Consular Gazette* 24, 1961 (March 10, 1905), p. 490.

12. *Zhongguo gaodeng xuexiao jianjie* (A short introduction to Chinese higher institutions) (Beijing: Jiaoyu Kexue Chubanshe, 1982), p. 231.

13. *Jiaotong daxue xiaoshi 1896-1949* (A history of Jiaotong University 1896-1949) (Shanghai: Jiaoyu Chubanshe, 1986).

14. Both the national press and the Shanghai press have abounded in articles on the Jiaoda reforms in recent years. Some of the most significant articles, together with a brief institutional history and copies of the major reform documents, have been conveniently assembled in *Shanghai Jiaoda de jiaoyu gaige* (The educational reform at Shanghai Jiaotong University) (Beijing: Renminchubanshe, 1985). For major newspaper articles, see *Renmin ribao* 4 (March 7, 21, 1983, February 29, March 7, 1984; *Guangming ribao*, January 27, March 7, June 4, 1983.

15. Interview with Dong Yinchang and Yang Dezhi, Academic Affairs Office, Jiaotong University, October 19, 1985.

16. *Shanghai Jiaoda de jiaoyu gaige*, pp. 51-58.

17. This is elucidated in an internal document, "Suggestions for the Reform of the Teaching Plan for Undergraduate Specializations," circulated by the Academic Affairs Office at Jiaoda, June 1985. A copy was given to the author in October 1985.

18. *Shanghai Jiaoda de jiaoyu gaige*, p. 57. This point was explained and given considerable emphasis in the interview with Dong Yinchang.

19. Wang Boqing, ed., *Shanghai Jiao Tong University General Catalogue*, pp. 62-75, 119-22.

20. Ibid., p. 15.

21. *Shanghai Jiaoda de jiaoyu gaige*, pp. 66-68.

22. Interview with Fan Yuanxing, vice-president, BUIST, September 17, 1985.

23. *Zhongguo gaodeng xuexiao jianjie*, pp. 18-20.

24. Interview with Yang Jingyan, head of the Academic Affairs Department, BUIST, September 17, 1985.

25. *Jiaoxue yanjiu*, no. 29, March 6, 1985.

26. Its journal is entitled *Gaodeng jiaoyu yanjiu* (Higher education research), and it

assists also in the planning and editing of *Gaodeng jiaoyu weilai yu fazhan* (The future and development of higher education) and *Gaodeng jiaoyuxue* (Journal of higher education), publications of the national society. Interview with Zhang Xing, head of the Higher Education Research Room, BUIST, September 17, 1985.

27. "Dongbei Gongxueyuan yange yu xianzhuang" (The development and present situation of Northeast University of Technology), in *Liaoning gaodeng xuexiao yange* (The evolution of Liaoning higher education), ed. Sun Huaqun (Shenyang: Liaoning Renmin Chubanshe, December 1983), pp. 233-34.

28. These observations came out of an illuminating day's seminar at NEUT with Professor Tao and about ten other members of the Liaoning Higher Education Research Society, September 24, 1985. For a full treatment of the problem of structural reform in higher education, see Tao Zengpian, *Gaodeng jiaoyu tizhi gaige jianlun* (An introductory discussion of structural reform in higher education) (Shenyang: Liaoning Renmin Chubanshe, 1985).

29. *XH* (London), June 21, 23, 1984.

30. *XH* (London), March 9, 1983.

31. *Zhongguo gaodeng xuexiao jianjie*, pp. 292-93.

32. Interview with Wu Zhaojing, head of the Academic Affairs Office, NAU, October 11, 1985.

33. Interview with Yuan Baomin, head of the department of agricultural economics and management, NAU, October 11, 1985.

34. *Zhongguo gaodeng xuexiao jianjie*, pp. 28-30.

35. "The History and Present Situation of Beijing Agricultural University," cyclostyled introduction provided by the university, September 1985.

36. Interview with Dai Shuhua, director of the President's Office, BAU, September 13, 1985.

37. Interview with Yun Zemin, academic responsible for the development of new graduate programs, School of Graduate Studies, BAU, September 13, 1985. See also Yun Zemin, "The Reform of Graduate Curricula in China," paper presented to the Annual Meeting of the Comparative and International Education Society, Toronto, March 15, 1986.

38. Interview with Chen Daxi, vice-president; Shang Hexiang, head of the Academic Affairs Office; Chen Xi, secretary of the foreign affairs department; and Chen Chuangu, chairman of the English department, Heilongjiang University, October 4, 1985.

39. *Zhongguo gaodeng xuexiao jianjie*, pp. 131-32; also "Liaoning daxue de yange yu xianzhuang" (Liaoning University's evolution and present conditions), in *Liaoning gaodeng xuexiao yange*, ed. Sun Huaqun, pp. 293-311.

40. Interview with Pei Yingchao, vice-director of the Academic Affairs Office, and Li Wu, deputy director of the Foreign Affairs Office, Liaoning University, September 23, 1985.

41. *Liaoning University* [Introductory Handbook], April 1985, pp. 11-12.

42. *Northeast University of Technology* [Introductory Handbook), p. 9.

43. *Zhongguo jiaoyu bao*, June 20, 1987.

44. Dai Shujun, "New-Style Vocational Universities," *Canadian and International Education* 16, 2 (June 1987). See also *Jianghan daxue xuebao* 1 (1983), pp. 15-20, for

an article depicting the unique characteristicsof the vocational university.

45. Interview with Yang Yonghong, vice-president, Shenyang Vocational University, September 25, 1985. For press reports of Shenyang University, see *Guangming ribao*, June 1, October 22, 1983.

46. For press accounts of Jinling, see *Renmin ribao*, June 26, 1981; *Guangming ribao*, November 12, 1982; *Jianghan daxue* xuebao 1 (1983), pp. 21-26.

47. Interview with Mr. Fan Yongxing, president, Jinling Vocational College, June 27, 1987.

48. Interview with Hu Renzhu, head of the Academic Affairs Office, and Dai Shujun, vice-head of the Higher Education Research Section, Jinling Vocational College, Nanjing, October 10, 1985.

49. See *Gaojiao zhanxian* 3 (1986), p. 39, for an article on the fever to go abroad that is touching even upper secondary students and affecting their study orientation even before they enter university.

50. Beijing, Xinhua News Service in Chinese, January 7, 1986, in FBIS, no. 6, January 9, 1986, p. K6.

Chapter 4

1. Michael Yahuda, *China's Foreign Policy After Mao* (London: Macmillan, 1983), chap. 5.

2. R. J. Holsti, *The Dividing Discipline* (Boston: Allen and Unwin, 1985), sees the recent rise of theories of global society and neo-Marxist approaches as the first serious challenges to the classical tradition in international relations. The behavioral revolution of American functionalism was well within the classical tradition, in his view.

3. Samuel Kim, *China, the U.N. and World Order* (Princeton: Princeton University Press, 1979), pp. 276ff.

4. Yahuda, *China's Foreign Policy*, pp. 51ff.

5. H. Harding, "China's Changing Role in the Contemporary World," in *China's Foreign Relations in the 1980s*, ed. H. Harding (New Haven: Yale University Press, 1984).

6. Samuel Kim, "Mao Zedong and China's Changing World View," chap. 2 in *China in the Global Community*, ed. J. Hsiung and S. Kim (New York: Praeger, 1980).

7. For a recent Chinese affirmation of the three worlds theory, see Chen Zhongjing, "Contemporary International Strategies," *Xiandai guoji guanxi*, no. 2 (April 20, 1986): 1-8, in JPRS-CPS-86-066, April 28, 1986, pp. 16-27.

8. Kim, *China, the U.N. and World Order*, p. 281.

9. Mao Zedong, "On Practice," in *Selected Works of Mao Tse-tung* (Beijing: Foreign Languages Press, 1975), pp. 295-309.

10. Ruth Gamberg, *Red and Expert* (New York: Schocken Books, 1976).

11. Roland Depierre, "Maoism in French Educational Thought and Action," in *China's Education and the Industrialized World*, ed. Hayhoe and Bastid.

12. Kim, *China, the U.N. and World Order*, pp. 276-79.

13. This comes across clearly in Deng Xiaoping's classic statement at the Twelfth Congress of the Chinese Communist Party in September 1982: "We will unswervingly follow a policy of opening to the outside world and actively increase exchanges with foreign countries on the basis of equality and mutual benefit. At the same time we will

keep a clear head, firmly resist corrosion by decadent ideas from abroad, and never permit the bourgeois way of life to spread in our country." *XH*, September 1, 1982.

14. The five principles basic to China's foreign policy are mutual respect for sovereignty and territorial integrity, mutual nonaggression, noninterference in each others' internal affairs, equality and mutual benefit, and peaceful coexistence. For a typical exposition see reports of Hu Yaobang's speech on Australia in the spring of 1985, *XH*, April 16, 1985, pp. 15-17.

15. Klaus Knorr and James Rosenau, *Contending Approaches to International Politics* (Princeton: Princeton University Press, 1969).

16. Robert Nisbet, *Social Change and History: Key Concepts in the Social Sciences* (Oxford: Oxford University Press, 1972).

17. M. Kaplan, "The Systems Approach to International Relations," in *New Approaches to International Relations*, ed. M. Kaplan (New York: St. Martin's Press, 1968).

18. David Singer, "In Defence of Systems Theory and a Science of International Politics," in *Contending Approaches to International Relations*, ed. Knorr and Rosenau, p. 66.

19. W. W. Rostow, *Stages of Economic Growth* (Cambridge: Cambridge University Press, 1960).

20. Irene Gendzier, *Managing Political Change: Social Scientists and the Third World* (Boulder: Westview Press, 1985).

21. See M. Oksenberg, "China Joins the World: Prospects and Implications," *Issues of Science and Technology* 1, 3 (1985) [National Academy of Sciences], for an example of the functionalist analytic approach that seems to make this kind of assumption.

22. World Order Models scholarship clearly owes a debt to dependency theory, yet I feel that the important distinctions between the two views of world order have been blurred in such applications to comparative education as Carnoy, *Education as Cultural Imperialism*, and P. Altbach, R. Arnove, and G. Kelly, *Comparative Education* (London: Macmillan, 1980). Martin McLean's article on "Educational Dependency" in *Compare* 13, 1, gives a thorough logical critique of the theoretical weakness of attempts made to develop a theory of educational dependency on the basis of economic dependency theory.

23. Johann Galtung, *The True Worlds: A Transnational Perspective* (New York: Freedom Press, 1980).

24. Samuel Kim, *The Quest for a Just World Order* (Boulder: Westview Press, 1984), chap. 5.

25. J. Galtung, "A Structural Theory of Imperialism," *Journal of Peace Research*, vol. 8 (1971).

26. Galtung, *The True Worlds*, chap. 4.

27. Hans Weiler, "Knowledge and Legitimation: The National and International Politics of Educational Research," paper presented at the Fifth Congress of Comparative Education, Paris, July 1984, p. 10. Quoted with permission from the author.

28. J. Galtung, "Is Peaceful Research Possible? On the Methodology of Peace Research," in *Peace: Research, Education, Action*, by J. Galtung (Copenhagen: Christian Ejlers, 1975), pp. 272-73.

29. Ali Mazrui, "The African University as a Multi-National Corporation," in *Political Values and the Educated Class in Africa*, by Ali Mazrui (London: Heinneman, 1978), pp. 282-319.

30. A. G. Frank, *Capitalism and Underdevelopment in Latin America* (New York: Monthly Review Press, 1979).

31. Galtung, *The True Worlds*, chap. 4.

32. Kim, *China, the U.N. and World Order*.

33. Kim, *The Quest for a Just World Order*.

34. Weiler, "Knowledge and Legitimation," p. 19.

35. Galtung, "Is Peaceful Research Possible?"

36. Mazrui, "The African University," pp. 306-18.

37. I am particularly indebted to Professor Brian Holmes for some understanding of how ideal types may be used in educational research. See Brian Holmes, *Comparative Education: Some Considerations of Method* (London: George Allen and Unwin, 1983).

38. I have found the work of Samuel Kim most illuminating in reflecting on this possibility. Some hopeful signs are identified in two of his recent articles: "Chinese Foreign Policy Behavior," in *China and the World*, ed. S. Kim (Boulder: Westview Press, 1984), and "Post-Mao Ch2ina's Development Model in Global Perspective," in *China's Changed Road to Development*, ed. N. Maxwell and B. McFarlane (Oxford: Pergamon Press, 1984).

39. Max Weber, *The Methodology of the Social Sciences* (New York: Free Press, 1949), pp. 94-95.

Chapter 5

1. An interesting debate on the relative applicability of European and American educational patterns to China's needs is found in C. H. Becker et al., *The Reorganization of Education in China* (Paris: Institute of Intellectual Cooperation, 1932), pp. 28ff., and S. Duggan, *A Critique of the League of Nations Mission of Educational Experts to China* (New York: Institute of International Education, 1933), pp. 16ff.

2. K. Shimohara, *Adaptation and Education in Japan* (New York: Praeger, 1979).

3. Shimbori Michiya, "The Sociology of a Student Movement: A Japanese Case Study," in *Learning to be Japanese*, ed. E. Beauchamp (Hamden, Conn.: Linnet Books, 1978), p. 298.

4. T. Kobayashi, *Society, Schools and Progress in Japan* (Oxford: Pergamon, 1976), p. 143.

5. Michiya, "The Sociology of a Student Movement," p. 290.

6. W. Cummings, "The Conservatives Reform Higher Education," in *Learning to be Japanese*, ed. Beauchamp, pp. 316-27.

7. G. Bereday, *Universities for All* (San Fransisco: Jossey-Bass, 1973), provides an interesting discussion of the achievement of mass higher education in Japan in comparison to the United States and the Soviet Union.

8. A lengthy and detailed article on the evolution of Sino-Japanese political relations appeared in *Renmin ribao*, October 27, 1985.

9. *XH*, September 12, 1984

10. *Renmin ribao*, overseas edition, January 17, 1986, in FBIS no. 15, January 23, 1986, pp. D2-D3; Deutches Institut für Wirtschaftforschung, *Wochenbericht* 29/86 (July 17, 1986): 374.

11. *XH*, November 24, 1984.

12. John Israel, *Student Nationalism in China* (Stanford: Stanford University Press, 1966), chap. 5.

13. These student protests were carefully watched from Hong Kong and analyzed in detail in the Hong Kong press. For translations of these comments and more subdued Chinese press accounts, see Hong Kong AFP in English, September 19, 1985, in FBIS, no. 182, September 19, 1985, p. D1; Beijing *Xinhua* in English, September 19, 1985, in FBIS, no. 183, September 20, 1985, p. D1; Hong Kong AFP in English, October 3, 1985, in FBIS, no. 193, October 4, 1985, pp. D1-D2; Tokyo Kyodo in English, March 23, 1985, in FBIS, no. 227, November 25, 1985, p. D1; Taipei International Service in English, December 5, 1985, in FBIS, no. 235, December 6, 1985, p. V11; Beijing *Zhongguo xinwenshe* in Chinese, December 9, 1985, in FBIS, no. 240, December 13, 1985, p. K1; Hong Kong *Chengming* in Chinese, no. 99, January 1, 1986, in FBIS, no. 3, January 6, 1986, pp. W3-W8.

14. For a discussion of the link between these two movements, see Suzanne Pepper, "Deng Xiaoping's Political and Economic Reforms and the Chinese Student Protests," *Universities Field Staff International Reports*, no. 30, Asia, available from 620 Union Drive, Indianapolis, Indiana 46202.

15. *XH*, March 19, 1983.

16. Hiroshi Abe, "Comparative International Experience: PRC Exchanges with Other Nations, Japan," paper presented at the Conference on Sino-American Cultural and Educational Exchange, East-West Center, Hawaii, February 18-22, 1985.

17. Interview with Makoto Nakamura, Embassy of Japan in Beijing, September 12, 1985.

18. Abe, "Comparative International Experience."

19. Ibid., p. 9. This is probably not as strong a bias for the growing number of students and scholars under private sponsorship, which jumped from 121 in 1981 to 294 in 1982 and 1,098 in 1983. See ibid., p. 11.

20. Interview with Makoto Nakamura, Japanese Embassy in Beijing, September 12, 1985.

21. "Dui Zhonghua Renmin Gongheguo Jishu Xiezu Shiji" (Achievements in technical cooperation with the PRC), JICA, February 1985. This brochure and other information about the program was provided in an interview with Mr. T. Yashima, resident representative of JICA, Beijing, September 16, 1985. A detailed rationale for all the work experience programs is given in JICA's brochure *Technical Training in Japan*.

22. Their numbers grew from 94 in 1980 to 191 in 1981, then 186 in 1982. See Abe, "Comparative International Experience," pp. 18-19.

23. *XH*, October 24, 1985.

24. *XH*, February 16, 1984

25. Interview with T. Yashima, September 16, 1985.

26. Interview with M. Nakamura, September 12, 1985.

27. See Hiroshe Abe, "Borrowing from Japan: China's First Modern Education System," in *China's Education and the Industrialized World*, ed. Hayhoe and Bastid.

28. F. Artz, *The Development of Technical Education in France* (Cambridge, Mass., and London: Society for the History of Technology and M.I.T. Press, 1966). Artz points out that in the early nineteenth century France was the only country in the world where engineering was clearly established as a learned profession.

29. Emile Durkheim, *The Evolution of Educational Thought* (London: Routledge and Kegan Paul, 1977).

30. Teng Ssu-yu, "Chinese Influence on the Western Examination System," *Harvard Journal of Asiatic Studies* 7, 4 (1942-43); I. Llasera, "Confucian Education Through European Eyes," in *China's Education and the Industrialized World*, ed. Hayhoe and Bastid.

31. Allen Linden, "Politics and Education in Nationalist China: The Case of the University Council," *Journal of Asian Studies* 28, 4 (August 1968): 763-76.

32. R. Hayhoe, "Catholics and Socialists: The Paradox of Sino-French Educational Interaction," in *China's Education and the Industrialized World*, ed. Hayhoe and Bastid.

33. Dick Wilson, "China and the European Community," *China Quarterly* 56 (October-December 1973): 647-66.

34. Jean-Luc Domenach, "Sino-French Relations: A French View," in *China's Foreign Relations: New Perspectives* (New York: Praeger, 1982).

35. See, for example, speeches by Giscard D'Estaing and Francois Mitterand while in China. *Documents d'Actualité*, no. 52 (December 29, 1980); no. 15 (August 1, 1983).

36. Jerome Ch'en, *China and the West* (London: Macmillan, 1979), pp. 166-68.

37. Depierre, "Maoism in French Educational Thought and Practice."

38. *XH*, April 13, 1985.

39. *XH*, April 17, 1985.

40. *XH*, April 12, 1985.

41. Beijing *Guoji shangbao* in Chinese, December 9, 1985, in FBIS, no. 249, December 27, 1985, p. G1.

42. Programme d'Echanges Culturels entre le Gouvernement de la Republique Française et le Gouvernement de la Republique Populaire de Chine pour les Années 1984-1985.

43. Interview with Mr. Shu Wenping, educational counsellor, Embassy of China in France, July 4, 1984.

44. Beijing *Xinhua* in English, November 10, 1987, in FBIS, no. 218, November 12, 1987, p. 8.

45. R. Hayhoe, "A Comparative Analysis of Chinese-Western Academic Exchange," *Comparative Education* 20, 1 (March 1984): 44.

46. Interview with M. Portiche, cultural counsellor, Embassy of France in China, September 10, 1985.

47. *XH*, April 5, 1984

48. *XH*, May 30, 1984.

49. *XH*, November 7, 1984.

50. *XH*, February 12, 1985.

51. *XH*, June 22, 1985.

52. Interview with Francois Gipouloux, commercial counsellor, Embassy of France in Beijing, September 10, 1985.

53. Beijing *Xinhua* in English, March 3, 1985, in FBIS, no. 44, March 6, 1985, p. G3; Beijing *Xinhua* in Chinese, March 3, 1985, in FBIS, no. 45, March 7, 1985, p. G1.

54. Habiba Cohen, *Elusive Reform: The French Universities 1968-1978* (Boulder: Westview Press, 1978).

55. R. Hayhoe, "Chinese, European and American Scholarly Values in Interaction," *L.A.C.E. Occasional Paper*, no. 13, London Association of Comparative Educationists, July 1984.

56. Kreissler, "Technical Education as the Key to Cultural Cooperation."

57. F. Kreissler, "L'Action culturelle allemande en Chine de la fin du XIXè siècle à la second guerre mondiale" (Doctoral thesis, Ecole des Hautes Etudes en Sciences Sociales, Paris, 1983).

58. W. Duiker, *Ts'ai Yüan-p'ei: Educator of Modern China* (University Park: Penn State University Press, 1977).

59. H. Peisert and G. Framheim, *Systems of Higher Education: Federal Republic of Germany* (International Council of Educational Development, 1978).

60. *Wochenbericht* 29/86 (July 17, 1986): 374.

61. Some evidence of German concern about this can be seen in a call by the German director of the Chinese section of the Federal German Oriental Economic Committee to German enterprises to import more semifinished products from China in order to keep trade at a balanced level between the two countries. See Beijing *Xinhua* in English, October 23, 1985, in FBIS, no. 205, October 23, 1985, p. G1.

62. Beijing *Xinhua* in English, June 10, 1985, in FBIS, no. lll, June 10, 1985, p. G7; *XH*, October 7, 1983, February 4, 1985.

63. "Report on Development Cooperation Activities in the P.R.C.," Beijing: UNDP Office, September 1985.

64. *Kulturaustausch Programm 1984/5 zwischen dem Bundesrepublik Deutschland und der Volksrepublik China*. I am indebted to Mr. Neumann of the DAAD for providing a copy of this document and answering questions concerning it during an interview in Bonn, April 30, 1984.

65. In a recent German study, a total of sixty-four German universities and Technische Hochschulen and four Fachhochschulen were identified as having partnerships with Chinese higher institutions that gain some financial support from either Land or federal agencies. See Erhard Louven and Monika Schädler, *Wissenschaftliche Zusammenarbeit zwischen der Volksrepublik China und der Bundesrepublik Deutschland* (Hamburg: Institut für Asienkunde, 1986), pp. 108-49.

66. *XH*, March 28, 1985.

67. These figures were given in an interview with Dr. Albrecht von der Heyden, cultural counsellor, Embassy of the FRG, Beijing, September 10, 1985.

68. Hayhoe, "A Comparative Analysis of Chinese-Western Academic Exchange," p. 46.

69. *XH*, December 5, 1985.

70. Hamburg DPA in German, October 11, 1987, in FBIS, no. 197, October 13, 1987, p. 10.

71. Beijing *Xinhua* in English, October 5, 1987, in FBIS, no. 193, October 6, 1987.

72. *Report on Development Cooperation in the PRC*, p. 91.

73. *China Daily*, September 13, 1985.

74. *XH*, February 3, June 5, and December 31, 1985.

75. Interview with Mrs. Theordore, German Consulate in Shanghai, October 23, 1985.

76. *China Daily*, September 7, 1985.

77. Report on Development Cooperation in the PRC, p. 90.

78. *XH*, April 7, 1984.

79. *XH*, July 14, 1984.

80. Louven and Schädler, *Wissenschaftliche Zusammenarbeit zwischen der Volksrepublik China und der Bundesrepublik Deutschland*, pp. 92-108.

81. Interview with Dr. Von der Heyden, September 10, 1985.

82. Kreissler, "Technical Education as the Key to Cultural Cooperation."

83. *XH*, October 11, 1984.

84. F. Ringer, *The Decline of the German Mandarinate* (Cambridge: Harvard University Press, 1969).

85. Papers of the International Assocation of Universities, *Problems of Integrated Higher Education: The Case of the Gesamthochschule* (Paris: rue Miollis, 1972); P. Stokes, "The German University: A View of Its Reform," *L.A.C.E. Occasional Paper*, no. 9, 1983.

86. Delia Davin, "Imperialism and the Diffusion of Liberal Thought: British Influences on Chinese Education," in *China's Education and the industrialized World*, ed. Hayhoe and Bastid; R. Hayhoe, "Chinese Universities and Western Academic Models," *Higher Education* (Amsterdam) (Spring 1989).

87. R. H. Wilkinson, "The Gentleman Ideal and the Maintenance of a Political Elite," in *Sociology, History and Education: A Reader*, ed. P. Musgrave (London: Methuen, 1970). This essay provides a provocative comparison between the Confucian and the Victorian "gentleman" ideal.

88. Teng Ssu-yu, "Chinese Influence on the Western Examination System," *Harvard Journal of Asiatic Studies* 7, 4 (1942) details the British debt to China for the idea of the civil service examinations.

89. *XH*, December 19, 1985.

90. *XH*, July 22, 1984.

91. Beijing *Xinhua* in English, December 17, 1985, in FBIS, no. 243, December 18, 1985, p. G1.

92. British Council, *Programme of Cultural, Educational and Scientific Exchanges between Britain and China, 1984-1986* (London, July 1984).

93. British Council, *Study and Research in the United Kingdom: Opportunities for Chinese Scholars at Postgraduate Level and Above* (London, April 1984).

94. Interview with Mrs. Beryl Barker, The British Council, August 15, 1983; April 1984.

95. Interview with Mr. Adrian Johnston, cultural attaché, British Embassy in Beijing, September 16, 1985.

96. Hayhoe, "Chinese-Western Academic Exchange," p. 45.

97. Royal Society, *A Summary of Royal Society Relations with China with Complementary Information on Other Relevant Agreements and Arrangements* (London, 1980).

98. *XH*, September 17, 1984.

99. Interview with Mr. Adrian Johnston, September 16, 1985.

100. Beijing *Xinhua* in English, March 2, 1985, in FBIS, no. 45, March 7, 1985, p. G1.

101. This project will be discussed in greater detail in chapter 7.

102. Beijing *Xinhua Domestic Service* in Chinese, September 15, 1984, in FBIS, no. 185, September 21, 1984, p. G2. A China-EEC trade agreement made originally in 1980 was renegotiated in 1984.

103. Beijing *Shijie zhishi*, no. 12, June 16, 1984, in FBIS, no. 142, July 23, 1984, pp. G1-G2.

104. Beijing *Xinhua* in English, March 3, 1985, in FBIS, no. 44, March 6, 1985, p. G3. See chapter 6 for further details about this institution.

105. *XH*, October 5, 1985.

106. *XH*, December 22, 1985.

107. W. Metzger, "The Age of the College," in *The Development of Academic Freedom in the United States*, by R. Hofstadter and W. Metzger (New York: Columbia University Press, 1955).

108. For the Morrill Act of 1862, see R. Hofstadter and W. Smith, eds., *American Higher Education: A Documentary History*, vol. 2 (Chicago: University of Chicago Press, 1961), p. 568.

109. J. Ben-David, *American Higher Education: Directions Old and New* (New York: McGraw Hill, 1972).

110. Jessie Lutz, *China and the Christian Colleges* (Ithaca: Cornell University Press, 1971).

111. This is the second point in ten clearly articulated for Sino-American educational exchange worked out by the Office of Science and Technology and the CSCPRC. See R. Clough, *A Review of the U.S. China Exchange Program* (Office of Research, International Communications Agency, 1981), p. 7.

112. Beijing *Zhongguo xinwenshe* in Chinese, July 24, 1985, in FBIS, no. 143, July 25, 1985, p. B9.

113. *China Exchange News* 16, 1 (March 1988): 26.

114. Interview with Dr. Karl Olsson, cultural affairs officer, U.S. Embassy in Beijing, September 10, 1985.

115. For a detailed articulation of the goals of the Fulbright program and a survey of American studies in China, see CSCPRC, *American Studies in China: Report of a Delegation Visit, October 1984* (Washington, D.C.: National Academy Press, 1985).

116. Its work can be followed in detail through its quarterly journal, *China Exchange News*.

117. "Report to the Governing Board of the National Research Council," December 7, 1985.

118. Interview with Peter Geitner of the Ford Foundation, Honolulu, February 18, 1985.

119. *New York Times*, April 29, 1987.

120. *New Horizons* 54, 1 (October 1986). This journal is a publication of the United Board for Christian Higher Education in Asia.

121. *China Education Exchange Annual Report Feb. 1, 1985 to Jan. 30, 1986* and

other background material available from China Education Exchange, 134 Plaza Drive, Winnipeg, Manitoba R3T 5K9.

122. Leo A. Orleans, *Chinese Students in America: Policies, Prospects and Numbers* (Washington, D.C.: National Academy Press, 1988).

123. R. Harris, *A History of Higher Education in Canada* (Toronto: University of Toronto Press, 1976). Harris made 1860 the starting point of his study "because it was not until approximately this date that one could conscientiously describe the Canadian university as having characteristics which clearly differentiated it from institutions in the several countries that provided the models for its first half-dozen degree-granting institutions. Prior to 1850, the Canadian universities were simply transplants from England, Scotland, the United States and France" (p. xix).

124. Martin Singer, *Canadian Academic Relations with the P.R.C. 1970-1983* (Ottawa: International Development Research Institute, 1985).

125. Jack Maybee, *The Chinese Program of the Canadian International Development Agency* (Ottawa: International Development Office, Association of Colleges and Universities of Canada, December 1985).

126. UNDP, "Report on Development Cooperation with the P.R.C." A few million dollars of the total have been provided by Canadian universities, hospitals, and other participating institutions.

127. (415)Interview with Ms. Alex Volkoff, first secretary, development, Canadian Embassy in Beijing, September 5, 1985.

128. Interview with Dr. Diana Lary, cultural attaché, Canadian Embassy in Beijing, September 5, 1985.

129. B. Burnaby, A. Cumming, and M. Belfiore, *Formative Evaluation Report of the China/Canada Human Development Training Program* (Toronto: Ontario Institute for Studies in Education, March 1986), p. 5.

130. Ibid., pp. 155-56.

131. K. Minden, "The Multiplication of Ourselves: Canadian Medical Missionaries in West China," in *China's Education and the Industrialized World*, ed. Hayhoe and Bastid.

Chapter 6

1. Hayhoe, "Towards the Forging of a Chinese University Ethos"; *Fudan Daxue zhi.*

2. West, *Yenching University and Sino-Western Relations.*

3. M. B. Bullock, "Promoting the American Way: Exchanges with China Revisited," paper presented at the Conference on Sino-American Educational and Cultural Exchange, East-West Center, Hawaii, February 18-22, 1985; *Qinghua Daxue xiaoshi gao* (Beijing: Zhonghua Shuju, 1981).

4. Kreissler, "L'action culturelle Allemande en Chine."

5. Hayhoe, "A Comparative Approach to the Cultural Dynamics of Sino-Western Educational Cooperation."

6. Depierre, "Maoism in French Educational Thought and Practice."

7. These reflections arise out of a series of interviews with about ten Canadian and American professors of management who have taught in cooperative projects in

China and an equal number of Chinese students studying in China in the autumn of 1984 and spring of 1985.

8. Visit to Wuhan University, July 30, 1980; *Wenhui bao*, July 15, 1984.

9. Most of the material in this section is drawn from an interview with Professor Liu Daoyu, then vice-president and now president of Wuhan University, Shanghai, October 24, 1985.

10. Interview with M. Portiche, cultural counselor, French Embassy in Beijing, October 24, 1985.

11. *XH*, June 26, 1982.

12. Much of the material in this section is drawn from a day spent at Tongji University, and talks with the dean, Professor Cao Shanhua, the head of the Academic Affairs Office, Professor Bi Jiaju, and others, October 16, 1985.

13. Detailed provision for the Tongji linkage is found in the *1984-85 Kulturaustausch-Programm*, copy kindly provided by Mr. Neumann, DAAD (Bonn, April 1984).

14. *XH*, December 8, 1985.

15. *Wenhui bao*, October 23, 1984.

16. Tsang Chiu-sam, *Society, Schools and Progress in China* (New York: Pergamon, 1968), p. 208.

17. *Renmin jiaoyu* 10 (October 1981): 64.

18. *XH*, November 3, 1983; March 15, 1984.

19. Hiroshi Abe, "Comparative International Experience," pp. 24-26.

20. *XH*, May 21, 1985.

21. "Third Plenary Session of Twelfth Central Committee of Communist Party of China," *XH* special issue, October 22, 1984, p. 7.

22. *Guangming ribao*, October 7, November 15, 1984.

23. *XH*, March 21, 1983.

24. "The National Center for Industrial Science and Technology Management Development (at Dalian), PRC, January, 1984" (Washington, D.C.: U.S. Department of Commerce, 1984).

25. Interview with Mr. Richard Lee, U.S. Department of Commerce, Washington, D.C., January 10, 1985.

26. "U.S. Visiting Team: National Center for Industrial S & T Management Development, Dalian, China, Feb. 14, 1985," U.S participation list provided in an interview with Christopher Marut, science and technology officer, U.S. Embassy in Beijing, September 10, 1985.

27. Interview with Professor Frank Jen, Jacobs School of Management, State University of New York at Buffalo, May 22, 1985.

28. "Interaction with the Dalian Alumni," unclassified U.S. Embassy telegram to the departments of State and Commerce, April 1985. Copy kindly provided by C. Marut.

29. *China Exchange News* 12 (September 1984): 22-23.

30. Interview with Professor William Fischer, East-West Center, Hawaii, February 20, 1985, and interview with Professor Frank Jen, Buffalo, May 22, 1985.

31. Speech of Mr. Zhang Yanning, vice-counselor of the SEC, at the fifth anniversary celebration, Dalian, April 1985. Copy kindly provided by C. Marut.

32. Fan Zhilong, "Can China Learn Anything from Western Techniques?" *China Reconstructs* (January 1984): 61. See also *China Daily*, September 23, 1983; July 7, 1984.

33. Interview with Professor Myron Gordon, faculty of management studies, University of Toronto, March 11, 1985.

34. *XH*, June 5, 1985.

35. Beijing *Xinhua* in English, March 3, 1985, in FBIS, March 6, 1985, p. G3.

36. *XH*, June 5, 1985.

37. Interview with Ms. Chen Derong, Chinese administrator of the center, and Mr. Jiang Yanzhu, English teacher, Beijing, September 16, 1985.

38. *XH*, October 6, 1983.

39. Interview with Ms. Alex Volkoff, first secretary development, Embassy of Canada in Beijing, September 5, 1985. Ms. Volkoff defined 80 percent of funding for CIDA-China projects as "tied aid".

40. L. McLean, *The Canada-China Enterprise Management Training Center: Report at the Transition from Phase I to Phase II* (Toronto: Ontario Institute for Studies in Education, February 1986).

41. Luke Chan and Zhian Guan, "Management Education in the PRC with Special Reference to Recent Support Projects by Foreign Countries," *Quantitative Studies in Economics and Population*, Research Report no. 111 (Hamilton: McMaster University, October 1984).

42. *China-Canada Management News: An Occasional Newsletter* (Ottawa: IDO, AUCC, September 1983; June 1984).

43. Doris Ryan and Thomas Fleming, *Evaluation of the Canada-China Management Education Program* (Toronto, OISE, March 1986).

44. Interviews with professors Wally Crowston and Tim Warner, and with three Chinese participants in the York-Nankai Linkage Program, Toronto, November 14, 1984.

45. This material is drawn from a two-day visit to the center and intensive discussions with its associate head, Mr. Xiong Chuanli, and many Chinese faculty members, October 2-3, 1985.

46. Interview with Zhao Shuming, director of international exchange programs, Foreign Affairs Office, Nanjing University, October 9, 1985.

47. Interview with Dr. William Speidel, Johns Hopkins University School of Advanced International Studies, Washington, D.C., December 12, 1984.

48. Interview with Professor Lin Zibin, Chinese academic director of the Center for Chinese-American Studies, Nanjing University, October 11, 1985.

49. Interview with Dr. Leon Slawecki and Mr. Wang Zhigang, directors of the center, June 24, 1987.

50. Interview with Professor Shi Weisan, vice-president, and Professor Huang Zhenhua, dean of the English department, University of International Business and Economics, Beijing, September 6, 1985.

51. Hiroshi Abe, "Borrowing from Japan: China's First Modern Educational System," in *China's Education and the Industrialized World*, ed. Hayhoe and Bastid.

52. Interview with Mr. Adrian Johnston, Embassy of Great Britain in Beijing, September 16, 1985.

53. Fang Houshu, article in *Third World Publishing*, ed. P. Altbach, A. Arboleda,

and S. Gopinthe (Portsmouth, N.H.: Heinnman Educational Books, 1985).

54. See *Nature* 318 (November 21, 1985) for a comprehensive assessment of the contribution of Chinese science and engineering to the global community. See also Otto Schnepp, "The Chinese Visiting Scholar Program in Science and Engineering," unpublished research paper funded by the National Science Foundation, Department of Chemistry, University of Southern California, Los Angeles, Spring 1985.

Chapter 7

1. George Psacharopoulos, "The World Bank and the World of Education: Some Policy Changes and Some Remnants," *Comparative Education* 17, 2 (June 1981).

2. World Bank, *Education Sector Policy Paper*, Washington, 1980.

3. Ibid., p. 93.

4. Peter Williams, "Education in Developing Countries: Halfway to the Styx," *Comparative Education* 17, 2 (June 1981).

5. Martin McLean, "The Political Context of Educational Development: A Comment on the Thesis of Development Underlying the World Bank Sector Policy Paper," *Comparative Education* 17, 2 (June 1981).

6. Williams, "Education in Developing Countries," p. 151.

7. G. Psacharopoulos, *Financing Education in Developing Countries* (Washington, D.C.: World Bank, 1985). For a critical commentary on this book, see Peter Atherton's review in *Canadian Universities in International Development* (Winter 1986-87): 9-12.

8. Teresa Hayter and Catherine Watson, *Aid: Rhetoric or Reality?* (London: Pluto Press, 1985); Cheryl Payer, *The World Bank: A Critical Analysis* (New York: Monthly Review Press, 1982).

9. Gilbert Gonzalez, "Educational Reform at the University of Colombia," *Comparative Education* 17, 2 (June 1981). This article gives a strong criticism of the Alliance for Progress in Colombia and the efforts of American AID and major American foundations to reform higher education by influx of money intended to bring it in line with American political and economics interests. The World Bank played a small role but is not singled out for comment.

10. *China: Long-Term Development Issues and Options* (Baltimore: Johns Hopkins University Press, 1985). This World Bank country economic report is steeped in this sort of argument for China's future economic development, and the examples of such socialist countries as Hungary, Rumania, and Yugoslaovia are often invoked.

11. Williams, "Education in Developing Countries."

12. William Feeney, "Chinese Policy in Multi-lateral Financial Institutions," in *China and the World: Chinese Foreign Policy in the Post-Mao Era* (Boulder: Westview Press, 1984), pp. 266-91.

13. *China: Socialist Economic Development* (Washington, D.C.: World Bank, 1981).

14. Ibid.

15. A remarkable rise in secondary provision from 14.6 million in 1965 to 67.5 million in 1977 was offset by falling enrolments in higher education and a serious reduction in the academic quality of programs as well as disruption of scientific research. See

Achievements of Education in China: Statistics 1949-1981 (Beijing: People's Education Press, 1985), pp. 50, 183, 207.

16. *XH*, April 7, 1986, SWB/FE no. 8239, C1/7-C1/10, April 22, 1986.

17. The way in which the keypoint system operates at primary and secondary level is analyzed by Billie Lo, "Primary Education: A Two-Track System for Dual Tasks" and Stanley Rosen, "New Directions in Secondary Education," in *Contemporary Chinese Education*, ed. R. Hayhoe (London: Croom Helm, 1984), pp. 47-92. The Chinese rationale for it is given in *Zhongguo jiaoyu nianjian* (Beijing: China Encyclopedic Press, 1985), pp. 130-32, 167-70.

18. *China: Long-Term Development Issues and Options*, pp. 125-26; *Annex I: Issues and Prospects in Education*, pp. 9-10.

19. Of 7.3 million examination competitors in 1979, only 250,000 were successful, a transition rate of 3.4 percent. By 1983, competitors were reduced to 2.4 million for 390,800 places, a transition rate of 16.3 percent, largely achieved through reducing the number of upper secondary graduates who qualified for the examination. See David Chambers and John Gardner, *Education Profile: China* (London: British Council, February 1985), p. A11.

20. Marianne Bastid, book review in *China Quarterly* 108 (December 1986): 725.

21. Interview with Dr. Barbara Searle, World Bank, Washington, D.C., March 16, 1987.

22. Interview with Dr. Robert Drysdale, World Bank, Washington, D.C., December 10, 1985.

23. Interview with Dr. Susan Cochrane, World Bank, Washington, D.C., March 16, 1987.

24. Interview with Dr. Barbara Searle, World Bank, Washington, D.C., March 16, 1987.

25. Interview with Dr. Frank Farner, World Bank, Washington, D.C., March 16, 1987.

26. The 15 research centers under Agricultural Research II are also mapped, though they are not included in the total of 183 higher institutions.

27. Interview with Dr. Frank Farner, World Bank, Washington, D.C., December 9, 1985. I am deeply indebted to Dr. Farner for the assistance he gave me in gaining access to materials that detail the World Bank projects depicted in this chapter.

28. A. Ter Weele, "China/World Bank University Development," *Prospects* 13, 4 (1983): 493-501.

29. Evaluation Report, Chinese University Development Project I, by the International Advisory Panel and the Chinese Review Commission (Washington, D.C., May 1986) (internal document).

30. I was responsible for an interim assessment of the project which involved reading and summarizing the reports of nearly one hundred specialists who took part in the project. Information on the final evaluation of the project was gained through talks with Mr. Ma Weixiang, deputy director of the loan office, Chinese State Education Commission, in March 1986, when he was a guest of the Higher Education Group at OISE.

31. Interview with Mr. Halsey L. Beemer, Jr., executive director of the International Advisory Panel, National Academy of Sciences, Washington, D.C., December 10, 1985.

32. R. McCormick, "The Radio and Television Universities and the Development of Higher Education in China," *China Quarterly* 105 (March 1986): 45-71.

33. I am grateful to Dr. Daniel Walker, team leader of the 1st Team, who provided information on the team's findings.

34. These amounts are broken down between Chinese and foreign funding as follows. Of the $48 million for faculty development, $14 million is in foreign currency; of the $16 million for specialist services, $12 million is in foreign currency; and of the $45 million for exchange programs, only $1 million is in foreign currency.

35. Interviews with Mr. Halsey L. Beemer, Jr., December 10, 1985; March 16, 1987.

36. Interview with Professor Jacob Siegel, Faculty of Management Studies, University of Toronto, October 20, 1987.

37. Interview with Dr. Arthur Bourns, chairman, International Advisory Panel, Toronto, June 11, 1986.

38. Interview with Ms. Veronica Li, World Bank, Washington, D.C., December 10, 1985.

39. The fourteenth key medical university, Beijing Medical University, was not included in this project because it was part of University Development I.

40. Dean Jamieson et al., *China: The Health Sector, A World Bank Country Study* (Washington, D.C.: The World Bank, 1984).

41. Interview with Dr. Mary Fanning, Toronto General Hospital, June 17, December 17, 1985.

42. H. Brown, "Teachers and the Rural Responsibility System in the PRC," *Asian Journal of Public Administration* (1985).

43. These ratios are calculated from statistics given in *Achievement of Education in China: Statistics 1949-1983*, pp. 198, 221; and *Achievement of Education in China: Statistics 1980-1985*.

44. In a final evaluation of University Development I carried out in March 1987, it was discovered that twenty of the twenty-eight universities had underspent their book budgets, in some cases by a wide margin, and these budgets represented only 2.4 percent of the total foreign funds available.

Postscript

1. Beijing *Xinhua* in Chinese, May 30, 1987, in FBIS, no. 104, June 15, 1987.

2. Hong Kong *Zhongguo xinwenshe* in Chinese, July 25, 1987, in FBIS, no. 143, July 27, 1987.

3. Beijing *Xinhua* in English, June 15, 1987, in FBIS, no. 115, June 16, 1987.

4. In early 1988 there were reports that universities were facing cutbacks in their budgets from government and being asked to strengthen their contract research and contract training activities, so coming to depend more and more on direct support from productive agencies. Details on the way market forces are affecting Chinese universities have not fallen within the scope of this volume, but they can be found in R. Hayhoe, "Shanghai as a Mediator of the Educational Open Door," *Pacific Affairs* 61, 2 (Summer 1988).

GLOSSARY OF CHINESE TERMS

benke	本科	muji	母机
Buwei soyouzhi	部委所有制	mulu	目录
daxue	大学	Shang Bu	商部
duanqi zhiye daxue	短期职业大学	shifan daxue	师范大学
jianjie	业暨	shuyuan	書院
jiaocha	交叉	xuefeng	學風
jiaoxue jihua	教学计划	xueyuan	学院
jiaowuchu	教务处	xueke zu	学科部
jiaoyan zu	教研组	zhishi mokuaimo	知识模块
jiaoyu ziliao hui	教育资料会	zhuanke	专科
jinshi	進士	zhuanye	专业
juren	舉人	zonghe daxue	综合大学
lao zhuanye dai 　chu xin zhuanye	老专业带出新专业	zonghe jishu daxue	综合技术大学

BIBLIOGRAPHY

Western Language Books and Articles

Abe, Hiroshi. "Borrowing from Japan: China's First Modern Educational System." In *China's Education and the Industrialized World: Studies in Cultural Transfer*, ed. R. Hayhoe and M. Bastid. Armonk, N.Y.: M. E. Sharpe, and Toronto: OISE Press, 1987.

_____. "Comparative International Experience: PRC Exchanges with Japan." Paper presented at the Conference on Sino-American Cultural and Educational Exchanges, East-West Center, Hawaii, February 1985.

Ahn, Byung-Joon. "Higher Education Policy and Politics after the Cultural Revolution." *Korea and World Affairs* 2, 3 (1978).

Alitto, Guy. *The Last Confucian: Liang Shu-ming and the Chinese Dilemma of Modernity*. Berkeley: University of California Press, 1978.

Albtach, P., A. Arboleda, and S. Gopinthe. *Third World Publishing*. Portsmouth, N.H.: Heinnemann Educational Books, 1985.

Altbach, P., R. Arnove, and G. Kelly. *Comparative Education*. London: Macmillan, 1980.

Artz, F. *The Development of Technical Education in France*. London and Cambridge, Mass.: Society for the History of Technology and MIT Press, 1966.

Ayers, William. *Chang Chih-tung and Educational Reform in China*. Cambridge: Harvard University Press, 1971.

Bady, Paul. *L'Ecole et la Revolution*. Paris: Project No. 84, 1974.

Barendsen, Robert. *The National College Entrance Examinations in the P.R.C.* Washington, D.C.: Office of Education, 1979.

Bastid, Marianne. *Aspects de la Réforme de l'Enseignement en Chine au début du XXè siècle d'aprés les écrits de Zhang Jian*. Paris: Mouton, 1971.

_____. "Chinese Educational Policies in the 1980s and Economic Development." *China Quarterly* 98 (1984): 189-219.

_____. "Economic Necessity and Political Ideals in Educational Reform during the Cultural Revolution." *China Quarterly* 42 (1970): 16-45.

_____. "Servitude or Liberation? The Introduction of Foreign Educational Practices and Systems to China since 1840." In *China's Education and the Industrialized World: Studies in Cultural Transfer*, ed. R. Hayhoe and M. Bastid. Armonk, N.Y.: M. E. Sharpe, and Toronto: OISE Press, 1987.

Baum, Richard. *Scientism and Bureaucratism in Chinese Thought: Cultural Limits of the Four Modernizations*. Lund: University of Lund Research Policy Institute, 1981.

Becker, C. H., et al. *The Reorganization of Education in China*. Paris: Institute of Intellectual Cooperation, 1932.

Ben-David, Joseph. *American Higher Education: Directions Old and New.* New York: McGraw Hill, 1972.

_____. *Centers of Learning.* New York: McGraw Hill, 1977.

_____. *Fundamental Research and the Universities.* Paris: OECD, 1968.

Bereday, George. *Universities for All.* San Fransisco: Jossey Bass, 1973.

Bernstein, Basil. *Class, Codes and Control: Towards a Theory of Educational Transmission.* 3 vols. London: Routledge and Kegan Paul, 1974-1977.

_____. "On the Classification and Framing of Educational Knowledge." In *Knowledge and Control*, ed. Michael Young. London: Collier Macmillan, 1971.

Bernstein, Thomas. *Up to the Mountains and Down to the Villages: The Transfer of Youth from Urban to Rural China.* New Haven: Yale University Press, 1977.

Bigelow, Karl. "Some Comparative Reflections on Soviet and Chinese Higher Education." *Comparative Education Review* 4, 3 (1960): 169-73.

Biggerstaff, Knight. *The Earliest Modern Government Schools in China.* Ithaca: Cornell University Press, 1961.

Borthwick, Sally. *Education and Social Change in China.* Stanford: Hoover Institution Press, 1983.

Brown, Hubert. "American Progressivism in Chinese Education: The Case of Tao Xingzhi." In *China's Education and the Industrialized World: Studies in Cultural Transfer*, ed. R. Hayhoe and M. Bastid. Armonk, N.Y.: M. E. Sharpe, and Toronto, OISE Press, 1987.

_____. "Politics and the 'Peking Spring' of Educational Studies in China." *Comparative Education Review* 26, 3 (1982).

_____. "Recent Policy Towards Rural Education in the P.R.C." *Hong Kong Journal of Public Administration* 3, 2 (1981): 168-88.

Bullock, Mary Brown. *An American Transplant: The Rockefeller Foundation and Peking Union Medical College.* Berkeley: University of California Press, 1980.

Carnoy, Martin. *Education as Cultural Imperialism.* New York: David MacKay, 1974.

Carnoy, Martin, and H. Levin. *Schooling and Work in the Democratic State.* Stanford: Stanford University Press, 1985.

Chaffee, John. *The Thorny Gates of Learning in Sung China.* Cambridge: Cambridge University Press, 1985.

Chambers, David. "Adult Education in Urban Industrial China: Problems, Policies and Prospects." In *Contemporary Chinese Education*, ed. R. Hayhoe. London: Croom Helm, 1984.

_____. "The 1975-1976 Debate over Higher Education Policy in the P.R.C." *Comparative Education* 13, 1 (1977): 3-14.

Chan, Sylvia, and Ronald Price. "Teacher Training in China: A Case Study of the Foreign Languages Department of Peking Teacher Training College." *Comparative Education* 14, 3 (1978): 243-52.

Chen Hsi-en, Theodore. *Chinese Education since 1949: Academic and Revolutionary Models.* New York: Pergamon Press, 1981.

_____. *The Maoist Educational Revolution.* New York: Praeger, 1974.

_____. *The Thought Reform of Chinese Intellectuals.* Hong Kong: Hong Kong University Press, and London: Oxford University Press, 1960.

Ch'en, Jerome. *China and the West: Society and Culture 1815-1937.* London: Macmillan, 1979.

Chen, Joseph. *The May Fourth Movement in Shanghai.* Leiden: E. J. Brill, 1971.

Cheng Chu-yuan. *Scientific and Engineering Manpower in Communist China 1949-1963*. Washington, D.C.: U.S. Government Printing Office, 1965.

China Educational Commission. *Christian Education in China*. New York: Committee of Referees and Council of the Foreign Missions Conference of North America, 1922.

Chow Tse-tsung. *The May Fourth Movement*. Stanford: Stanford University Press, 1960.

"Chronology of the Two-Road Struggle in the Educational Front in the Past Seventeen Years." *Chinese Education* 1, 1 (1968): 3-58.

Chu, Don-chean. *Chairman Mao: Education of the Proletariat*. New York: Philosophical Library, 1980.

Chung Shih. *Higher Education in China*. Hong Kong: Union Research Institute, 1953.

Cleverley, John. *The Schooling of China*. London: George Allen and Unwin, 1985.

Chuang Chai-hsuan. *Tendencies Towards a Democratic System of Education in China*. Shanghai: Commercial Press, 1922.

Cohen, Habiba. *Elusive Reform: The French Universities 1968-1978*. Boulder: Westview Press, 1978.

Covell, Ralph. *W.A.P. Martin: Pioneer of Progress in China*. Washington, D.C.: Christian University Press, 1978.

Cowan, R., and M. McLean. *International Handbook of Educational Systems*. Vol. 3. London: John Wiley and Sons, 1984.

Crozier, Brian. *The Man Who Lost China*. London: Angus and Robertson, 1977.

Davin, Delia. "Imperialism and the Diffusion of Liberal Thought: British Influences on Chinese Education." In *China's Education and the Industrialized World: Studies in Cultural Transfer*, ed. R. Hayhoe and M. Bastid. Armonk, N.Y.: M. E. Sharpe, and Toronto: OISE Press, 1987.

Dean, Genevieve C. *Science and Technology in the Development of Modern China: An Annotated Bibliography*. London: Mansell, 1979.

_____. *Technology Policy and Industrialization in the P.R.C.* Ottawa: International Development Research Centre, 1979.

Deng Xiaoping. *Selected Works*. Beijing: Foreign Languages Press, 1985.

_____. "Speech at the National Education Work Conference." *Beijing Review* 21, 18 (1978): 6-13.

Depierre, Roland. "Maoism in French Educational Thought and Action." In *China's Education and the Industrialized World: Studies in Cultural Transfer*. Armonk, N.Y.: M. E. Sharpe, and Toronto: OISE Press, 1987.

Duggan, Stephen. *A Critique of the Report of the League of Nations Mission of Educational Experts*. New York: Institute of International Relations, 1933.

Duiker, William. *Ts'ai Yüan-p'ei: Educator of Modern China*. University Park: Pennsylvania State University Press, 1977.

Durkheim, Emile. *The Evolution of Educational Thought*. London: Routledge and Kegan Paul, 1977.

Education and Science. Beijing: Foreign Languages Press, 1983.

Education in China: The Past Five Years. Beijing: Ministry of Education, 1983.

"Educational Policy after the Gang of Four." *Chinese Education* 11, 1 (1978): 3-174.

Emerson, John Philip. *Administrative and Technical Manpower in the P.R.C.* Washington, D.C.: U.S. Department of Commerce, 1973.

_____. "Manpower Training and Utilisation of Specialized Cadres, 1949-1968." In *The*

City in Communist China, ed. John Willis. Stanford: Stanford University Press, 1971.

_____. "Urban School-Leavers and Unemployment in China." *China Quarterly* 93:1-16.

Epstein, Irving. "The Politics of Curricular Change." In *Education and Social Change in the PRC*, ed. John Hawkins. New York: Praeger, 1983.

Fairbank, John. *Chinese Thought and Institutions*. Chicago: University of Chicago Press, 1964.

_____, ed. *The Missionary Enterprise in China and America*. Cambridge: Harvard University Press, 1974.

Fairbank, John, and Teng Ssu-yu, eds. *China's Response to the West: A Documentary Survey 1839-1923*. Cambridge: Harvard University Press, 1954.

Fairbank, Wilma. *America's Cultural Experiment in China 1942-1949*. Washington, D.C.: Bureau of Cultural Affairs, U.S. Department of State, 1976.

Fenn, William Purvance. *Christian Higher Education in Changing China 1880-1950*. Michigan: W. B. Eerdmans, 1976.

Fingar, Thomas. *Higher Education and Research in the P.R.C.: Institutional Profiles*. Washington, D.C.: U.S.-China Clearinghouse, 1980.

_____. *Higher Education in the P.R.C.* Stanford: Northeast Asia-United States Forum on International Policy, 1981.

_____, ed. *China's Quest for Independence: Policy Evolution in the 1970's*. Boulder: Westview Press, 1980.

Fingar, Thomas, and Linda Reed. *Survey Summary: Students and Scholars from the P.R.C. in the U.S.* Washington: CSCPRC and National Association for Foreign Students Affairs, 1981.

Fitzgerald, C. P. *Floodtide in China*. London: Cresset Press, 1958.

Folsom, K. *Friends, Guests and Colleagues: The Mu-fu System in the late Ch'ing Period*. Berkeley: University of California Press, 1968.

Frank, André Gunnar. *Capitalism and Underdevelopment in Latin America*. New York: Monthly Review Press, 1979.

Franke, Wolfgang. *The Reform and Abolition of the Traditional Examination System*. Cambridge: Harvard University Press, 1960.

Fraser, Stewart. "Notes on Sino-Soviet Cooperation in Higher Education 1950-1960." In *Melbourne Studies in Education 1961-62*, ed. E. L. French. Melbourne: Melbourne University Press, 1964.

Fraser, Stewart. "Sino-Soviet Educational Relations." In *Changing Dimensions in International Education*, ed. R. F. Paulsen. Tuscon: University of Arizona Press, 1969.

_____, ed. *Chinese Communist Education: Records of the First Decade*. Nashville: Vanderbilt University Press, 1965.

_____, ed. *Education and Communism in China: An Anthology of Commentary and Documents*. London: Pall Mall Press, 1971.

Furth, Charlotte. *Ting Wen-chiang: Science and China's New Culture*. Cambridge: Harvard University Press, 1970.

Galt, Howard. *A History of Chinese Educational Institutions*. London: Arthur Probsthain, 1951.

Galtung, Johann. *Peace: Education, Research, Action*. Copenhagen: Christian Ejliers, 1975.

_____. "A Structural Theory of Imperialism." *Journal of Peace Research* 8 (1971).

_____. *The True Worlds: A Transnational Perspective.* New York: Freedom Press, 1980.

Gamberg, Ruth. *Red and Expert.* New York: Schocken Books, 1977.

Gardner, John. *Chinese Politics and the Succession to Mao.* London: Macmillan, 1982.

_____. "Chou Jung-hsin and Chinese Education." *Current Scene* 15 (1977).

_____. "Study and Criticism: The Voice of Shanghai Radicals." In *Shanghai: Revolution and Development in an Asian Metropolis,* ed. Christopher Howe. London: Cambridge University Press, 1981.

Gardner, John, and Idema Wilt. "China's Educational Revolution." In *Authority, Participation and Cultural Change in China.* London: Cambridge University Press, 1973.

Gendzier, Irene. *Managing Political Change: Social Scientists and the Third World.* Boulder: Westview Press, 1985.

Goldman, Merle. *China's Intellectuals: Advise and Dissent.* Cambridge: Harvard University Press, 1981.

Goodman, David. *Beijing Street Voices: The Poetry and Politics of China's Democracy Movement.* London: Marion Boyas, 1981.

Gray, Jack, and Gordon White. *China's New Development Strategy.* London: Academic Press, 1982.

Gregg, Alice. *China and Educational Autonomy: The Changing Role of the Protestant Missionary in China 1807-1937.* New York: Syracuse University Press, 1941.

Grieder, Jerome. *Hu Shih and the Chinese Renaissance.* Cambridge: Harvard University Press, 1970.

_____. *Intellectuals and the State in Modern China.* New York: The Free Press, 1981.

Gruson, Pascale. *L'Etat Enseignant.* Paris: Mouton, 1978.

Gu Mingyuan. "The Development and Reform of Higher Education." *Comparative Education* 20, 1 (1984): 141-49.

Hao Keming. "Research on Higher Education in China Today." *Comparative Education* 20, 1 (1984): 149-54.

Harding, Harry, ed. *China's Foreign Relations in the 1980s.* New Haven: Yale University Press, 1984.

Harris, Robin. *A History of Higher Education in Canada.* Toronto: University of Toronto Press, 1976.

Hawkins, John. *Education and Social Change in the PRC.* New York: Praeger, 1983.

_____. "Educational Exchanges and the Transformation of Higher Education in China." In *Bridges to Knowledge: Foreign Students in Comparative Perspective,* ed. E. Barber, P. Altbach, and R. Myers. Chicago: University of Chicago Press, 1984.

_____. *Mao Tse-tung and Education: His Thoughts and Teachings.* Connecticut: Linnet Books, 1970.

Hayhoe, Ruth. "Catholics and Socialists: The Paradox of Sino-French Educational Interaction." In *China's Education and the Industrialized World: Studies in Cultural Transfer,* ed. R. Hayhoe and M. Bastid. Armonk, N.Y.: M. E. Sharpe, and Toronto: OISE Press, 1987.

_____. "China, Comparative Education and the World Order Models Project." *Compare* 16, 1 (1986): 65-80.

_____. "China's Higher Curricular Reform in Historical Perspective." *China Quarterly* 110 (June 1987).

_____. *Chinese, European and American Scholarly Values in Interaction*. London: London Association of Comparative Educationists, 1984.

_____. "A Comparative Analysis of Sino-Western Academic Exchange." *Comparative Education* 20, 1 (1984): 39-56.

_____. "A Comparative Analysis of the Cultural Dynamics of Sino-Western Educational Cooperation." *China Quarterly* 102 (December 1985).

_____. " Intellectual Freedom and the Chinese University." *Canadian and International Education* 15, 1 (1986).

_____. "Past and Present in China's Educational Relations with the Industrialized World." In *China's Education and the Industrialized World: Studies in Cultural Transfer*, ed. R. Hayhoe and M. Bastid. Armonk, N.Y.: M. E. Sharpe, and Toronto: OISE Press, 1987.

_____. "Penetration or Mutuality? China's Educational Cooperation with Europe, Japan and North America." *Comparative Education Review* 31, 4 (1986): 532-59.

_____. "Shanghai as a Mediator of the Educational Open Door." *Pacific Affairs* 61, 2 (Summer 1988).

_____. "Sino-Western Educational Cooperation: History and Perspectives." *Prospects* 15, 2 (1985).

_____. "Towards the Forging of a Chinese University Ethos: Zhendan and Fudan 1903-1919." *China Quarterly* 92 (June 1983).

_____, ed. *Contemporary Chinese Education*. Armonk, N.Y.: M. E. Sharpe, and London: Croom Helm, 1984).

_____, ed. "Chinese Educators on Chinese Education." Special Issue of *Canadian and International Education* 16, 1 (1987).

Hayter, Teresa, and Catherine Watson. *Aid: Rhetoric or Reality?* London: Pluto Press, 1985.

Henze, Juergen. "Alphabetisierung in China." *Bildung und Erziehung* 36, 3:295-313.

_____. "Begabtenforderung im Bildungwesen der VR China: Das System der 'Schwerpunkt-Schulen.' " *Asien* 4 (1982): 29-58.

_____. *Bildung und Wissenschaft in der Volksrepublik China zu Beginn der Achtziger Jahre*. Hamburg: Institut für Asienkunde, 1983.

_____. "Developments in Vocational Education since 1976." *Comparative Education* 20, 1 (1984): 117-40.

_____. "Educational Modernization as a Search for Higher Efficiency." In *China's Education and the Industrialized World: Studies in Cultural Transfer*, ed. R. Hayhoe and M. Bastid. Armonk, N.Y.: M. E. Sharpe, and Toronto: OISE Press, 1987.

_____. "Higher Education: The Tension Between Quality and Equality." In *Contemporary Chinese Education*. ed. R. Hayhoe. Armonk, N.Y.: M. E. Sharpe, and London: Croom Helm, 1984.

Hinton, William. *Hundred Day War: The Cultural Revolution at Tsinghua University*. New York: Monthly Review Press, 1972.

Ho Ping-ti. *The Ladder of Success in Imperial China: Aspects of Social Mobility 1368-1911*. New York: Columbia University Press, 1962.

Ho, Samuel, and Ralph Huenemann. *China's Open Door Policy: The Quest for Foreign Technology and Capital*. Vancouver: University of British Columbia Press, 1984.

Hofstadter, R., and W. Metzger. *The Development of Academic Freedom in the United States*. New York: Columbia University Press, 1955.

Holmes, Brian. *Comparative Education: Some Considerations of Method*. London: George Allen and Unwin, 1983.

Holsti, K. J. *The Dividing Discipline*. London: George Allen and Unwin, 1985.

Hsiao, Theodore. *The History of Modern Education in China*. Shanghai: Commercial Press, 1935.

Hsiung, J., and S. Kim, eds. *China in the Global Community*. New York: Praeger, 1980.

Hsu, Immanuel C. Y. "The Reorganization of Higher Education in Communist China 1949-1961. " *China Quarterly* 19 (1964): 128-60.

Hsüeh Chün-tu. *China's Foreign Relations: New Perspectives*. New York: Praeger, 1982.

Hu Chang-tu. "The Historical Background: Examinations and Controls in Pre-Modern China." *Comparative Education* 20, 1 (1984): 7-27.

Hu Chang-tu. *Chinese Education Under Communism*. New York: Teachers College Press, 1962.

_____. "The Chinese People's University: Bastion of Marxism-Leninism." In *The World Yearbook of Education: Universities Facing the Future*, ed. R. F. Butts and W. B. Niblett. London: Evans Bros. 1972.

Hu Shiming and Eli Seifman, eds. *Towards a New World Outlook: A Documentary History of Education in the P.R.C. 1949-1976*. New York: AMS Press, 1976.

Huang Shiqi. "Contemporary Educational Relations with the Industrialized World: A Chinese View." In *China's Education and the Industrialized World: Studies in Cultural Transfer*, ed. R. Hayhoe and M. Bastid. Armonk, N.Y.: M. E. Sharpe, and Toronto: OISE Press, 1987.

_____. "On Some Vital Issues in the Development and Reform of Higher Education." *Higher Education in Europe* 10, 3 (1985): 63-75.

Israel, John. *Student Nationalism in China 1927-1937*. Stanford: Hoover Institution Press, 1960.

Kaplan, M., ed. *New Approaches to International Relations*. New York: St. Martin's Press, 1968.

Keenan, Barry. *The Dewey Experiment in China*. Cambridge: Harvard University Press, 1977.

Kim, Samuel. *China, the U.N. and World Order*. Princeton: Princeton University Press, 1979.

_____, ed. *China and the World*. Boulder: Westview Press, 1984.

_____. *The Quest for a Just World Order*. Boulder: Westview Press, 1984.

Knorr, Klaus, and James Rosenau. *Contending Approaches to International Politics*. Princeton: Princeton University Press, 1969.

Kobayashi, T. *Society, Schools and Progress in Japan*. Oxford: Pergamon Press, 1976.

Kothari, Rajni. *Footsteps into the Future: Diagnosis of the Present World and Design for an Alternative*. New York: Free Press, 1974.

Kreissler, Françoise. "Technical Education as the Key to Cultural Cooperation: The Sino-German Experience." In *China's Education and the Industrialized World: Studies in Cultural Transfer*, ed. R. Hayhoe and M. Bastid. Armonk, N.Y.: M. E. Sharpe, and Toronto: OISE Press, 1987.

Kuo Ping Wen. *The Chinese System of Public Education*. New York: Teachers College Press, 1915.

Kwong, Julia. *Chinese Education in Transition: Prelude to the Cultural Revolution*. Montreal: McGill-Queens University Press, 1979.

Llasera, Isabelle. "Confucian Education Through European Eyes." In *China's Education and the Industrialized World: Studies in Cultural Transfer*, ed. R. Hayhoe and M. Bastid. Armonk, N.Y.: M. E. Sharpe, and Toronto: OISE Press, 1987.

Lampton, David. *A Relationship Restored: Trends in U.S.-China Educational Exchange 1978-1984*. Washington, D.C.: National Academy Press, 1986.

Latourette, Kenneth. *A History of Christian Missions in China*. London: Society for Promoting Christian Knowledge, 1929.

Levenson, Joseph. *Confucian China and Its Modern Fate: The Problem of Intellectual Continuity*. London: Routledge and Kegan Paul, 1958.

_____. *Confucian China and Its Modern Fate: The Problem of Monarchical Decay*. London: Routledge and Kegan Paul, 1964.

_____. *Confucian China and Its Modern Fate: The Problem of Historical Significance*. London: Routledge and Kegan Paul, 1965.

Li, Anthony. *The History of Privately Controlled Higher Education in China*. Westport, Conn.: Greenwood Press, 1977.

Lin Pao-tchin. *L'Instruction Feminine en Chine*. Paris: Librairie Geuthner, 1926.

Linden, Allen. "Politics and Education in Nationist China: The Case of the University Council 1927-28." *Journal of Asian Studies* 28, 4 (1968): 395-422.

Lindsay, Michael. *Notes on Educational Problems in Communist China*. New York: Institute of Pacific Relations, 1950.

Liu, Adam Yuen-ching. *The Hanlin Academy: Training Ground for the Ambitious*. Connecticut: Archon Books, 1981.

Liu Shaoqi. *Collected Works*. 3 vols. Hong Kong: Union Research Institute, 1969.

Liu Wenxiu. "Developments and Interrelationships of Higher Education in New China." *Canadian and International Education* 14, 2 (1985): 59-71.

Lo, Billie L. C. "Primary Education: A Two-Track System for Dual Tasks." In *Contemporary Chinese Education*, ed. R. Hayhoe. Armonk, N.Y.: M. E. Sharpe, and London: Croom Helm, 1984.

_____. *Research Guide to Education in China After Mao*. Hong Kong: Centre of Asian Studies, University of Hong Kong, 1983.

_____. "Teacher Education in the Eighties." In *Contemporary Chinese Education*, ed. R. Hayhoe. Armonk, N.Y.: M. E. Sharpe, and London: Croom Helm, 1984.

Löfstedt, Jan-Ingvar. *Chinese Educational Policy*. Stockholm: Almqvist and Wiksell, 1980.

_____. "Educational Planning and Administration in China." *Comparative Education* 20, 1 (1984): 57-72.

Louie, Kam. "Salvaging Confucian Education, 1949-1983." *Comparative Education* 20, 1 (1984): 27-38.

Louven, Erhard, and Monica Schädler. *Wissenschaftlicher Zusammenarbeit zwischen der Volksrepublik China und der Bundesrepublik Deutschland*. Hamburg: Institut für Asienkunde, 1986.

Lucas, AnElissa. *Chinese Medical Modernization: Comparative Policy Continuities 1930s-1980s*. New York: Praeger, 1984.

Lutz, Jessie. *China and the Christian Colleges*. Ithaca: Cornell University Press, 1971.

Mao Zedong. "Comrade Mao Tse-tung On Educational Work." *Chinese Education*, vols. 2-6 (1969-1973).

_____. *Selected Works*. 5 vols. Beijing: Foreign Languages Press, 1975, 1977.

Mason, E., and R. Asher. *The World Bank since Bretton Woods*. Washington, D.C.: Brookings Institute, 1973.

Maxwell, N., and B. McFarlane, eds. *China's Changed Road to Development*. Oxford: Pergamon Press, 1984.

Mazrui, Ali. *Political Values and the Educated Class in Africa*. London: Heinneman, 1978.

McCormick, R. "Central Broadcasting and Television University." *China Quarterly* 81 (1980): 129-36.

McLean, Martin. "Educational Dependency: A Critique." *Compare* 13, 1 (1983).

Menzel, Joanna. *The Chinese Civil Service: Career Open to Talent?* Boston: D. C. Heath, 1963.

Meskill, John. *Academies in Ming China*. Tuscon: University of Arizona Press, 1982.

Minden, Karen. "The Multiplication of Ourselves: Canadian Medical Missionaries in West China." In *China's Education and the Industrialized World: Studies in Cultural Transfer*, ed. R. Hayhoe and M. Bastid. Armonk, N.Y.: M. E. Sharpe, and Toronto: OISE Press, 1987.

Miyazaki, Ichisada. *China's Examination Hell: The Civil Service Examinations of Imperial China*. New York: Weatherhill, 1971.

Moulder, Frances. *Japan, China and the Modern World Economy: Towards a Reinterpretation of East Asian Development ca 1600 to ca 1918*. Cambridge: Cambridge University Press, 1979.

Munro, Donald. *The Concept of Man in Contemporary China*. Ann Arbor: Center for Chinese Studies, University of Michigan, 1977.

Nathan, Andrew. *Chinese Democracy*. New York: Alfred A. Knopf, 1985.

Nee, Victor. *The Cultural Revolution at Peking University*. New York: Monthly Review Press, 1969.

Needham, Joseph. *A Shorter Science and Civilization in China*, ed. Colin Ronan. Cambridge: Cambridge University Press, 1978.

Neugebauer, Ernst. *Anfänge Pädagogische Entwicklungshilfe unter dem Völkerbund im China 1931 bis 1935*. Hamburg: Institute für Asienkunde, 1971.

Nisbet, Robert. *Social Change and History*. Oxford: Oxford University Press, 1872.

Ogden, Suzanne. "The Politics of Higher Education in the P.R.C." *Chinese Law and Government* 11, 3 (1982).

Orleans, Leo A., "China's Science and Technology: Continuity and Innovation." In *P.R.C.: An Economic Assessment*, ed. Joint Economic Committee. Washington, D.C.: U.S. Government Printing Office, 1972.

_____. "Chinese Students and Technology Transfer." *Journal of North East Asian Studies* 4, 4 (October 1985).

_____. *Chinese Students in America: Policies, Issues and Numbers*. Washington, D.C.: National Academy Press, forthcoming.

_____. *Manpower for Science and Engineering in China*. Washington, D.C.: Committee for Science and Technology, U.S. House of Representatives, 1980.

_____. *Professional Manpower and Education in Communist China*. Washington, D.C.: U.S. Government Printing Office, 1960.

_____. "Soviet Influences on Chinese Higher Education." In *China's Education and the Industrialized World: Studies in Cultural Transfer*, ed. R. Hayhoe and M. Bastid. Armonk, N.Y.: M. E. Sharpe, and Toronto: OISE Press, 1987.

_____. *The Training of Scientific and Engineering Manpower in the P.R.C.* Washington, D.C.: U.S. Government Printing Office, 1983.

_____, ed. *Science in Contemporary China*. Stanford: Stanford University Press, 1980.

Papers of the International Association of Universities. *Problems of Integrated Higher Education: The Case of the Gesamthochschule*. Paris: Rue Miollis, 1972.

Parish, William, ed. *Chinese Rural Development: The Great Transformation*. Armonk, N.Y.: M. E. Sharpe, 1985.

Parker, Franklin, and Betty June Parker. *Education in the People's Republic of China Past and Present: An Annotated Bibliography* New York: Garland, 1986.

Payer, Cheryl. *The World Bank: A Critical Analysis*. New York: Monthly Review Press, 1982.

Payne, Robert. *Chiang Kai Shek*. New York: Weybright and Talley, 1969.

Peake, Cyrus. *Nationalism and Education in Modern China*. New York: Columbia University Press, 1932.

Peisert, H., and G. Framheim. *Systems of Higher Education: F.R.G., U.S.A.* International Council of Educational Development, 1978.

Pepper, Suzanne. *China's Universities: Post-Mao Enrollment Policies and their Impact on the Structure of Secondary Education*. Ann Arbor, Michigan: Center for Chinese Studies, 1984.

_____. "China Universities: New Experiments in Socialist Democracy and Administrative Reform." *Modern China* 8, 2 (1982): 147-204.

_____. "Chinese Education After Mao: Two Steps Forward and Two Steps Back and Begin Again?" *China Quarterly* 81 (1980): 1-65.

_____. "Deng Xiaoping's Political and Economic Reforms and the Chinese Student Protests." *Universities Field Staff International Reports*, no. 30 Asia.

_____. "Education and Political Development in Communist China." *Studies in Comparative Communism* 3, 3-4 (1970): 132-57.

_____. "Education and Revolution: The 'Chinese Model' Revisited." *Journal of Asian Studies* 18, 9 (1978): 847-90.

Petit, Joseph. *Engineering Education in the P.R.C.* Washington, D.C.: National Academy Press, 1983.

"Physics, Chemistry and Mathematics Education in China." *Chinese Education* 13, 1-2 (1980): 1-165.

Prewitt, Kenneth. *Research Opportunities in China for American Humanists and Social Scientists*. Washington, D.C.: Social Science Research Council, 1981.

Price, Ronald. "Convergence or Copying? China and the Soviet Union." In *China's Education and the Industrialized World: Studies in Cultural Transfer*, ed. R. Hayhoe and M. Bastid. Armonk, N.Y.: M. E. Sharpe, and Toronto: OISE Press, 1987.

_____. *Education in Communist China*. New York: Praeger, 1970.

_____. "Labor and Education." *Comparative Education* 20, 1 (1984): 81-92.

_____. *Marxism and Education in China and Russia*. London: Croom Helm, 1977.

Purcell, Victor. *Problems of Chinese Education*. London: Kegan Paul, Trench, Trubner and Co., 1936.

Rankin, Mary. *Early Chinese Revolutionaries*. Cambridge: Harvard University Press, 1971.

Rawski, Evelyn. *Education and Popular Literacy in Ch'ing China.* Ann Arbor: University of Michigan Press, 1979.

Regulations Concerning Academic Degrees in the P.R.C. Beijing: Chinese Education Association for International Exchanges, 1982.

Ridley, Charles. *China's Scientific Policies: Implications of International Cooperation.* Stanford: Hoover Institution Press, 1976.

Ridley, Charles, Paul Godwin, and Dennis Doolin. *The Making of a Model Citizen in Communist China.* Stanford: The Hoover Institution Press, 1971.

Rosen, Stanley. "New Directions in Secondary Education." In *Contemporary Chinese Education,* ed. R. Hayhoe. Armonk, N.Y.: M. E. Sharpe, and London: Croom Helm, 1984.

_____. "Obstacles to Educational Reform in China." *Modern China* 8, 1 (1982): 3-40.

_____. "Recentralization, Decentralization and Rationalization: Deng Xiaoping's Bifurcated Educational Policy." *Modern China* 11, 3 (1985).

_____. *Red Guard Factionalism and the Cultural Revolution in Guangzhou.* Boulder: Westview Press, 1983.

Scalapino, Robert, ed. *Elites in the People's Republic of China.* Seattle: University of Washington Press, 1972.

Schram, Stuart. *Mao Tse-tung Unrehearsed.* Harmondsworth, England: Penguin Books, 1977.

Schwartz, Benjamin. *In Search of Wealth and Power: Yen Fu and the West.* Cambridge: Harvard University Press, 1964.

Science and Technology in the P.R.C. Paris: OECD, 1977.

Selden, Mark. *The Yenan Way in Revolutionary China.* Cambridge: Harvard University Press, 1971.

Seybolt, Peter. ed. *Revolutionary Education in China: Documents and Commentary.* New York: International Arts and Sciences Press, 1971.

_____. *The Rustification of Urban Youth in China: A Social Experiment.* Armonk, N.Y.: M. E. Sharpe, 1975.

_____. "The Yenan Revolution in Mass Education." *China Quarterly* 48 (1971): 641-69.

Shih Ch'ing-chih. *The Status of Science and Education in Communist China and a Comparison with that of U.S.S.R.* Kowloon: Union Research Institute, 1962.

Shimohara. K. *Adaptation and Education in Japan.* New York: Praeger, 1979.

Shirk, Susan. *Competitive Comrades: Career Incentives and Student Strategies in China.* Berkeley: University of California Press, 1982.

Singer, Martin. *Canadian Academic Relations with the People's Republic of China since 1970.* 2 vols. Ottawa: International Development Research Centre, 1986.

_____. *Educated Youth and the Cultural Revolution in China.* Ann Arbor: Center for Chinese Studies, 1971.

Spence, Jonathan. *To Change China: Western Advisors in China 1620-1960.* Boston: Little, Brown, 1969.

Stauffer, Milton, ed. *The Christian Occupation of China.* Shanghai: China Continuation Committee, 1922.

Sun Yat-sen. *San Min Chu I: The Three Principles of the People.* Shanghai: Commercial Press, 1929.

Suttmeier, Richard. *Research and Revolution.* Lexington, Mass.: Lexington Books, 1974.

_____. *Science, Technology and China's Drive for Modernization*. Stanford: Hoover Institution Press, 1980.

Swetz, Frank. *Mathematics Education in China: Its Growth and Development*. Cambridge: M.I.T. Press, 1974.

Taylor, Robert. *China's Intellectual Dilemma: Politics and University Enrollment 1949-1975*. Vancouver: University of British Columbia Press, 1981.

_____. *The Sino-Japanese Axis*. London: Athlone Press, 1985.

Teng Ssu-yu. "Chinese Influence on the Western Examination System." *Harvard Journal of Asiatic Studies* 7, 4:267-312.

Ter Weele, Alexander. "China-World Bank and University Development." *Prospects* 13, 4 (1983): 493-502.

Ting Wang. "Propaganda and Political Struggle: A Preliminary Case Study of Hsüeh-hsi yu P'i-p'an." *Issues and Studies* 13, 6 (1977).

Tsang Chiu-sam. *Society, Schools and Progress in China*. London: Pergamon Press, 1968.

Unger, Jonathan. "The Chinese Controversy over Higher Education." *Pacific Affairs* 53, 1 (1980): 29-47.

_____. *Education under Mao: Class and Competition in Canton Schools 1960-1980*. New York: Columbia University Press, 1982.

_____. "Severing the Links between School Performance and Careers: The Experience of China's Urban Schools 1968-1976." *Comparative Education* 20, 1 (1984): 93-102.

Wang Feng-gang. *Japanese Influence on Educational Reform in China*. Beiping: Authors Book Store, 1933.

Wang Hsueh-wen. *Chinese Communist Education: The Yenan Period*. Taiwan: Institute of International Relations, 1975.

_____. "The 'Two Estimates': A Great Debate on the Educational Front." *Issues and Studies* 14, 2 (1978): 22-36.

Wang, Y. C. *Chinese Intellectuals and the West: 1872-1949*. Chapel Hill: University of North Carolina Press, 1966.

Weber, Max. *The Methodology of the Social Sciences*. New York: Free Press, 1949.

Weiler, Hans. "Knowledge and Legitimation: The National and International Politics of Educational Research." Paper presented at the 5th World Congress of Comparative Education, Paris, July 1984.

West, Philip. *Yenching University and Sino-Western Relations 1916-1952*. Cambridge: Harvard University Press, 1976.

White, Gordon. "Higher Education and Social Redistribution in a Socialist Society: The Chinese Case." *World Development* 9, 2 (1981): 149-66.

_____. *Party and Professionals: The Political Role of Teachers in Contemporary China*. Armonk, N.Y.: M. E. Sharpe, 1981.

_____. *The Politics of Class and Class Origin: The Case of the Cultural Revolution*. Canberra: Australian National University Press, 1976.

White, Lynn. *Careers in Shanghai: The Social Guidance of Personal Energies in a Developing Chinese City*. Berkeley: University of California Press, 1979.

Whyte, Martin. "Educational Reform: China in the 1970s and Russia in the 1920s." *Comparative Education Review* 18, 2:112-28.

Wilkinson, R. H. "The Gentleman Ideal and the Maintenance of a Political Elite." In *Sociology, History and Education: A Reader*, ed. P. Musgrave. London: Methuen, 1970.

Wilson, Richard, and Amy Wilson. "The Red Guards and the World Student Movement." *China Quarterly* 42 (1970): 88-104.

Wu Yuan-li and Robert Sheeks, eds. *The Organization and Support of Scientific Research and Development in Mainland China*. New York: Praeger, 1970.

Yahuda, Michael. *China's Foreign Policy After Mao*. London: Macmillan, 1983.

Yin Chi-ling. *Reconstruction of Modern Educational Organizations in China*. Shanghai: Commercial Press, 1924.

Young, Michael. *Knowledge and Control*. London: Collier-Macmillan, 1971.

_____. "The Schooling of Science." In *Explorations in the Politics of School Knowledge*, ed. M. Young and G. Whitty. London: Nafferton Books, 1976.

Zhao Bao-heng. "Education in the Countryside Today." *Comparative Education* 20, 1 (1984): 103-106.

Western Language Documents and Reports

Achievements in Technical Cooperation with the PRC. Japan International Cooperation Agency, February 1985.

Burnaby, B., A. Cumming, and M. Belfiore, M. *Evaluation Report of the China-Canada Human Resources Training Program*. Toronto, OISE, March 1986.

Chambers, D., and J. Gardner. *Education Profile: China*. London: The British Council, February 1985.

Chan, Luke, and Guan Zhiang. *Management Education in China with Special Reference to Recent Support Programmes by Foreign Countries*. Research Report no. 111, QSEP. Hamilton: McMaster University, 1984.

Clough, Ralph. *A Review of the U.S.-China Exchange Program*. Washington, D.C.: Office of Research, International Communications Agency, 1981.

Committee for Scholarly Cooperation with the People's Republic of China. *American Studies in China: Report of a Delegation Visit, October 1984*. Washington, D.C.: National Academy Press, 1985.

Evaluation Report. Chinese University Development I, by the International Advisory Panel and Chinese Review Commission. Washington, D.C.: National Academy of Sciences, 1986.

Kulturaustausch Programm 1984/5 zwischen dem Bundesrepublik Deutschland und der Volksrepublik China. Bonn, 1984.

Maybee, Jack. *The China Program of the Canadian International Development Agency*. Ottawa, International Development Office, AUCC, 1985.

McLean, L. *The Canada-China Enterprise Management Training Center: Report at the Transition from Phase I to Phase II*. Toronto: OISE, February 1986.

_____. *Overview of the Development of the China/Canada Enterprise Management Training Centre at Chengdu, Sichuan*. Toronto: OISE, July 1986.

National Center for Industrial Science and Technology Management Development (at Dalian, PRC), July 1984. Washington, D.C.: U.S. Department of Commerce, 1984.

Programme d'Echanges Culturels entre le Gouvernement da la République Française et le gouvernement de la République Populaire de Chine pour les années 1984-1985.

Programme of Cultural, Education and Scientific Exchange between Britain and China 1984-1986. London: The British Council, 1984.

Report of Development Cooperation Achievements in the PRC. Beijing: UNDP Office, September 1985.

Ryan, D. *Final Report: Evaluation of the Canada-China Management Education Program*. Toronto: OISE, January 1987.

Ryan, D., and T. Fleming. *Evaluation of the Canada-China Management Education Program*. Toronto: OISE, March 1986.

Science and Technology Cooperation between the U.S. and China. Washington, D.C.: Committee on Energy and Commerce, U.S. House of Representatives, 1984.

Study and Research in the U.K.: Opportunities for Chinese Scholars at Postgraduate Level and Above. London: The British Council, 1984.

A Survey of Royal Society Relations with China and Other Relevant Agreements and Arrangements. London: The Royal Society, 1980.

Technical Training in Japan. JICA brochure, 1985.

University Administration in China. University of East Anglia, Conference of Registrars and Secretaries and Conference of University Administrators, 1983.

World Bank. *China: Issues and Prospects in Education*. Washington, 1985.

_____. *China: Long-term Development Issues and Options*. Baltimore: Johns Hopkins University Press, 1985.

_____. *China: Management and Finance of Higher Education*. Washington, D.C., May 15, 1986.

_____. *China: Socialist Economic Development, The Social Sector, Population, Health, Nutrition and Education*. Washington, D.C., 1983.

World Bank. *Education Sector Policy Paper*. Washington, D.C.: 1980, 1985.

Western Language Serial Publications

Alternatives [India]
Asian Journal of Public Administration [Hong Kong]
Asien [West Germany]
Beijing Review [Beijing]
Britain-China: Newsletter of the Great Britain-China Center [London]
Canadian and International Education [Calgary]
Canadian Universities in International Development [AUCC, Ottawa]
China Daily [Beijing]
China Exchange News [CSCPRC, Washington]
China News Analysis [Hong Kong]
China Quarterly [London]
China Reconstructs [Beijing]
China-Canada Management News: An Occasional Newsletter [AUCC, Ottawa]
Chinese Education [Armonk, New York]
Chinese Law and Government [Armonk, New York]
Comparative Education [Britain]
Comparative Education Review [U.S.]
Compare [Britain]

Current Scene [Hong Kong]
Documents d'Actualité [Paris]
Foreign Broadcast Information Service Daily Report China (FBIS) [Virginia]
Harvard Journal of Asiatic Studies [U.S.]
Issues and Studies [Taiwan]
Issues of Science and Technology [U.S.]
Joint Publications Research Service, China Political Sociological (JPRS-CPS) [Virginia]
Journal of Asian Studies [U.S.]
Journal of Northeast Asian Studies [U.S.]
Journal of Peace Research
Modern China [U.S.]
Nature
Prospects [Paris]
Summary of World Broadcasts, the Far East (SWB/FE) [Britain]
Wochenbericht [Deutches Institute für Wirtschaftforschung]
Xinhua News Agency [London]

Chinese Language Books

Beijing Normal University Editing Group. *Beijing Shifan daxue xiaoshi* (A history of Beijing Normal University). Beijing: Beijing shifan daxue chubanshe, 1982.

Central Committee of the Chinese Communist Party and the Literature Research Unit of the CPC. *Zhishi fenzi wenti* (Problems of intellectuals). Beijing: Renmin chubanshe, 1983.

Chen Dongyuan. *Zhongguo jiaoyu shi* (A history of Chinese education). Shanghai: Shangwu yinshua guan, 1937)

Chen Jingpan, ed. *Zhongguo jindai jiaoyu shi* (A history of Chinese education in recent times). Beijing: Renmin jiaoyu chubanshe, 1979, 1983.

Chen Qingzhi. *Zhongguo jiaoyu shi* (A history of Chinese education). Shanghai: Shangwu yinshua guan, 1936.

Chen Wangdao wenji (Selected writings of Chen Wangdao). 3 vols. Shanghai: Renmin chubanshe, 1979.

Chen Xuexun, ed. *Zhongguo jindai jiaoyu wenxuan* (Essays of recent Chinese educational history). Beijing: Renmin jiaoyu chubanshe, 1983.

Cheng Yangwu. *Zhanhuo zhong de daxue: cong Shaanbei gongxue dao Renmin daxue de huigu* (A university in the firing line: Looking back on the transition from Shaanbei Public Institute to People's University). Beijing: Renmin jiaoyu chubanshe, 1982)

China Metallurgical Higher Education Society and BUIST Higher Education Research Unit, eds. *Rencai yuce lunwenji* (Selected essays on manpower forecasting). Beijing: China Metallurgical Higher Education Society and BUIST Higher Education Research Unit, 1984.

Dangdai Zhongguo Congshu Jiaoyu Juan Pianjishi, ed. *Dangdai Zhongguo gaodeng shifan jiaoyu ziliao xuan* (Selected materials on contemporary Chinese higher normal education). Shanghai: Huadong Shifan daxue chubanshe, 1985.

East China Teachers University Department of Education, ed. *Jiaoyuxue cankao ziliao*

(Reference materials on education). Beijing: Renmin jiaoyu chubanshe, 1981.

East China Teachers University Department of Education and Center for Educational Research, eds. *Zhongguo xiandai jiaoyu shi* (A history of contemporary Chinese education). Shanghai: Huadong shida chubanshe, 1983.

Fudan University Higher Education Research Center, ed. *Fudan daxue de gaige yu tansuo* (Fudan University's reforms and explorations). Shanghai: Fudan daxue chubanshe, 1987.

Fudan daxue zhi (A record of Fudan University). Shanghai: Fudan daxue chubanshe, 1985.

Gaodeng xuexiao gongke benke zhuanye jianjie (A brief introduction to regular engineering specializations in higher institutions). Beijing: State Education Commission 2nd Department of Higher Education, 1985.

Gu Shusen. *Zhonguo lidai jiaoyu zhidu* (China's historical educational system). Nanjing: Jiangsu renmin chubanshe, 1981.

Huang Meizhen, Shi Yuanhua, and Zhang Yun, eds. *Shanghai daxue shiliao* (Historical materials on Shanghai University). Shanghai: Fudan daxue chubanshe. 1983.

Hunan diyi shifan xiaoshi (Institutional history of Hunan No. 1 Teachers College). Shanghai: Jiaoyu chubanshe, 1983.

Jiaoyu faling (Educational regulations). Shanghai: Zhonghua shuju, 1947.

Jiaotong daxue xiaoshi 1896-1949 (A history of Jiaotong University 1896-1949). Shanghai: Jiaoyu chubanshe. 1986.

Liang Rongruo. *Zhongri wenhua jiaoliu shilun* (Essays on Sino-Japanese cultural interaction). Beijing: Shangwu yinshua guan, 1985.

Qinghua University History Editing Group. *Qinghua daxue xiaoshi gao* (Draft history of Qinghua University). Beijing: Zhonghua shuju, 1981)

Renmin Jiaoyu Chubanshe, ed. *Lao jiefangqu jiaoyu gongzuo jingyan pianduan* (Excerpts from the educational experience of the old liberated areas). Shanghai: Shanghai jiaoyu chubanshe, 1979.

Shanghai Jiaoda de jiaoyu gaige (The educational reforms at Shanghai Jiaotong University). Beijing: Renmin chubanshe, 1985.

Sheng Langxi. *Zhongguo shuyuan zhidu* (The Chinese shuyuan system). Shanghai: Zhonghua shuju, 1934)

Shu Xincheng. *Jindai Zhongguo liuxue shi* (A history of contemporary Chinese study abroad). Shanghai: Zhongguo shuju, 1927.

_____, ed. *Zhongguo jindai jiaoyu shi ziliao* (Documents of recent Chinese educational history). 3 vols. Beijing: Renmin jiaoyu chubanshe, 1979.

Sun Huaqun, ed. *Liaoning Gaodeng xuexiao yange* (The evolution of Liaoning higher education). Shenyang: Liaoning renmin chubanshe, 1983.

Tao Zengpian. *Gaodeng jiaoyu tizhi gaige jianlun* (An introductory discussion of structural reform in higher education). Shenyang: Liaoning renmin chubanshe, 1985.

_____. *Gaodeng jiaoyu xingzheng guanli* (Management and administration of higher education). Shenyang: Liaoning renmin chubanshe, 1984.

Wang Yun, ed. *Gaodeng xuexiao guanli* (The management of higher education institutions). Beijing: Beijing City Higher Education Society, 1985.

Xiao Chaoran et al. *Beijing daxue xiaoshi* (A history of Beijing University). Beijing: Renmin chubanshe, 1979.

Yu Li, ed. *Daxue guanli gainian* (Concepts in higher education management). Shanghai: Fudan daxue chubanshe, 1985.

_____. *Xiandai jiaoyu sixiang yinlun* (Discussions on contemporary educational thought). Shanghai: Huadong shifan daxue chubanshe, 1986.

Xiong Mingan. *Zhongguo gaodeng jiaoyu shi* (A history of Chinese higher education). Chongqing: Chongqing chubanshe, 1983.

Yan'an Ziran Kexueyuan Shiliao Bianxiezu, ed. *Yan'an ziran kexueyuan shiliao* (Historical materials on Yan'an College of Natural Sciences). Beijing: Zhonggong dangshi ziliao chubanshe and Beijing Gongye daxue chubanshe, 1986.

Zhang Liuquan. *Zhongguo shuyuan shihua* (The evolution of Chinese shuyuan). Beijing: Jiaoyu kexue chubanshe, 1981.

Zhang Qiyun. *Zhonghua minguo daxue zhi* (A record of universities in the Chinese Republic). Taiwan: Zhonghua wenhua chuban shiye weiyuanhui, 1954.

Zhongguo jiaoyu chengjiu: tongji ziliao 1949-1983 (Achievement of education in China: Statistics 1949-1983). Beijing: Renmin chubanshe, 1984.

Zhongguo jiaoyu chengjiu: tongji ziliao 1980-1985 (Achievement of education in China: Statistics 1980-1985). Beijing: Renmin jiaoyu chubanshe, 1986.

Zhongguo jiaoyu nianjian (Chinese education yearbook). Shanghai: Kaiming shudian, 1934.

Zhongguo jiaoyu nianjian (Chinese education yearbook). Shanghai: Commercial Press, 1948.

Zhongguo jiaoyu nianjian 1949-1981 (Chinese education yearbook 1949-1981). Beijing: Zhongguo dabaike quanshu chubanshe, 1984.

Zhongguo jiaoyu nianjian 1982-1984 (Chinese education yearbook 1982-1984). Changsha: Hunan Education Press, 1986.

Zhongguo jiaoyu nianjian. Difang jiaoyu (Chinese education yearbook, local education). Changsha: Hunan Education Press, 1986.

Zhongguo renmin gongheguo jiaoyu dashi ji 1949-1982 (A record of important educational events in the People's Republic of China 1949-1982). Beijing: Jiaoyu kexue chubanshe, 1983.

Zhonguo gaodeng jiaoyu jianjie (A brief introduction to Chinese higher institutions). Beijing: Jiaoyu kexue chubanshe, 1981.

Zhou Yutong. *Zhongguo xiandai jiaoyu shi* (History of contemporary Chinese education). Shanghai: Liangyou tushu yinshua gongsi, 1934.

Zhu Jiusi. *Gaodeng jiaoyu chuyi* (Modest opinions on higher education). Wuhan: Huazhong xueyuan chubanhe, 1984.

Chinese Language Serial Publications

Daxue jiaoyu (University education), renamed *Gaodeng jiaoyu* (Higher education) (People's University excerpt service)

Fudan jiaoyu (Fudan education) (Shanghai)

Fudan xuebao (The Fudan journal) (Shanghai)

Gaodeng jiaoyu yanjiu (Higher education research) (Beijing)

Gaodeng jiaoyu xue (The study of higher education) (Beijing)

Gaodeng jiaoyu weilai yu fazhan (The future and development of higher education) (Beijing)

Gaojiao zhanxian (The higher education front) (Beijing), renamed *Zhongguo gaodeng jiaoyu* (Chinese higher education) from July 1986
Guangming ribao (Enlightenment daily) (Beijing)
Heilongjiang gaojiao yanjiu (Heilongjiang higher education research) (Harbin)
Hongqi (Red flag) (Beijing)
Jianghan daxue xuebao (Jianghan University journal) (Wuhan)
Jiaoxue yu yanjiu (Education and research) (People's University, Beijing)
Jiaoyu kexue yanjiu (Research in educational science) (Wuhan)
Jiaoyu yanjiu (Educational research) (Beijing)
Jiefang ribao (Liberation daily) (Shanghai)
Liaoning shangzhuan xuebao (Liaoning commerce journal) (Shenyang)
Renmin jiaoyu (People's education) (Beijing)
Renmin ribao (People's daily)
Shanghai gaodeng jiaoyu yanjiu (Shanghai higher education research)
Shanxi daxue xuebao: Shekeban (Shanxi University journal for the social sciences)
Shenzhou xueren (China's scholars abroad)
Shijie jingji daobao (The world economic newspaper) (Shanghai)
Tianjin shiyuan xuebao (The Tianjin Teachers College journal) (Tianjin)
Waiguo jiaoyu (Foreign education) (Beijing)
Waiguo jiaoyu dongtai (Foreign educational trends) (Beijing)
Waiguo jiaoyu ziliao (Foreign educational materials) (Shanghai)
Wenhui bao (Shanghai)
Wenzhai bao (Beijing)
Wuhan shifan xueyuan xuebao (Wuhan Teachers College journal)
Xuexi yu pipan (Study and criticism) (Fudan University journal 1973-1976)
Zhongguo fazhi bao (Chinese law newspaper) (Beijing)
Zhongguo jiaoyu bao (Chinese education newspaper) (Beijing)

INDEX